GREAT BLACK AMERICANS

GREAT BLACK AMERICANS

Second Revised Edition

Formerly titled *Great American Negroes*

BEN RICHARDSON
AND
WILLIAM A. FAHEY

HarperCollins*Publishers*

Acknowledgments

The poem by James Weldon Johnson on page 127 is from *Along This Way* (The Viking Press, 1933).

The quotation by Langston Hughes on page 137 is from *Shakespeare in Harlem* (Alfred A. Knopf, Inc., 1942).

Library of Congress Cataloging-in-Publication Data
Richardson, Ben Albert. Great Black Americans.
1. Negroes—Biography. I. Fahey, William A. II. Title.
E185.96.R5   920'.073   75-12841
ISBN 0-690-00994-1.—ISBN 0-690-04791-6 (lib. bdg.)

10

Preface

Great Black Americans (formerly titled *Great American Negroes*)
is designed to serve as an introduction to some of the
accomplishments of the Afro-American. It is not a comprehensive survey, for such a work would run to many volumes.
However, it does attempt to indicate the continuous involvement of the black man in significant aspects of American life
from the beginning down to the present time and to demonstrate the importance of that involvement not only for black
men and women but for all Americans—indeed, for all
humanity. Dr. Charles Drew's work on the storage and
transfusion of blood brought credit to him and to his race, but
the result of his work was the extension of hope to suffering
man wherever he bleeds and dies. Marian Anderson's singing
gave voice to the heart of her people, bringing to renewed life
the great black tradition of the spiritual. But anyone, of
whatever color, who has heard her around the world has been
encouraged, literally had "heart put into" him, by her song.
Martin Luther King's "We shall overcome . . ." specifically
reflected the aspiration of the black man to overcome bigotry
and prejudice and take his rightful place in American society,

an overcoming no less profitable to the bigot than to the subject of that bigotry. King's crusade for freedom was a great human crusade. His death diminishes us all.

Since 1956, when this book was last revised, many things have happened affecting the lives of black people. The great civil rights campaigns in the South have been fought and won. The extension of voter registration has resulted in the election of more black public officials across America than during any period since Reconstruction. The long hot summers of the sixties, when anguish exploded in fire and smoke in the nation's blighted ghettos, have left their legacy of gutted cities and angry men. Watts has become a name for the violence of despair. Consciousness of blackness as a value rather than a stigma, voiced long ago by W. E. B. Du Bois, has achieved general recognition.

Great Black Americans, almost completely rewritten in its present form, attempts to express these changes as they are reflected in the lives of the men and women whose accomplishments are here set forth. But it is with the men and women themselves, and their accomplishments, that the book is mainly concerned.

Walt Whitman wrote—
America . . . I sing
Langston Hughes answered—
I, too, sing America

Here, in part, is the America Hughes sang—the great black America that gave him voice, subject, reason for singing. Ample voice, large subject, reason enough for song.

William A. Fahey

Contents

Music

"The music of the American Negro," says a historian of music, "is at once the most readily recognized and the least understood of our national traditions . . . rich and varied, . . . it has played a basic role in our musical culture." Dating back to the days of slavery and before, the work songs, ballads, and "shouts," the spirituals, dance tunes, and reels of the Afro-American have their origins in the sorrows and joys of an oppressed but enduring people. "Slides from one note to another and turns and cadences not in articulated notes" were characteristic of this music. And the authors of *Slave Songs of the United States*, published shortly after the Civil War, confessed that "the odd turns made in the throat, and the curious rhythmic effect produced by single voices chiming in at different irregular intervals, seem almost as impossible to place on the score as the singing of birds or the tones of the Aeolian Harp."

This early black music was communal in nature, created by people as they worked, or danced, or sent up praise to God. Sometimes, of course, the hand of a single author is apparent in the music. Many of the spirituals are based upon identifiable hymns. But almost always, the tune has been modified by the singers, given its distinctive form by them.

So too with the later music: ragtime, Dixieland, the blues, jazz. Though W. C. Handy, the father of the blues, was the composer of such songs as the "St. Louis Blues," he confessed that each one of his blues was "based on some old Negro song of the South. . . . the blues that are genuine," he said, "are really folk songs." And when Bessie Smith, the greatest of all blues singers, sang, she paid little attention to the notes, or even the words, of the printed version. The song became hers, as she molded it in the singing.

The great jazz musicians have been improvisers, weaving complex musical patterns out of a given tune. The best jazz has been created by small groups of sympathetic instrumentalists whose thematic elaborations have blended in great "renditions" of oftentimes commonplace songs.

Spirituals, the blues, jazz, are great black contributions that have profoundly affected the course of American music. In addition, individual black men and women have enriched popular music, opera, the symphony, chamber music, choral song, in fact, the whole range of music, as creators and performers. Here are a few of them.

WILLIAM GRANT STILL

William Grant Still was born on May 11, 1894. Three months later his father, who had been a schoolteacher and an amateur musician, died. Shortly thereafter, his mother took him to the farm where she had grown up, just outside Little Rock, Arkansas, to live with her mother and sister. Everybody in the little home sang or played instruments. As a toddler William used to tag along behind his grandmother as she went about her housework. She constantly sang black spirituals and old folk tunes. When she was able to take a minute out to rest, she would play with the boy and teach him the songs too. The two were great friends. In the afternoons when his grandmother went to the back porch and called the chickens to her for feeding, William went with her. He called the chickens too. The sudden onrush of the flock frightened him at first but he gradually grew used to them. He loved to feed the baby chicks; they were such funny little puffs of yellow fuzz.

Mrs. Still married again when William was nine years old. Charles B. Shepperson was a devoted husband and a sympathetic father. He had a great love for operatic music, and because his job as a postal employee paid him adequately, he was able to save enough money to buy a phonograph and a large collection of classical records.

William learned to play the phonograph and spent every spare moment with the records. His neglected chores reflected

William Grant Still

this devotion. He learned to understand and love the music on the records. His stepfather had splendid taste and only the best records came into his collection.

His parents took him to see the various operas that came to Little Rock. His stepfather bought the librettos and explained the stories to him. He explained the music too. When they returned home, the whole family discussed the performance. What William had to say was as important as the comments of his elders. They treated him that way. It gave him confidence, pride, and a drive to learn more.

William learned to identify the instruments in the orchestra. The violin was his favorite.

The family indulged in considerable speculation one week when knives and tools from Mr. Shepperson's tool chest disappeared. By the middle of the week curiosity ran high. If William was making a boat, he certainly would be finished by that time. No inkling of what went on in the privacy of his "workroom" in the shed came until he emerged at the end of the week with a handmade violin. It lacked the line and finish of a Stradivarius, but it was varnished, it had twine strings, and it played—or at least made a sound.

William was proud of his handiwork. He played the great concertos on the phonograph and accompanied the recording artists on his violin. He was in earnest. His parents respected his wishes and immediately arranged for him to study the violin. No thought was given, however, to his making music a life's work.

A teacher at the local grammar school, William's mother had her son in her class. She knew everyone expected her to favor him, so she exacted a very full measure of learning from William and he benefited from it in the end. When he was graduated from high school at sixteen years of age, he was the class valedictorian.

The possibilities for a black musician to succeed in his chosen profession were slight when William finished high school. Even today, in spite of the great popularity many enjoy, actual financial security is won by relatively few. Therefore, when William informed his parents that he wanted to make music his life's vocation, they objected.

He enrolled at Wilberforce University, a Reconstruction Era church college in Xenia, Ohio. His parents suggested that he place his major emphasis on science. William disagreed— still, he obeyed.

As a grade and high school student, William had written music. A little band made up of his friends played his "scores." He thought of music in that way; he loved to hear it, to play it, and to write his own.

At Wilberforce, William followed his science courses faithfully, but he seized every opportunity to play or write music. He helped to form a string quartet, and when the pieces they selected did not meet with his approval, he wrote new ones.

When he brought them to rehearsal, the group welcomed the digression from the ordered music. William's arrangements often broke the accepted laws of instrumentation—and sometimes parts were missing because the composer's zeal got the better of his proofreading—but his compositions were usually interesting.

William proved to be a valuable man in the college orchestra, too. He learned to perform creditably on several instruments—the oboe, the baritone, the piccolo, and some others. When players failed to attend rehearsals or concerts, William substituted for them. He was also able to instruct other members of the orchestra when parts perplexed them. This varied knowledge enabled him to orchestrate and arrange effectively. The group played his arrangements and in time William was elected leader.

He understood clearly that a sound foundation of music information was necessary for any success in the field. So William spent every available dollar on books, scores, and other material. He continued to attend concerts and operas in nearby cities. His teachers looked kindly on his efforts at composition, and on several occasions the band and orchestra played programs made up entirely of his music.

Samuel Coleridge-Taylor, the black English composer, was his idol. He bought and studied his music until he felt at one with that great man. His wanting to emulate Coleridge-Taylor had its more dramatic aspects. The English genius wore his hair in a vertical shock straight up on his head. The fibers of his hair were coarse and strong and made this coiffure possible. William's hair was soft and therefore refused to stand up. All efforts to comb, brush, or set it in that mode failed. William then decided to be great enough in his own right to wear his hair in any style that suited him.

The summer vacation months were months of creation for William. He endlessly composed serious classical music and submitted his pieces to contests all over the country. His successes were few. Usually the returned manuscript brought a note of explanation. The music was such a departure from convention that the judges were unable to understand what either the music or the composer was trying to say.

By this time it was clear to his mother that William was intent on making music his career. He even asked to be allowed to transfer to Oberlin College in Ohio. Its music school was and still is celebrated.

The two sat down and talked the matter over. William described his successes with the quartet and the orchestra. He told of his arrangements and orchestrations. He spoke about the concerts of his music as a final argument—but all to no avail.

His mother was proud of his achievements and wished him every continued success—but she remained firm in her insistence that he return to Wilberforce and complete his scientific courses. Her apprehensions were twofold. First, she felt that a certain moral laxity went with itinerant musical careers, and her second fear arose from her realistic facing of the fact that most black musicians were (and still are) economically insecure.

William went back to Wilberforce. His regular courses were uninteresting but he managed to get fairly good grades. His music was his real interest and he worked hard at it.

Two months before graduation, William left Wilberforce and started out to make a way in life for himself. William C. Handy, the father of the blues, was in the publishing business in Memphis, Tennessee. Later, when he was enjoying a wave of prosperity in his new firm in New York City, he hired William to make arrangements for him and to travel on the road in his band.

The work of a band on the road was not nearly as pleasant as it seemed to those who made up its audiences. Segregation made black performers a homeless lot of talented aliens in most communities. They had to find lodging in the black or "colored" section, as the segregated part of town where black people lived was then called. Since there were few if any public accommodations available to them, they generally roomed as best they could with whatever private families could make space for them. Restaurants refused to serve them, so their chances of eating were very precarious. They played until late hours and when they weren't playing before an audience, they were rehearsing. The pay they received was rarely commensurate with their skill, or labors.

Even though William soon tired of the discomforts caused by discrimination in transportation and lodging, he managed to continue in the business for nearly six years. Then he decided to do something he had wanted to since childhood. He went to Oberlin College for a year and studied composition.

After this period of pleasant, fruitful study, William returned to New York where he accepted a job as the recording director of the Black Swan Phonograph Company.

Some time later Edgard Varèse, the famous modern composer, was looking for a young, talented black man to whom he could extend a scholarship in composition. One of the officials of the company recommended William. He got the scholarship and was exposed to the modernism that helped to shape the character of his compositions for some time thereafter. Through Varèse he got a chance to hear his music played by recognized orchestras.

The next portion of his life found him playing in orchestras in theaters and nightclubs and working as an arranger of popular music for some of the most important artists in the musical world. The list of those who sought his talent includes Earl Carroll, Sophie Tucker, Paul Whiteman, Don Voorhees, and Willard Robison.

He was associated with radio stations of the Columbia Broadcasting System and the National Broadcasting Company and was the first black man to conduct a radio station orchestra when the men of the orchestra on WOR elected him to lead them.

Today William Grant Still devotes most of his time to the composition of symphonic music. He has received repeated Guggenheim Fellowships as fitting gestures of appreciation and help. Three of his most famous compositions are entitled "Africa," the Afro-American Symphony, and Symphony in G-Minor.

"Africa" is a symphonic poem in three movements. It represents an Afro-American's fanciful conception of the beginnings of his race. It is built on folklore that has come down through the years. "Africa" is easily one of his most celebrated compositions. Its three movements are entitled "Land of Peace," "Land of Romance," and "Land of Superstition." It is dedicated to the eminent flautist Georges Barrère and was performed by Barrère in New York in 1930. It has since been played by the Rochester Philharmonic Orchestra and by orchestras in Europe. In 1936 the composer directed its presentation by the Hollywood Bowl Orchestra in California.

The Afro-American Symphony was performed by the New York Philharmonic Symphony Orchestra under Hans Lange and by the Philadelphia Symphony under Leopold Stokowski. In Berlin an audience broke a twenty-year tradition and clamored for an encore of the scherzo from this symphony. Later when Karl Krueger conducted it in Budapest, his audience did the same thing.

The last composition of the three is the Symphony in G-Minor, subtitled "Song of a New Race." Still was earnestly requested by Dr. Leopold Stokowski, who introduced it with the Philadelphia Orchestra in Philadelphia in December 1937, to give it this name.

Gradually Still abandoned those characteristics of modern music upon which his earlier works were based. The more traditional aspects of musical form came to seem increasingly important to him with the passing of the years. However, his work lost none of its vitality; witness "Fanfare for the 99th Squadron," his tribute to the first all-black air force squadron; "And They Hanged Him on a Tree," a fine choral work; and "In Memoriam," subtitled "A Tribute to the Colored Soldiers Who Died for Democracy," one of the most impressive pieces of music to come out of World War II.

William Grant Still has written works for large symphony orchestra, for small orchestra, for band, for piano, for chorus, and a great number of pieces for voice, single instrument, and chamber groups. He has also written ballets—*Lenox Avenue*, *La Guiablesse*, and *Sahdji*—and operas. Over the years a flood of harmonious sound has come from Still, whose life has been devoted to the creation and performance of music. Advancing age shows no sign of stemming that flood.

In 1972, reviewing his new opera, *Highway 1, U.S.A.*, *Newsweek* magazine called him the "77-year-old doyen of American black composers" and praised the work as performed by Opera/South, an exciting, new, predominantly black company sponsored by three southern colleges in Jackson, Mississippi. "The Music of William Grant Still," a two-record album released by Orion in 1974, contains a generous sampling of the later work of the man described by *The New Yorker* magazine as "America's pioneer black symphonic composer." The records, in addition to some shorter pieces, contain "Danzas of Panama," "Ennanga," and "Songs of Separation," a suite for violin and piano, singled out by music critic Winthrop Sargeant for their "originality and nobility."

Those words might well be used to characterize not only the suite and the album but all of the music of Still. Considering the volume of his work and the number of forms it has taken, two words might be added to complete the characterization: "various" and "copious." As his career rounds toward the close like a great symphonic poem—original and noble, various and full—William Grant Still can, with all of us, take delight in his life in music.

DUKE ELLINGTON

"Now, once again, Edward. One, two, three, and four. Never mind trying to get so much 'expression' into it—just play it up to tempo. This is a scale, not a sonata." Mr. Henry Grant had to remind his pupil of this every time they met.

Edward insisted on playing even the common scale of C major slowly, with great expression. He wanted to play the chords he heard inside himself. And he did play them. They were strange and unconventional, but they sounded fine to the boy. However, Mr. Grant was a wise man, and he knew that his pupil must learn the rudiments of music before he could take flight and create. He insisted that Edward apply himself to the routine of practice in a systematic way.

So Edward applied himself—at least for a time. But he was constantly drifting off, chasing musical moods of his own down strange harmonic paths. In any case, the piano lessons, which had begun when Edward was seven, were soon broken off. That was the end of the formal musical education of one of the great masters of American music.

Edward Kennedy Ellington was born in Washington, D.C., on April 29, 1899, to Daisy Kennedy Ellington, an indulgent mother who saw in her son several potentialities and nurtured them all. His father, James Edward Ellington, was a blueprint maker in the Navy Department who also worked occasionally as a butler, sometimes in the White House. He little thought

Duke Ellington

then that his son would one day play at the White House, but that was to be the case. In fact, Ellington was to play there before four American Presidents, and on one such occasion, in 1969, at a celebration of his seventieth birthday, he was awarded the Presidential Medal of Freedom. But by then he had become what his friend Leonard Bernstein was later to describe as "himself a significant chapter in the history of American music."

In his early years, however, young Ellington was as much interested in art as in music—more so, in fact. And his liking for fancy clothes outdid his other interests. So flamboyant was he in manner and dress that his classmates in grammar school began to call him "Duke." The name—and the manner—was to stick with him all his days. Even in his sixties and seventies, he was to affect collarless jackets in brilliant rainbow colors, with contrasting shirts, befeathered velour hats, "jive" shoes, elaborate cuff links, and all the accouterments of the man who really "dressed." And despite a generally suave attitude and "cool" demeanor, he could assert himself with ducal authority, particularly when the interpretation of his music was in question.

An illustration of the attitude was provided at the University of Wisconsin in 1972 at a public rehearsal of his orchestra for the first performance of one of his new compositions, beginning in the key of E.

"E," said Ellington, indicating the key signature. But only half the band responded properly.

"No! E! E! E as in Ellington," Duke shouted. "E as in Edward! . . . E as in excellence! E as in elegance! . . . E! E as in all good things! Edward . . . Ellington . . . excellence . . . elegance!"

As John S. Wilson reported in an obituary article in *The New York Times* on May 25, 1974, the musicians all hit E.

Excellence and elegance were lifelong pursuits for Duke, in music, in life—in all things. Aiming high, he headed for a career in art, winning a poster contest sponsored by the National

Association for the Advancement of Colored People when he was still in school. Then in 1917, upon graduating from high school, he was offered a scholarship by the Pratt Institute of Applied Art in New York. It was a tempting offer, but he turned it down to follow music. *Music Is My Mistress* he was to call his autobiography, written in 1973. His love affair with it began even before he finished high school.

It started in the Poodle Dog Café, where young Duke worked after school as a soda jerk, for the café had a soda fountain as well as a bar, a poolroom, and a dance floor. Its piano was battered, with sticking keys. Its musicians were a pick-up group, paid, if at all, from a kitty atop the piano. Some were known to drink. In fact, the pianist spent more time at the bar than at the piano, and when he couldn't make it back to the piano, a failure that occurred quite often, Edward Kennedy Ellington sat in.

His early piano lessons came in handy, to be sure, but mostly he played by ear. And he learned by listening to other piano players, players of the "two-fisted" school, such as Sticky Mack, Doc Perry, James P. Johnson, and Willie "the Lion" Smith, who played around Washington at the time. Thus, the affair developed. How serious it was to be soon became evident when young Ellington declared himself with his first composition. It was called "Soda Fountain Rag."

After graduating from high school, Duke continued to work in Washington. That is, he worked when he could, sitting in with whoever would hire him. But his own creativity precluded regular employment. On one occasion, for example, he was hired by Russell Wooding, who had organized a huge orchestra featuring five pianos. Duke was to play one. And he did, in his own inimitable way, weaving colorful arabesques around the other four pianists in a piece scored to be played in unison—as the other pianists played it. The effect was electric. And the audience applauded. But Mr. Wooding was not pleased, and at intermission, Mr. Ellington left—urged on his way by the irate conductor.

On another occasion Duke was hired to play for a formal affair and told to dress accordingly. But he was working on a piece of his own when the date came up and he hurried off to make the engagement dressed as he was. The band was already on the bandstand when Duke dashed into the ballroom. He wormed his way through the crowd and leaped onto the bandstand—clad in a loud plaid suit. It was elegant, but decidedly not formal. The conductor substituted at the piano that evening. Another piano player was later hired.

Soon Duke organized his own band and began to play dates in and around Washington. The band was popular, and by the time Duke was twenty, he was making $150 a week, playing at parties and dances. The drummer in that band was Sonny Greer, who was to remain with Duke until 1950, setting a pattern of enduring association that was to characterize many of Ellington's sidemen in the various bands that he put together over the years. For the band was important to Duke, and if he made great demands on their musicianship, he treated the members well, encouraging them to develop as musicians and providing them with musical opportunities they could get nowhere else. As Billy Strayhorn, another longtime associate, once put it: "Ellington plays the piano, but his real instrument is his band."

In 1922 Duke, Sonny Greer, and three other members of the Washingtonians, as the band was called, went to New York. However, unseasoned musicians like themselves had difficulty finding work there, and they spent most of their time listening to other groups play. Nevertheless, the trip was not without profit. For in addition to absorbing the music of Willie "the Lion" Smith and Fats Waller—both of whom were to be important influences on Duke's piano technique—he made friends with them and after a brief return to Washington got a call from Waller, who had found an opening for Duke's band.

Back in Harlem in 1923, they played at Barron's. Then they moved downtown to the Hollywood Club, as it was then called (it was later known as the Kentucky Club), at 49th Street and Broadway. The engagement lasted four and a half years, with the Washingtonians making their first recordings and radio broadcasts under Duke's direction.

In 1927 the Cotton Club opened in Harlem. It was to be a colorful showplace, featuring music, dancing, and a lavish, gaudy review that would attract hordes of tourists anxious to have a look at "uninhibited" Harlem. "King" Oliver and his band were scheduled to appear, but at the last minute Oliver declined, feeling that he had not been offered enough money. Ellington was asked to fill in and accepted, expanding his group to ten men for the large club. It was a turning point in his career, for there was a nightly radio broadcast from the Cotton Club. Soon "East St. Louis Toodle-Oo," which Ellington wrote and used as his theme song, was being heard across the country. And Ellington's "jungle" style, rich in tonal color and featuring the growling trumpet of Bubber Miley, was attracting musicians as well as tourists to the Cotton Club.

During the thirties the Ellington band broadened its horizons, appearing in such motion pictures as *Check and Double Check*, *Murder at the Vanities*, *Belle of the Nineties*, and *The Hit Parade*. They also made extended tours, in 1933 and 1939, of Britain and the Continent, initiating a practice that Ellington would continue throughout his long career.

A fallow period followed for Ellington, during which his band was overshadowed by the big swing bands: Benny Goodman, Artie Shaw, the Dorseys, and Glenn Miller. But as the swing era faded, in the early forties, Duke's band came into its own: Cootie Williams' searing, growling trumpet; the virtuoso trombone of Tricky Sam Nanton, with its startling mute effects; Johnny Hodges' brilliant improvisations on the alto sax; the haunting, glowing clarinet of Barney Bigard; Harry Carney's rugged baritone sax combined in the clear ambience of Duke's piano to produce an intermingling that was, in Ellington's favorite expression of excellence, "beyond category." And the group's renewed popularity as performers was matched by an incredible upsurge of creativity on the part of their leader, who was to produce more than six thousand pieces during his lifetime, including such standard popular repertory numbers as "Solitude," "Sophisticated Lady," "In a Sentimental Mood," "I Let a Song Go Out of My Heart," and "I Got It Bad."

In addition to his popular dance tunes, Duke wrote such instrumental pieces as "Black and Tan Fantasy," "The Mooche," "Creole Love Call," and "Mood Indigo," which were soon established as part of the jazz repertory. In fact, Ellington made important contributions to the development of jazz, extending the usual twelve- or thirty-two-bar chorus, for example, as in his "Reminiscing in Tempo," a twelve-minute work written in 1934.

However, Duke Ellington did not consider himself a jazz musician and consistently rejected the term "jazz" as applied to his music. Reflecting on his work in an interview in 1965, Ellington said, "In the 1920s I used to try to convince Fletcher Henderson that we ought to call what we're doing 'Negro music.' But it's too late for that now. The music has become so integrated that you can't tell one part from the other so far as color is concerned. Well, I don't have time to worry about it. I've got too much music on my mind."

The music that he had on his mind included extended compositions intended for the concert hall that evoked comparison with the work of Debussy, Delius, and Ravel. Ellington's first effort in this genre came in 1943 when he wrote "Black, Brown and Beige," a fifty-minute tone poem that he introduced at a concert at Carnegie Hall in New York. Thereafter, during the forties, Duke played an annual concert at Carnegie Hall, featuring such new compositions as his musical suites, "The Deep South" and "The Perfume Suite," "Symphonia," "Night

Creature," "Controversial," and "New World a-Comin'," the latter piece based on themes suggested by Roi Ottley's novel of that name.

There were other performances in such strongholds of serious music as the Chicago Civic Opera House, San Francisco's Philharmonic Hall, the Philadelphia Academy of Music, and the Metropolitan Opera House in New York. For his appearance at the Metropolitan in 1951 he played his "Harlem," a descriptive tone poem commissioned by the NBC Symphony Orchestra. Other concert pieces written by Duke include "Liberian Suite," commissioned by the Republic of Liberia to celebrate its one-hundredth anniversary; "Togo Brava," for the black state of Togo; "Such Sweet Thunder," inspired by *A Midsummer Night's Dream* as staged at the Shakespeare Festival in Stratford, Ontario, in 1957; and "Suite Thursday," growing out of his interest in Steinbeck's novel *Sweet Thursday* and commissioned by the Monterey Jazz Festival in 1960.

The 1950s were bad years for bands. Interest dropped off, and most big bands simply went out of business. Those that remained toured widely to earn money, and when there were no engagements, the musicians were "at liberty," unsalaried. But Duke kept his band together despite the economic pinch. "It's a matter of whether you want to make music or make money," he observed, as Mr. Wilson reports. "I like to keep a band so I can write and hear the music the next day. The only way you can do that is to pay the band and keep it on tap fifty-two weeks a year. If you want to make a real profit, you go out for four months, lay off for four, and come back for another four. Of course, you can't hold a band together that way and I like the cats we've got. So, by various little twists and turns, we manage to stay in business and make a musical profit. And a musical profit can put you way ahead of a financial loss."

The musical profits, over the years, were enormous. (So, by the way, were the financial ones, one report placing Ellington's worth in excess of $20 million.) And inevitably, with music of such quality as Duke played, popularity would return. As indeed it did. In 1956, Duke performed at the Newport Jazz Festival. And one of his "cats," Paul Gonsalves, had the audience dancing in the aisles to a twenty-seven-chorus tenor sax solo in "Diminuendo and Crescendo in Blue," which Duke had written twenty years earlier. Meanwhile, there were world tours, a number of them under the auspices of the State Department, which sent him to Africa several times, South America, the Far and Middle East, as well as Europe, which Ellington visited frequently. On one such visit, in Paris, he was presented with the Legion of Honor by President Pompidou of France.

Wherever he went, Duke took an electric piano along, for hardly a day—or night—went by that he wasn't composing something. "You know how it is," he once said. "You go home expecting to go right to bed. But then on the way, you go past the piano and there's a flirtation. It flirts with you. So, you sit down and try out a couple of chords and when you look up, it's 7 A.M."

The results of these "flirtations" took many forms. In addition to his dance and concert music and his contributions to the jazz repertory, Duke wrote the scores for five motion pictures—*Paris Blues, Anatomy of a Murder, Assault on a Queen, Change of Mind,* and *Janus,* a German film. He also did a musical, *Jump for Joy,* produced in Los Angeles in 1941. He adapted John Gay's *Beggar's Opera* for performance on Broadway as *Beggar's Holiday* in 1947. In 1963 he wrote a pageant of black history, *My People,* presented in Chicago. And in 1970 he did *The River,* a ballet, for Alvin Ailey and the American Ballet Theatre.

The work that Ellington considered "the most important thing I've ever done" marked his entry into a new field in 1965. This was a concert of sacred music of his own composition, given in Grace Cathedral in San Francisco. Performed with a company that included his own full orchestra, three choirs, a dancer, and several vocalists, the concert was repeated twice during the same year in New York at the Fifth Avenue Presbyterian Church. Pursuing his new interest, Duke gave a Second Sacred Concert at the Cathedral of St. John the Divine in New York in 1968. And a Third Sacred Concert was performed at Westminster Abbey in London in 1973.

From the profane to the sacred, from the dance floor to the concert hall, on the motion picture sound track and in the fluid movements of the choreographer, from "Soda Fountain Rag" to "Liberian Suite," Duke Ellington poured a flood of music into the world. Upon his death, at the age of seventy-five, on May 24, 1974, after more than half a century of making music, tributes came from all over the world. Perhaps Sarah Vaughan, who had often sung with him, expressed best what people felt. "He has made us all happier and richer by having lived among us," she said. "He will not be easily replaced on this earth."

LOUIS ARMSTRONG

Down in New Orleans at the turn of the century jazz was being born. It combined rhythmic elements from the spirituals of shoutin' congregations and the syncopations of ragtime. It made use of the plaintive five-tone scale of the blues, a musical form based on primitive folk music dating back to the days of slavery and before. It was nurtured, in that cosmopolitan city, by such famous Creole musicians as Celestine, Emmanuel Perez, Alphonse Picou, "Papa" Laine, and Bouboule Augustin —men whose brass marching bands played at picnics and at funerals, joyous affairs once the coffin was lowered into the grave.

It grew up in the black honky-tonks of the Battlefield, as the wildest section of New Orleans' infamous Third Ward was called, fostered by such outstanding instrumentalists as "Mad" Buddy Bolden, Bunk Johnson, and King Oliver. Later it began to spread, first to Storyville, where Jelly Roll Morton improvised ingeniously on a huge white piano in old Mahogany Hall; then it invaded the French Quarter with Kid Ory's orchestra. Soon it was heard on the riverboats, up and down the Mississippi. Eventually it reached Chicago, carried by men like Freddy Keppard and Jimmy Noone. By 1916 jazz had reached New York, introduced by a New Orleans cornet player known as "Nick" La Rocca. Soon jazz was king throughout the

Louis Armstrong

country, and its hot licks were beginning to excite young European musicians.

Louis Armstrong, whose musical career was to follow the path blazed by jazz, was born where and while jazz was being born, in New Orleans on July 4, 1900. His parents were poor, hardworking people. His father, Willy Armstrong, was a laborer in a turpentine factory. His mother, Mary Ann—or Mayann as she was called—cooked for a white family in the French Quarter, working until shortly before Louis was born and returning to her job even before he was christened. Home was a single room on the second floor of a dilapidated tenement. The room, reached by an outside staircase, was rented for fifty cents a month. It contained, by way of furniture, an oil lamp, a table, a straw mattress, a chest, and two or three wooden chairs. The walls were decorated with pictures torn from the Sunday supplement of the newspaper by some previous tenant.

Since both of young Louis' parents worked all day to earn the meager income which enabled them to get along, the child was taken care of by his grandmother Josephine Albert. And when his sister Beatrice—later nicknamed "Mama Lucy"—was born two years after Louis, Grandma minded her too. But at night the family crowded together in the small, ugly room for dinner, which usually consisted of bread and red beans. The grinding poverty which produced these conditions led, inevitably, to quarrels. Louis' parents fought with one another, separated, made up, fought and separated again. Louis was left with Grandma for longer and longer periods of time. Finally, when Louis was five years old, his mother and father separated permanently. Since both of his parents remarried, Louis remained with his grandmother for some time. But as he grew older he went to live with his mother, who had moved away from James Alley and set up home with her new husband on Perdido Street, a street later made famous by Duke Ellington's song.

Life on Perdido was a joyous affair for Louis, despite the

fact that the neighborhood was dominated by a dingy old gas storage plant and the forbidding Parish Prison. For one thing, there was the Fisk School, which Louis attended and where he soon made many friends. "Sweet Child," "Coochie," "Little Mack," and "Big Nose" were the names his new pals were known by, and Louis' wide, grinning mouth and generously proportioned lips soon won him the nickname "Dippermouth." For variety he was sometimes called "Satchelmouth," an epithet later abbreviated to the well-known "Satchmo."

And then there was music. The neighborhood was amply supplied with honky-tonks—Segretta's, Ponce's, Matranga's—and nearby stood the Funky Butt Dance Hall. On warm summer nights Perdido would throb with music. Louis, standing beneath the windows of one of the cabarets for hours, would stomp his foot in time with Bob Lyon's hypnotic bass or try to follow the dizzying glide of the trumpet when Buddy Bolden took a "break." When he got a little older, "Dipper" and some of his friends organized a quartet and sang at busy street corners or in front of bars and taverns, passing the hat when they finished.

Of course, life was not all music for Louis. His stepfathers—six of them, over the years—were poor, hardworking men, and young Dipper had to pitch in and help support the family. At the age of seven he started selling papers for a news vendor, often staying out until ten or eleven o'clock at night to earn a half-dollar. On such nights he would find the family in bed when he returned, for their working day started early. Then he would warm the pot of red beans and sit down to his late supper alone.

When he was nine years old Louis left school for a full-time job. He worked on Konowski's Coal Truck, filling coal buckets for the driver between stops. With tips, he earned between seventy-five cents and a dollar a day.

Louis Armstrong regarded an incident that took place when he was thirteen years old as a turning point in his life. It occurred on New Year's Eve—with a .38 pistol he found in an old trunk in his mother's room, he shot up the street in Wild West fashion, contributing his share to the noisy festivities. As he stood in the middle of the street with the smoking gun in his hand, the sheriff appeared on the scene. The boy was arrested, tried, and sentenced to an indefinite term at the Colored Waifs Home. The fault had been grievous and the punishment was severe. But Louis made the best of a bad situation. And later he looked back on the episode without bitterness. "I do believe," he said, "that my whole success goes back to that time I was arrested as a wayward boy at the age of thirteen. Because then I *had* to quit running around and began to learn something. Most of all, I began to learn music."

Louis spent more than a year and a half in the Waifs Home. And he did learn something about music as a member of the institution's band. Starting with the lowly tambourine, he was later transferred to the drums and eventually became bugler. Before he left the home, he was playing the cornet and had been made leader of the band.

Naturally, when Dippermouth left the home the cornet remained behind. Soon he was back on the coal wagon again. A driver, now that he was fifteen, he hauled five loads of coal a day, getting about seventy-five cents for his backbreaking efforts. There seemed to be little chance of his ever playing a horn again. Then Louis got a break. The cornet player in Henry Ponce's cabaret failed to appear for work one night and Satchmo was offered the job. He snatched at the opportunity to earn $1.25 a night plus tips while playing on a borrowed cornet. But such a job offered little security and Louis was ambitious. So he kept his coalman's job too. Working in Ponce's until four in the morning, he would rush home and tumble into bed when he was through. Then, after three hours' sleep, he would report to the Andrews Coal Company at seven and work until five in the evening. It was a grueling schedule, but Louis was making money at last. And he was playing the cornet!

Every now and then Louis sought better-paying, less-taxing work. He tried dishwashing and delivering milk. He worked as a junkman and as a member of a gang of house razers. For a while he worked on the docks as a stevedore, unloading banana boats. But he always went back to the coal cart.

It was while delivering coal in the French Quarter that Louis met the famous King Oliver, who was playing there with Kid Ory's orchestra. King had heard about Louis' playing, and he made friends with the boy. One night he went to Ponce's place to hear Satchmo blow his horn. Impressed with the boy's ability, Oliver invited him to his home. Learning that Louis did not have an instrument of his own, Oliver gave him one of his old cornets. He got Louis engagements in some of the better clubs, sending him occasionally as a replacement for himself. Most important of all, he taught Louis something of his own technique. "Papa Joe," as Louis came to call Oliver, helped to make Louis Armstrong into a musician in his own likeness. He could have done no greater favor for the aspiring young jazzman, for he was, as Satchmo has said, "the finest trumpeter who ever played in New Orleans."

Encouraged by King Oliver, Louis spent more and more time playing his horn. In 1918 he quit his job as coalman forever and devoted his energy exclusively to music. He played in various honky-tonks in New Orleans and its environs, including a stint in Gretna, a river town that Louis called "the toughest place" he ever played. Perhaps then it was more than mere coincidence that threw the belligerent Daisy Parker, his first wife, into his path in Gretna. At any rate, after several years of feuding, Daisy and Louis separated permanently.

Before he divorced Daisy, however, Louis tried to determine whether or not distance would cause her to grow fonder—and less pugnacious. He joined Fate Marable's orchestra on the riverboat *Sydney*, and for a year or so he sailed the Mississippi, providing music for the passengers. Daisy failed to respond to the treatment, but Satchmo profited from the experience nonetheless. The food on the boat was excellent, and Louis, weighing 140 pounds when he joined the *Sydney*, was soon wearing fat men's trousers. More important, he became friendly with David Jones, the band's melophone player, a highly trained musician who taught him how to read music.

Louis played in Tom Anderson's cabaret on Rampart Street for a while after he left the *Sydney*. But the river had given him wanderlust; and when "Papa Joe" Oliver, who had left New Orleans, invited Louis to join him at the Lincoln Garden in Chicago, where he had his own band, Satchmo headed north immediately. He played second cornet in Oliver's band and, with the King blasting away on the trumpet, a very subordinate position it was. But he was allowed free rein in his singing. And his songs, delivered in a deep, husky half-growl, were an immediate success. Soon, too, he had mastered the so-called "Chicago style" of jazz, and under pressure from the band's pianist, Lil Hardin, who was to become Louis' second wife, King Oliver permitted Louis to share the spotlight with him more and more frequently. Before long the former pupil was outshining his aging teacher. And Chicago was rocking to the furious Armstrong renditions of "Muskrat Ramble," "Tiger Rag," and "Basin Street Blues."

A nationwide tour with Oliver's band helped to spread Satchmo's fame across the country. And recordings served the same end. An incident connected with one of those early recordings illustrates the power of the lungs with which Louis blew himself to musical fame. The record in question is "Chimes Blues," which Oliver's band made for the Gennett Studios in 1924. For the trumpet break on that record the sound engineer placed Louis next to Joe Oliver in front of the band. The playback revealed that only Armstrong's trumpet could be heard against a blurred, indistinct background. To get a successful recording, it was necessary to place Louis and his horn ten feet behind the rest of the group!

Fletcher Henderson, who was playing at the Roseland

Ballroom on Broadway in New York, asked Louis to join his band in 1924. Louis leaped at the chance to join so fine a group of musicians, for among the players were men like Buster Bailey, Don Redman, Coleman Hawkins, and others of the same caliber. For more than a year and a half Louis played with "Smack" Henderson and his boys, winning many new fans in the East.

Chicago had won Louis' heart, however, and back he went, as soon as he could, to the cabarets on Calumet and Thirty-fifth streets, where the capital of jazz was then located. There he met Joe Glaser, who became his manager and remained so for many years, until Glaser's death in 1969.

To this period belongs Louis Armstrong's Hot Five—Lil Hardin at the piano, Johnny St. Cyr playing the banjo, Kid Ory on the trombone, Johnny Dodds on the clarinet, and Satchmo himself, of course, blowing the trumpet. And the records of this group are Chicago jazz classics; "Gut Bucket Blues," "Yes, I'm in the Barrel," "Heebie Jeebies," and "Sunset Café Stomp" are some of them. Later, when Louis and Lil separated, Earl Hines' huge and skillful hands pounded and shaped the rhythm from the piano, and Zutty Singleton beat the drums behind Louis in a perfect frenzy. With the addition of Jimmy Noone, Don Redman, or Jimmy Strong, the Hot Seven, as Louis' group was now known, issued such great records as "St. James Infirmary," "No One Else But You," "Basin Street Blues," and "I Can't Give You Anything But Love."

And the flood of music—raucous, hot, blue; smoking with the passions Louis had experienced; burnished bright by the magic trumpet—continued to flow. Some of the music was composed by the great trumpeter himself. Louis wrote twenty-odd tunes, including his favorites, "If We Never Meet Again" and "Struttin' with Some Barbecue."

Of course, there were disappointments and upsets in Louis' life. He was divorced several times. Musicians occasionally failed him when he needed them to play dates. A dance hall that Louis, Zutty, and "Fatha" Hines opened in Chicago closed very quickly and left them all broke. But there was acclaim, too, and profit, and satisfaction. There were triumphs like the *Hot Chocolates* revue, in New York, in which Louis played Fats Waller's "Ain't Misbehavin'." And there was the occasion upon which Louis received a wristwatch inscribed with best wishes "from the musicians on Broadway." There was success in Hollywood, with records like "Body and Soul," "Memories of You," "You're Driving Me Crazy," "Shine," and others to prove that it was deserved. There was Europe—Paris, Berlin, Madrid, Brussels, Oslo, Copenhagen, Stockholm, Rotterdam, Geneva—for Louis to sweep through in triumph, the New World king of a new kingdom—Jazz!

Later there were worldwide tours that took "Pops," as he was affectionately called, through Latin America, the Middle East, and Africa, winning him the unofficial title of "America's ambassador of goodwill." On his tour of Africa in 1960, one hundred thousand people in Accra, Ghana, came to hear him blow his magic horn. And in Léopoldville thousands of admirers lifted him onto a canvas throne and carried him into the city stadium where he was to play.

Over the years, the great showman with the wide grin made so many recordings that he lost count of the exact number. But his brilliant trumpet and his husky voice, which has been described as "a piece of sandpaper calling to its mate," have appeared on more than fifteen hundred records, with sidemen from three generations of jazz musicians.

For almost sixty years Louis Armstrong made music, altering the shape of jazz in the course of his career from an art of ensemble improvisation to one dominated by brilliant solo performances, with his virtuoso trumpet leading the way. Before his death, on July 6, 1971, shortly after his seventy-first birthday, Louis said, "My life has been my music."

Indeed it had been, to the enrichment of us all.

MARIAN ANDERSON

Marian Anderson was born on Webster Street, in South Philadelphia, on February 27, 1903, in a room her parents had rented when they were married. Her mother, Annie, who came from Virginia, where she had been a teacher before her marriage, was a tiny woman. Her father, on the other hand, was well over six feet tall. One of Marian's earliest recollections is of her mother reaching up on tiptoe to tie her father's tie and he, laughing heartily, urging her to get a newspaper to stand on to make herself a little taller.

John Anderson had grown up in Philadelphia, and he worked there in the Reading Terminal Market. Another of Marian's early memories is of the long, golden bar of pound cake he would bring home from the market almost weekly. On those occasions, she says in her autobiography, *My Lord, What a Morning*, "my appetite for all other food would vanish."

When Marian was about two years old, the family moved in with her father's parents, who had a house on Fitzwater Street. There her sister Alyce was born. Then, with the birth of a second sister, Ethel, they moved again, to a small house that they rented on Colorado Street, not too far from Grandmother's.

It was in the Colorado Street house that Marian, "la-la-la-ing a vocal accompaniment" to a rhythm she beat out on the kitchen table, gave voice to what she says people might describe

Marian Anderson

as the first signs of music in her. It was then, too, she remembers hearing her father sing, as he dressed, "Bits of 'Asleep in the Deep,' never finishing it."

Mr. Anderson, who sold coal and ice and had other jobs in addition to his work in the market, was close to his family and enjoyed taking them on outings. The biggest, Marian recalls, was the annual excursion each spring to see the Barnum and Bailey Circus. He would also bring home little presents for the girls, never forgetting new bonnets, which he picked out himself, at Easter. But Mr. Anderson's great pride was his work at the Union Baptist Church, where he was in charge of the ushers. There he took Marian every Sunday from her earliest years. By the time she was six, she was singing in the junior choir, where Alexander Robinson, the choirmaster, recognizing her ability, encouraged her by assigning her solos or parts in duets and quartets.

When Marian was about eight years old, her father bought a piano from his brother, who had no use for it. Marian was delighted with the instrument, and, though there was no money for lessons, with the help of a card marked with the notes she learned to play some simple melodies. Then, seeing a violin in a pawnshop window, she had the urge to play that instrument, too. Saving up the nickels she earned scrubbing neighbors' steps, she bought the violin for $3.98. The pawnbroker assured her it was just short of a Stradivarius. However, considerably short of that, the instrument soon succumbed to inexpert handling and ended as a total wreck long before Marian learned to play it.

Marian's father died when she was twelve years old. The family went back to live with the grandparents on Fitzwater Street, later moving with them into a large house on Christian Street, where Grandmother Anderson boarded three or four children whose mothers had to work. Since Marian's aunt and two cousins also shared the house, there were always plenty of people about, and Marian learned early how to get along with other people and to respect their rights and privileges. Grand-mother Anderson, a large, authoritative woman, who liked to remind people that she was part Indian, insisted on that. And she was boss, at least during the day, while Marian's mother went out to work in domestic service or did laundry at home, which Marian and her sisters often delivered.

When she was thirteen years old, Marian was asked to join the senior choir at the Union Baptist Church, which was well-known for the excellence of its music. Since her voice had a wide range and was particularly rich in the lower registers, Mr. Williams, the leader of the senior choir, frequently called upon her to fill in for absent soloists. Soon she was being sent out with quartets or duets or even as soloist to represent the church at recitals in neighboring churches. Once she and several other members of the choir went as far as New York City, where they sang at the Abyssinian Baptist Church in Harlem.

It was at the Union Baptist Church that Marian met Roland Hayes, the celebrated black tenor, who gave an annual concert there. She even got to sing with him on one of his appearances and impressed him so that he paid a visit to Marian's grandmother, urging her to send her granddaughter to Boston for professional voice training. But the Andersons could not afford the great expense of such training, and besides, Marian's grandmother objected. If the girl could sing naturally, what was the need of lessons?

At home, in Philadelphia, Marian's rich, deep contralto voice continued to call itself to the attention of people interested in music. Singing one day at the William Penn High School, where she was enrolled in a commercial course, Marian was heard by a visitor, Dr. Rohrer, who said, "I don't understand why this girl is taking shorthand and typewriting. She should have a straight college preparatory course and do as much as possible in music." His advice was followed. Marian transferred to the South Philadelphia High School, whose principal, Dr. Lucy Wilson, took a personal interest in her, encouraged her singing, and introduced her to people who could help her toward a career in music.

Mary Saunders Patterson, a black woman with a magnificent soprano voice, was Marian's first voice teacher. After hearing Marian sing, she offered to waive her usual fee of a dollar a lesson when she learned that the Andersons could not afford that sum. It was Mrs. Patterson who provided Marian with the "all-important foundation of singing style," teaching her how to project her voice and how to conserve it, how, consciously, to produce a particular note, how to breathe correctly, and other basics of the singer's craft.

Having provided Marian with a good foundation, Mrs. Patterson recommended that she continue her studies with Agnes Reifsnyder, a contralto, like Marian, and therefore better equipped than a soprano to teach her. Miss Reifsnyder "was not interested in fireworks or vocal gymnastics," says Marian, "but she concentrated a great deal on breathing and gave me exercises further to set the voice." She also introduced the young singer to the songs of Brahms, among others, and helped her to prepare whole programs for concerts.

Shortly before graduating from high school, Marian was introduced to Giuseppe Boghetti, a world-famous voice teacher. The interview did not go well. Mr. Boghetti had more pupils than he wanted and was not interested in acquiring new ones. However, reluctantly, he agreed to listen to Marian. When she sang "Deep River" for him, his attitude changed at once. "I will make room for you right away," he said when she had completed the song. Thus began a relationship that was to last many years, with occasional interruptions, until Boghetti's death.

Meanwhile, Marian's singing engagements increased in number and she began to receive sizable sums for each performance. Soon she was able to help her mother buy a small house on South Martin Street.

So successful a performer had Marian become by the age of about twenty that she felt ready for the big time, and when someone proposed a concert at Town Hall in New York City Marian agreed. That was a mistake. Marian was still an unknown singer, and the concert was ill attended. The sparsely filled auditorium made her nervous. Moreover, she included several German songs in the program, and her German was weak. The performance was unsatisfactory, the reviews were unfavorable, and Marian was so disheartened she was ready to abandon singing as a career.

However, with the help of her mother Marian threw off her discouragement and returned to music again. In 1923 she became the first black woman to win first prize in a voice contest sponsored by the Philadelphia Harmonic Society. Then, two years later, competing against three hundred singers in New York City, she won the Lewisohn Stadium Concert Award and appeared with the New York Philharmonic Orchestra at the stadium on August 26, 1925. A few years after that she received a Rosenwald Foundation Fellowship, enabling her to go to Germany, where she studied *Lieder*, German art songs, that were to be, along with spirituals, so important a part of her repertory.

Marian Anderson's career was on firm footing now. Concert tours in the Scandinavian countries, where she was an enormous success, were followed by tours on the Continent, with major concerts in Paris, Brussels, Geneva, Vienna, and Salzburg, among other cities. In Salzburg, Maestro Arturo Toscanini, the distinguished conductor, was in the audience. During intermission he came backstage to compliment the singer. She was so nervous at his appearance that she mumbled, "Thank you, sir, thank you very much," without having heard a word he said. Only later did she learn that Maestro Toscanini's words were: "Yours is a voice such as one hears once in a hundred years."

Returning to New York just before Christmas 1935 for an

American tour that was to begin with a concert at Town Hall, Miss Anderson fell down a companionway of the ship in rough seas and broke her ankle. Remembering the bitter disappointment of her first appearance at Town Hall, more than ten years earlier, the singer was determined to make a success of it this time, broken ankle notwithstanding. So on December 30, with her leg in a cast, she hobbled onstage, propped herself against the piano, gave her crutches to an attendant, arranged her long skirt to conceal her cast, signaled for the curtain to be raised, and sang—triumphantly. There was some pain involved, but Miss Anderson scarcely felt it. The occasion was too exhilarating.

Miss Anderson's tour schedule increased year by year, with foreign tours sandwiched in between her American appearances and acclaim meeting her everywhere. In Moscow, Stanislavski, the famous theatrical director, asked her to do *Carmen* with him, a request that she later regretted having refused. Joseph Stalin heard her sing. In Denmark, the widow of Edvard Grieg, the great composer, invited her to tea. At his home near Helsinki, Finland's most famous composer, Jean Sibelius, prepared to serve her coffee. When she sang one of his songs for him—"Im Wald ein Mädchen singt"—he embraced her heartily, saying, "My roof is too low for you." Then turning to his wife, who was making the coffee, the seventy-year-old composer shouted, "Not coffee, but champagne."

Despite her world renown, however, there was one famous concert platform on which Marian Anderson could not appear —Constitution Hall, in Washington, D.C. Scheduled to sing in our nation's capital, Miss Anderson was denied the use of the hall by its owners, the Daughters of the American Revolution. America was shocked by this act of discrimination. Mrs. Franklin D. Roosevelt resigned her membership in the D.A.R. in protest against it and worked to provide an alternative platform, turning the event into a *cause célèbre*. A platform was built before the Lincoln Memorial, and there, on Easter Sunday

1939, Marian Anderson sang before a vast throng that stretched over the Mall from the Lincoln Memorial to the Washington Monument. She sang "America," "Ave Maria," and a group of spirituals, including "My Soul Is Anchored in the Lord." It was her answer to bigotry and prejudice.

During that same year, Marian Anderson was awarded the Spingarn Medal, given annually to the black American who "shall have made the highest achievement . . . in any honorable field of endeavor." In 1941 she was presented with the Bok Award, a $10,000 prize bestowed upon "an outstanding citizen of Philadelphia." The prize forms the basis of the Marian Anderson Award, instituted by the singer "to help young people to pursue an artistic career." It is granted "without regard to race, creed, or color."

In 1943 Miss Anderson was married to Orpheus H. Fisher, the architect, and the couple built a home on a large farm near Danbury, Connecticut. However, the singer was to enjoy domestic life there only intermittently, between concert tours, for many years. Regularly, until her retirement as a recitalist in 1965, she gave as many as sixty or more concerts a year, visiting Europe, Asia, and South America and traveling all over the United States to do so.

Having a repertory of more than two hundred songs, including, in addition to spirituals, Bach, Brahms, Handel, Saint-Saëns, Schubert, and others, Miss Anderson further extended her musical activities in 1955, when she fulfilled a lifelong dream. Singing the role of Ulrica in Verdi's *A Masked Ball*, the great contralto made her debut at the Metropolitan Opera House in New York. She was thus the first black woman to become a member of the company at the famous old opera house.

In the fall of 1957 Miss Anderson made a twelve-nation concert tour of the Far East, traveling more than thirty-five thousand miles under the auspices of the State Department as an ambassadress of goodwill for the United States. The tour, on which she was greeted everywhere with acclaim, won many friends for the United States. It was the subject of an hour-long television report called "The Lady From Philadelphia," released in America upon her return. In 1958 this Lady from Philadelphia was appointed alternate delegate in the United States Mission to the United Nations, an appointment that enabled her to continue her efforts toward international understanding.

Despite her worldwide fame and the honors that have come to her, Marian Anderson remains a humble person. She often speaks of herself in the first person plural when talking of her singing because she has always regarded her accompanist as a full partner and because her humility extends to the great gift of song with which she has been blessed. Speaking of her audience several years before she retired from the concert stage, Miss Anderson said, "There was a time when I was very much interested in applause and the lovely things they said. But now," she continued, "we are interested in singing so that somebody in the audience will leave feeling a little better than when he came."

Marian Anderson gave her last public recital on Easter Sunday 1965. When she had taken her final bows on the stage at Carnegie Hall in New York, Irving Kolodin, music critic for the *Saturday Review*, commented, "never has a performer done more to earn them—as an artist, as a person, as a public figure."

DEAN DIXON

The tones of the New York Philharmonic Orchestra filled Carnegie Hall. A rapt audience listened, among them, high up in the third balcony, a sweet-mannered black woman with a squirming three-year-old child on her lap. Finally, he fidgeted into a position that suited him and soon was fast asleep. It was 1918. The woman was Mrs. Henry Charles Dixon. The boy was Dean Dixon, who would one day lead that famous orchestra.

All through his childhood Mrs. Dixon continued to take Dean to Carnegie Hall. The balcony was a long way up, but the tickets were cheap, the acoustics were excellent, and the New York Philharmonic was one of the best symphony orchestras in the world. Having learned that Dean had the rare gift of absolute pitch, his mother was determined that he be exposed to fine music and that he have the opportunity to make something of his gift.

At the age of three Dean was started on the violin. His mother arranged for lessons, encouraged him to practice, and delighted in playing games with him that tested and trained his ability to differentiate between the sounds of the notes. She took him to the Metropolitan Opera House on Saturday afternoons. The visits to Carnegie Hall continued. As Dean grew older, he learned to understand the music he heard and came to know the various conductors who led the orchestra. He

Dean Dixon

no longer slept through the program. He couldn't. The music thrilled him now.

At first Mrs. Dixon had no thought that her son would become a professional musician. It was a question of culture. She wanted him to know the best music. And it was a question of economy. His gift of perfect pitch should not be wasted. As for a profession, like many poor people with high aspirations and dreams of meaningful lives for their sons, Mrs. Dixon hoped that Dean would become a doctor. She had even decided on the school—Edinburgh University, in Scotland, where racial discrimination was not so apt as it was in America to cut short a black mother's hopes of seeing her son become a doctor.

The Dixons were poor people. Mr. Dixon had died while Dean was still a small child. They lived simply and frugally in a small apartment in uptown New York. Dean attended a nearby public school and went to the Episcopal Mission Church on Edgecombe Avenue with his mother on Sundays. But daily practice and weekly lessons made the violin the center of young Dean's life. Mrs. Dixon saw to that, sometimes to Dean's annoyance, as when practice interfered with a stickball game in the streets. However, Dean was content on the whole, for his mother was diplomatic about urging him to practice and never pushed him too far. She encouraged his other interests, too, and was delighted to have his friends in the house. In any case, Dean was soon so deeply interested in music that he required little urging to keep up with his violin lessons.

However, when Dean was eleven years old, his violin teacher advised against continuing with the instrument. Mrs. Dixon was told that Dean was an apt pupil but that by nature he was not a violinist. Mrs. Dixon questioned the judgment, thanked the teacher for his kindness in returning a part of the money she had advanced for Dean's lessons, but insisted that Dean continue his violin studies with someone else.

At DeWitt Clinton High School Dean played in the school

orchestra, work he enjoyed very much. It meant being excused early from classes to attend rehearsals. It also provided a stock excuse for all lateness to classes. But more than these advantages, there was for Dean the actual joy of playing the music he had come to know and love.

Mr. Harry Jennison was the music teacher in charge of the orchestra, and he and Dean used to stay after rehearsal and talk about the selections on the next program. They analyzed the score of each and discussed the composer and his technique of composition. Dean showed an amazing understanding of these aspects of music. He was interested in the instrumentation, the voicing of parts, and the structural movements of the scores. His interests were, in fact, the interests of a budding conductor.

Because Dean wanted to have more experience in music generally, he organized a little symphony orchestra in the theater of the Harlem Y.M.C.A. At the outset the orchestra comprised a pianist, another violinist, and Dean, who alternated between conducting and playing the other violin part. His baton was a lead pencil.

Gradually his orchestra grew larger, until it numbered more than fifty persons. It was indeed a mixed group. Men, women, and children, black and white, all were part of its enthusiastic membership. Some players were highly skilled. Others had to count aloud the rests and tap their feet to keep the tempo. But Dean was patient with their limitations. He was informed and in his modest way, teacher-like, he informed them. They worked happily together.

Shortly after his graduation in 1932, Dean and his mother talked with Mr. Jennison about Dean's future. Mrs. Dixon still had visions of her son as a doctor and mentioned her plans to help him study medicine at Edinburgh University. Mr. Jennison was firm in his belief that Dean would make an accomplished musician. His firmness was no match for Mrs. Dixon's however, and it required the help of George Gartlan, the head of music in the city's public school system, to convince her that Dean should audition for the Institute of Music and Arts of the Juilliard School of Music.

The audition was an awesome affair, presided over by Dr. Walter Damrosch, who was one of the chief musical educators of his day. Tall, exacting, furiously moustached, and terribly German, Dr. Damrosch listened attentively and then scribbled off a note to the admissions office—in German. When Dean presented the note to the admissions office, the registrar commented, "You must have been very good." He was admitted to the Institute of Music and Arts as a student of the violin.

After a short period of study Dean met some former high school classmates, who were enrolled in the newly organized course in music education. This work led to a degree. Dean talked with his mother by telephone. They both agreed that it would be a good idea to take this course and continue his violin also. When Dean entered the music education course, fifty-two pupils were enrolled in it. Four years later seventeen were graduated, Dean among them.

One of his courses at the institute, conducting, was taught by Adolph Schmid, a demanding teacher, particularly so with promising students. Dean was very promising, and Schmid soon recognized his aptitude. The recognition resulted in hard work, but it also provided Dean with many opportunities to develop his skill in handling an orchestra, opportunities that were to be the basis of his later success.

In 1936 he was awarded a bachelor of science degree, and because his work was so good, he was given a fellowship to study conducting in the Juilliard School proper. Albert Stoessel was to be his teacher. The opportunity was unique. A black man had never undertaken conducting as a profession. In fact, no black man had ever been accepted in a major symphony orchestra. Hence the role of conductor seemed like a wildly impossible one. Nevertheless, Dean accepted the fellowship and enrolled concurrently in Columbia University to work toward a master's degree.

At the same time he continued his work with his orchestra. The group named itself the Dean Dixon Symphony Society and now boasted seventy members. A committee of sympathetic women led by his mother interested the community in Dean's concerts. His name became synonymous with the strivings of the black musician to gain entrance to a field heretofore closed to him. The black community took pride in Dixon's efforts.

In 1938, while he was still studying at Juilliard and at Columbia, the opportunity came to conduct the Chamber Orchestra of the League of Music Lovers at Town Hall. Soon after he was invited to be guest conductor with the New York Chamber Orchestra, an organization made up of musicians from the great symphony orchestras who work in this smaller unit for sheer enjoyment and relaxation.

The following year Columbia University awarded Dixon the master of arts degree. He had proved his academic qualifications for the work he chose to do. It remained for the world of musicians and music lovers to accept him—a black man.

The next few years were difficult. Encouragements were mostly verbal. Actual opportunities to use his skills were few. But neither Dean nor Mrs. Dixon despaired in the face of this obvious discrimination. Eventually his good work with the limited material of his orchestra came to the notice of Eleanor Roosevelt, who accepted an invitation to attend one of his concerts. On May 18, 1941, the auditorium of the Heckscher Theater at 104th Street and Fifth Avenue was crowded. People of all races were there. They came to hear the orchestra, but more to see Dean Dixon conduct it through its imposing program. They came to see Dean Dixon succeed.

He did succeed, conducting his musicians through a program that included Hadyn, Bach, Tchaikovsky, and Beethoven. Critics acclaimed the event, and Dixon was invited to be guest conductor with the NBC Summer Symphony.

In January 1942 Dixon conducted the NBC Orchestra over its nationwide network of radio stations. Public acclaim was overwhelming.

Dixon was then invited to conduct the New York Philharmonic Orchestra in one of its Lewisohn Stadium concerts. This orchestra, which his mother had taken him to hear regularly as a child, had played under the direction of such great conductors as Arturo Toscanini, Serge Koussevitzky, Bruno Walter, and others of similar stature. Now it was Dixon's turn. On August 10, the Sunday night of the concert, Dixon scored another triumph. The critics again lavished praise on his work. Dean Dixon was now established as a conductor worthy enough to work alongside the masters.

Further triumphs lay ahead for the young man, including his debut at Carnegie Hall and guest appearances with the Boston and Philadelphia symphony orchestras. In 1948 he won the Alice Ditson Award as "outstanding American conductor." But despite his great ability, prejudice prevented him from gaining a full-time conducting post in the United States. Discouraged, Dixon left the United States for Europe in 1949. "I suppose I should have enlisted the help of the teeth people—NAACP and Urban League," Dixon said in an interview many years later, "but I wanted my music, not my color, to open doors."

In Europe his music did open doors, a few at first, then more and more. Thus, in 1951, he gave nine European concerts. In 1952 he gave sixty. As Dixon describes his acceptance in terms of critical notices, he says that headlines referred to him in his first appearances as "Negro American Conductor." Later the notices announced, "Negro Conductor." Then, successively, he was headlined, "Dean Dixon, Conductor," "Dixon, Conductor," and finally just "Dixon." When the newspapers started calling him just "Dixon," "that's when I knew I had made it," says the conductor.

Making it has included concert tours that have taken him to

all of the major cities of Europe and guest appearances with the finest symphony orchestras in the world. He has served, in Sweden, as music director of the Göteborg Symphony, and for ten years he was music director of one of West Germany's major radio orchestras in Frankfurt. For three of those years, beginning in 1964, he simultaneously held the Frankfurt post and headed the Sydney Symphony, in Australia, making music on a truly global scale. Despite the fact that Dixon's talents have won greater rewards for their possessor abroad than at home, the conductor has not been embittered by this circumstance.

The music critic Virgil Thomson has called Dixon "our most assiduous ambassador of American music." Dixon has introduced more than fifty contemporary works to European audiences, thirty of these works being first performances and most of them by American composers. Indeed, he is known as an exponent of an enlightened program policy, for he avoids, in his concerts, the overworked, standard musical selections and presents in their place fresh new music in the idiom of today. His "career is proof," as one of his admirers has said, "that contemporary audiences are not at war with contemporary music."

When Dixon returned to America in 1970, after twenty-one years abroad, seventy-five thousand people turned out to hear him conduct the New York Philharmonic at a concert in Central Park. Other concerts followed, including one at Lincoln Center and a televised Young People's Concert of the New York Philharmonic. But the triumph of that first concert was sweetest. The program that night in Central Park concluded with Brahms' Second Symphony. When the last note had sounded, seventy-five thousand people rose as one to give a standing ovation to the black man from New York who had established a worldwide reputation as a conductor. Dean Dixon had come home.

CHARLIE PARKER

"Bird," they called him. The name is invoked now with awe, as if to describe a phenomenon, a new species of being. In fact, Charlie Parker was a legend in his own lifetime. And after his death, in 1955, graffiti began to appear around the spots that he had haunted in Harlem and Greenwich Village, announcing, "Bird Lives." While he was actually alive, Birdland, the big jazz palace of the fifties on Broadway in New York, was named for him, a fact that points up the impact of his music and suggests the strangeness of his life. For "birdland," like Cloud Cuckoo-Land, suggests not a place for ordinary human beings but a special place, remote and inaccessible, whimsically unusual, verging on the absurd. Indeed, Charlie Parker's music was called "inhuman," "inaccessible," and "absurd" by a number of contemporary musicians and critics who failed to recognize what he was about. But those are judgments that have since been reversed as the true nature of Bird's genius has become evident.

Charlie Parker was no exotic creature of a season but a musician with roots in the music of the Southwest, centering in Kansas City, where he grew up. The downtown entertainment district, an area of clubs, bars, honky-tonks, and dance halls that came to rival New Orleans as one of the great formative centers where jazz was made, was Charlie Parker's training ground. His school and his college were places with names like

Charlie Parker

the College Inn, the Reno, the Sunset, the Cherry Blossom, and Lucille's Bandbox. And his teachers were the great Kansas City jazzmen, particularly those who played the horn and made K.C. the center of saxophone country: Prof. Smith, Budd Johnson, Jimmy Keith, Eddie Barefield, Tommy Douglas, and at the top of the pyramid, Herschel Evans, Ben Webster, and the incomparable Lester Young.

The inspiring force behind the musical revolution of the forties, Charlie Parker was, like most revolutionary leaders, thoroughly schooled in the tradition he overthrew. Moreover, like all true leaders, he was an enormously fertile source of ideas that would be exploited by others after he passed from the scene. But it was Bird who turned American popular music around, shifting its melodic base, while helping to found a movement—bop—and establishing the saxophone as the dominant instrument of jazz for generations to come. It was he who revealed the potential of its great range and flexibility.

Bird was born on August 29, 1920, across the Kaw River from Kansas City, Missouri, in suburban Kansas City, Kansas. He was named after his father, a traveling song-and-dance man from Memphis, Tennessee, who had worked the vaudeville circuits as an entertainer. Stranded in Kansas City, a turn-around point for a number of vaudeville routes, Charles, Sr., had met and married a seventeen-year-old local girl by the name of Addie Boyley. Vaudeville was on its last legs in those days. It would be further crippled and finally killed during the 1920s by increasing competition from radio and the newly invented sound motion picture. There were occasional tours for Charlie's father, mostly with small traveling circuses playing the dusty prairie towns of the Midwest. At home, he played the piano or listened to the phonograph: Louis Armstrong, Ma Rainey, Bessie Smith, and Duke Ellington. Thus from his earliest years Charlie was immersed in black music.

When Charlie was eight or nine years old, the family moved across the Kaw into Kansas City proper, renting a house at

1516 Olive Street, in the heart of the black ghetto, close to K.C.'s entertainment district. The purpose of the move was to put Charlie's father in closer touch with the entertainment world, for Kansas City was a regional booking center for touring companies. Although the move was to have far-reaching consequences for Charlie, Jr., it didn't help his father's career. He was soon forced to abandon the vaudeville stage for work as a railroad Pullman chef. Frequently away from home for long periods of time, he saw less and less of his wife and son. Finally, around 1931, he left them altogether, drifting out of their lives.

With the disappearance of her husband, Addie Parker became "mother, father, everything to Charles." And Charlie became "Mama's little man," doted upon and pampered by his hardworking mother, who earned a living as a domestic. Reflecting on her son's early years, in an interview in *Jazz Review* in 1960, Addie recalled, "He never worked like the other little boys in the neighborhood. He wanted to carry the papers, but I wouldn't let him. I thought I could take care of him until he was a man." In fact, while he was but a schoolboy in the Crispus Attucks Grammar School, where his quick mind and good memory made him a first-rate student, his mother nourished dreams of him as a doctor and managed to put by a little money from her paycheck each week for his later education.

However, Lincoln High School, which Charlie entered at thirteen, was ill-staffed and overcrowded. Like all too many ghetto schools, it simply kept its students marking time. At first, Charlie complained, "They don't teach you anything there, Mama. The teachers are no good." Then, neither stimulated nor challenged, he simply marked time—without advancing a single grade.

The one exception to the sense of apathy and hopelessness was the music department. Run by Alonzo Lewis, a professional musician, it provided competent training for its students.

Moreover, the students knew that job possibilities lay open to blacks in music as in no other field.

Naturally enough, Charlie Parker tried out for the band and made it. His instrument was the tuba. "All I did was play *coop, coop—coop, coop,*" Charlie was later to say. It was not a very satisfying musical experience. "He was given a tuba to play," his mother was later to comment. "I didn't go for that; it was so heavy and funny coiled around him with just his head sticking out. So I got him another instrument."

The savings for Charlie's medical education—$45—went for the instrument, one not especially appropriate for the school's marching band. But by this time Charlie had become interested in the Deans of Swing, a dance band organized by his fellow students. Charlie's instrument was the saxophone. Tootie Clarkin, who operated a nightclub where Charlie later worked, described the horn as "an old sax, made in Paris in 1898, that was like nothing." Festooned with rubber bands which held the broken parts in place and patched here, there, and everywhere with glistening bits of cellophane tape to cover holes and split seams, Charlie's horn was a musical joke. The valves were always sticking. The pads didn't fit and leaked air. He had to hold it sideways to make it blow. But Charlie blew it. And since it came without a case, his mother made one for it from blue-and-white striped pillow ticking.

Kansas City was a sprawling, vigorous, rapidly growing city in those days, raucous, lively, and uninhibited. A great wheat and cattle market, it was the commercial center for an area stretching from Houston, Texas, to Denver, Colorado. By day its streets teemed with cowboys and cattle barons, grain dealers and farm machinery salesmen, draymen, railroad men, wheat ranchers and farmhands, buying, selling, hiring and trading, contracting for workers, produce, hides, grain, and other goods and services. At night other commodities were sought—liquor, women, food, drugs, entertainment. All were available in the neon-lit bars and cabarets, the flashy brothels and smoky gambling halls of K.C., provided by a crime syndicate operating under the protection of Mayor Tom Pendergast and his corrupt political machine. Between the political coup that put him in power in 1928 and his conviction on tax fraud charges in 1939, Boss Pendergast ran a wide-open city. Prostitution flourished. The Volstead Act, which put teeth into Prohibition, was unenforced in K.C., where bootleg liquor ran in streams. The city was the center of the illicit drug trade throughout the Southwest. And such gangsters as Johnny Lazia, "the Al Capone of Kansas City," Pretty Boy Floyd, Adam Ricketti, and Frank Nash, who was killed in the Union Station Massacre of 1933, roamed the streets freely, fearing not the police but one another.

Musicians also thrived. The pay was not high, but the work was steady. The conventions of polite society, with its expectations of decorum, pallid good taste, and pleasant prettiness, were totally lacking. And innovation was at a premium in the bars and cabarets where bands blew all night and often well into the morning for the "dancing pleasure" of hard-drinking, coarse-grained but lively and responsive customers. The musicians were mostly black, and the blues and the jazz that grew out of it were based on age-old rhythmic patterns going back to the African homeland.

Jazz flourished in Kansas City, where it took on vital regional hallmarks. One of these was the riff, a relatively short musical phrase repeated over a pattern of changing chords based on the blues. The resulting clash gave a satisfyingly rough texture to the music, a feeling of imbalance, change and incompletion, requiring more. More came, pell-mell, as other instrumentalists took the riff skittering over tumbling chords at an "up" tempo, fast and loud. Audiences roared their approval. They roared their approval, too, for the prolonged and intricate solos of the outstanding instrumentalists, who would try to outdo one another in complex thematic invention and execution, particularly in informal after-hours jam sessions.

Charlie studied the great soloists. As a matter of fact, he studied the whole musical scene very carefully, wandering about the district by night while his mother worked. Since, at fourteen, he was big for his age, he managed, without too much difficulty, to get into the late night spots where the really hot playing didn't start until midnight. A long black slicker and a slouch hat helped disguise his youthful appearance.

He learned a great deal about music during his rambles, but his technique was inadequate to perform the complex playing he hoped to do when he got his first chance to jam. That chance came one night at an obscure little club called the High Hat. Lawrence Keyes and James Ross—who had graduated from Lincoln High and the Deans of Swing and were working at the club—invited him to the bandstand. And it was a disaster. Believing that everything was played in one key, Charlie tried a difficult improvisation in a chorus from "Body and Soul" at double time and the whole thing came apart. He was laughed off the bandstand. Afterward his friends let him in on the secret. There was no single, universal key. Rather, there were a dozen major ones, each following the other, half a tone apart, up the piano keyboard. They neglected to point out that of the twelve scales based on those keys only about three or four were regularly used in jazz. So Charlie went home and began to memorize all twelve scales, "woodshedding," or practicing industriously, on each of them until he had them note perfect. Much of the work was, of course, unnecessary for all practical purposes. But Charlie didn't know that—happily, as it turned out. For the mastery he acquired gave him a range and flexibility that few working musicians had and was to provide the basis for his amazing versatility as a soloist.

Lincoln High had done little for Charlie. At fourteen he dropped out and joined Local 627 of the American Federation of Musicians. Then he acquired, in rapid order, a job, a wife, and a son. The union card, admitting him to the status of professional and allowing him to work at his music for pay, was a necessity. In order to get it he had to advance his age by four years to meet the minimum age requirement of eighteen. The job he found was nothing much, paying only $1.25 a night, but he was playing his horn. The wife was Rebecca Ruffing, a high school girlfriend who, shortly after Charlie and she settled in with Addie at 1516 Olive Street, brought her mother, brothers, and sisters to join them. Charlie's son, Leon, was born in 1936. But already, with a mother, a mother-in-law, a wife who had little if any interest in his musical career, and a second, ready-made family in residence, Charlie was bored with family life. He was soon spending most of his time with his musician friends. Two years after the birth of their son, Rebecca and Charlie were divorced.

In the fall of 1936 Charlie was in an automobile accident. He escaped without serious injury but was awarded several hundred dollars as part of the insurance settlement. More money than he had ever had at one time in his life, the settlement enabled him to get rid of his old $45 horn and buy a brand-new "ax," a Selmer E-flat alto saxophone. That was a big step forward in his musical career. Then he went to work with the Tommy Douglas orchestra. Douglas, who had studied at the Boston Conservatory and was thought the best-trained musician in the Southwest, tutored Charlie, who also studied musical theory with Carrie Powell and Efferge Ware. With the aid of Prof. Smith, an old pro on the alto sax, Charlie worked on his technique. Perhaps an even more important source of Charlie's musical development was his collection of Lester Young records, which he carried around with him and played on his portable phonograph, wearing the grooves down to powder as he absorbed "The President's" style.

Musical jobs were not so easy to come by in New York, where Charlie drifted next, as in K.C., and for a while he scoured pots at Jimmy's Chicken Shack in lower Harlem. He hated the job, but something good came of it. For Art Tatum, the greatest of jazz pianists, was playing at the Chicken Shack, and Charlie studied his playing intensely, absorbing the flood of musical ideas that came from the fingers of this great innovator and master harmonist. From Tatum Charlie picked up a way of working little quotations from popular tunes into changes that he played on a melody. Tatum's uncanny speed, accuracy of touch, and complex, controlled rhythmic patterns gave Charlie goals to strive for on the saxophone. For he felt that if Tatum's dazzling speed and rhythmic patterns could be reproduced on the more versatile horn, where a column of air could be shaped and bent with a subtlety that the piano was incapable of, something could indeed be achieved that had not been done before. Charlie would in fact reach that difficult goal, but not at once.

When he was nineteen he joined the great Jay McShann Orchestra, traveling widely throughout the country. The band's first recording session took place in Dallas on April 30, 1941, where they made six sides for Decca, including "Hootie Blues," with an inspired solo by Charlie that broke new musical ground and helped to establish Parker's fame as one of the great new talents in jazz.

When the McShann Orchestra headed back to Kansas, Charlie remained behind in New York. Without a regular job, he frequently sat in at Monroe's Uptown House and at Minton's Playhouse, cabarets in Harlem, working with such musicians as Dizzy Gillespie and Thelonius Monk, Young Turks of jazz who were creating an intense, discordant music that would soon be called bop.

Married again, briefly, to Geraldine Scott, and broke, Charlie pawned his horn. Then he teamed up with Earl "Fatha" Hines, who gave him a tenor sax and featured him, along with Dizzy Gillespie and Sarah Vaughan, in his big band. Later, together with Dizzy and Miss Vaughan, Charlie toured with another big band formed by singer Billy Eckstein.

But the small, flexible jazz combo was replacing the big band as the vehicle of popular music of the forties. On The

Street, a string of clubs and bars on 52nd Street in New York, musical history was being made. So Charlie settled in at The Three Deuces with a quintet consisting of himself on alto, Dizzy Gillespie playing trumpet, Stan Levy on drums, Curly Russell on bass, and Al Haig at the piano. There, where the soloist became composer, improvising elaborate off-beat harmonic structures with blues overtones running against strong counter-rhythms, the bop revolution was accomplished. Often stridently atonal, the result was neither hot, as in early jazz, nor mellow, like the music of the great swing bands, but cool—knowing, technically brilliant, self-contained, satirical in its complex use of earlier musical material. The numbers were "Round About Midnight," "Epistrophy," "Scrapple from the Apple," and "Swingmatism," among others. Somewhat later came Bird's own "Ornithology," "Yardbird Suite," and "Moose the Mooche."

Drugs were becoming an increasingly serious problem for Charlie Parker, who had been experimenting with them since his adolescent days in K.C. They almost destroyed him on a West Coast trip that started in December 1945 and ended in Camarillo State Hospital, a mental institution in California to which he was consigned for six months. Released, he turned to alcohol, for which he had an enormous capacity, and then back to drugs as well. Later there was to be a suicide attempt, followed by voluntary commitment to Bellevue Hospital in New York. Diagnosis: acute alcoholism and undifferentiated schizophrenia. Released and back on the street, Charlie missed dates and played badly. There were ulcer attacks. His "cabaret card," a license to perform issued by the New York State Liquor Authority, was lifted because of narcotics addiction. He suffered from cirrhosis of the liver. Finally, in 1955, when he should have been at the peak of his powers, he died, worn out by his excesses, his body overwhelmed by drugs and alcohol. The coroner estimated his age at fifty-three. He was actually thirty-four years old.

California was the beginning of the end for Charlie Parker. In fact, a prizewinning short story by Elliot Grennard, based on Bird's destructive experience there, is called "Sparrow's Last Jump." There were, however, a good many more jumps in Bird before the end. There were, for example, two more wives: Doris Syndor and Chan Richardson. There were several musical tours, including three European ones. There were new groups to play with, including, happily, a revived quintet with Max Roach, the incomparable drummer, and young Miles Davis, on trumpet, and, less happily, Charlie Parker with strings. There were, of course, records, on which "Klactoveesedstene," "Chasing the Bird," "Parker's Mood," "Relaxin' at Camarillo," and other Parker originals were saved for posterity. There was, in the last nine years of his life, a flood of music that was to help form a generation of great horn players—John Coltrane, Ornette Coleman, Eric Dolphy, Sonny Rollins, Archie Shepp— and to change the shape of jazz. The events leading up to Camarillo did not in fact constitute "Sparrow's Last Jump." But following that time, one could say, in lines from the *Rubáiyát* that Charlie was fond of quoting:

> *The Bird of Time has but a little way*
> *To flutter—and the Bird is on the Wing.*

Happily, through his records, his influence upon other musicians, his transformation of jazz, one can still say, "Bird is on the Wing." Charlie Parker is dead. Bird lives.

Theater

The first minstrels in America were black slaves. Many plantations had groups of talented slaves who played music, told jokes, and rattled castanet-like bones made from the ribs of a sheep or some other small animal. These troupes of minstrels were the pride of their rich masters and were called on to entertain guests on special occasions.

Later, and still prior to the Civil War, white men blackened their faces and played black parts in their versions of minstrel troupes. Indeed, black performers were not allowed to act in these shows, and it was not until many years later that black people were permitted even to appear on a stage with a white performer.

The stereotype created by the white minstrels worked great harm to the black American because he was regularly portrayed as an irresponsible, jig-dancing, dialect-speaking buffoon. As the minstrels increased in popularity, this portrayal found greater currency. The harm done has not been offset to this day.

It was, however, in musical comedy, which grew out of these crude beginnings, that some of the greatest strides were made by the black man in the theater. Bert Williams was one of the foremost comedians on the American stage. With his partner, George Walker, he made history on Broadway. Together with two ladies, they resurrected the plantation dance favorite, the Cake Walk. They became the first of a long line of fine black dancers, among the greatest of whom was Bill "Bojangles" Robinson.

And what the ebullient "Bojangles" was to the lighter side of the dance, Katherine Dunham is to its more serious side. Whether considered as entertainment or as art, the dance has been graced with many outstanding black performers, including, in recent years, Pearl Primus, Alvin Ailey, and Judith Jamison.

The comic theatrical tradition dating back to Williams has, of course, been sustained in modern times by such humorists as Red Foxx, Bill Cosby, Flip Wilson, and Dick Gregory.

Nor has the more serious side of acting been neglected by black actors. Ira Aldridge, a black American who studied in London with the celebrated actor Edmund Kean and played before the royalty of Europe, was one of the great tragedians of his time. Before the Civil War started, he was famous for his performance of Shakespeare's *Othello*.

In modern times the black stock companies that formed and acted in the early years of the twentieth century in the Lincoln and Lafayette theaters in Harlem deserve notice as pioneers. Their work has been continued by Robert Hooks, who, as the director of the Negro Ensemble Company, has established a black repertory theater, staged the work of new black writers, and provided a continuing opportunity for black actors to develop and display their talents.

In recent years many fine black actors and actresses have won critical acclaim and popular support for the roles they have created. They include Charles Gilpin, James Earl Jones, Moses Gunn, Ossie Davis, Ruby Dee, Cicely Tyson, and, of course, Paul Robeson, to name but a few.

PAUL ROBESON

"Paul, you can sing." It was his brother Bill, interrupting an impromptu after-dinner songfest of three of the Robeson brothers, Paul, Ben, and himself. They had started with gusto on "Down by the Old Mill Stream." As Ben recounts the episode, in an interview published in Paul's book, *Here I Stand*, "Paul was bearing down . . . with boyish glee; in fact, all of us were. Out of all the discord, Bill yelled: 'Wait a minute, hit that note again, Paul.' Paul hit it out of the lot, and Bill said: 'Paul, you can sing.'"

The boys broke off for a sandlot baseball game, "the perfect end to every fair day," as Ben remembers. When darkness fell and the boys returned to the house to settle down for the night, Bill insisted that his young brother give them "Annie Laurie," by way of confirming his musical discovery. "Paul had to satisfy him to have any peace," Ben recalls. So Paul, sweaty from baseball but anxious to please his big brother, sang. "Bill listened as he warbled, and concluded: 'Paul, you *can* sing.'"

Indeed, he could sing. And Bill's discovery of that fact was the beginning of a career that led Paul Robeson around the world, singing the songs of his people in concert halls and theaters, in drawing rooms and public squares to kings and princes, before great statesmen and artists, and, more importantly, to the common men of all countries.

Actually, the real beginnings of Paul Robeson's career were

Paul Robeson

buried even further in the past. For the deep resonance of his voice was his heritage from his father, born on a slave owner's plantation in Martin County, North Carolina, some sixteen years before the start of the Civil War.

Paul's father, William, had known slavery but had not borne it readily. At the age of fifteen, he had escaped north on the Underground Railroad, returning twice thereafter, dangerously, to visit his mother, Sabra, before she died. Free, he had worked his way through Lincoln University in Pennsylvania. In 1876, shortly after graduating, he married Maria Louisa Bustil, a Philadelphia schoolteacher whose great-grandfather Cyrus had baked bread for George Washington's troops during the Revolutionary War. The couple settled in Princeton, New Jersey, where William became pastor of the Witherspoon Street Presbyterian Church, a position he held for more than twenty years.

Paul was born in Princeton, on April 9, 1898, the youngest of the Robeson children. There were four others living at the time of his birth: William D., Jr., age seventeen; Reeve, who was called Reed in the family, twelve; Benjamin, six; and Marian, his only sister, who was four. Shortly after Paul's birth, his father was ousted as pastor of the Witherspoon Street Church in a factional dispute among members of the congregation. A gentle, scholarly man, who had served the church well and was already middle-aged with a good-sized family to support, the Reverend Robeson took his displacement without bitterness. He bought a horse and wagon and began to earn his living hauling ashes for the townsfolk. Paul's earliest memories are of the growing pile of ashes in the backyard at 13 Green Street and of the mare named Bess, whom he loved.

Later, with growing children to educate, the Reverend Robeson added hack-driving to his work, taking students from the university around town or on trips to the nearby seashore. Thus William, Jr., went off to Lincoln University, his father's school, to begin the long preparation that would make him a physician. Benjamin went to Biddle University in North Carolina, where he played football and trained for the ministry. And Marian left for Scotia Seminary, also in North Carolina, where she studied to become a teacher. At first Reed remained at home, driving a cab like his father. But his independent spirit brought him into frequent conflict with his often arrogant customers in a Princeton that had close ties with the South and treated black people with disdain. After several brushes with the law for putting disrespectful riders in their place—flat on their backs in the public road—Reed, too, left home.

However, before most of the children were ready for college, an accident occurred that left the family desolate. Paul was six at the time. His mother, who was ill and whose eyesight was failing, was in the house alone. No one is certain of what happened. Perhaps, with her poor vision, Maria Louisa brushed too close to the stove or stumbled into it as she passed through the kitchen. Suddenly there was a burst of bright flame and acrid smoke engulfing her. When Paul's father returned, he found her barely conscious. She died in his arms.

The house was lonely indeed after that. But in their loneliness and sorrow Paul and his aging father drew close together. They would sit for hours together bent over the checkerboard in the parlor, engrossed in their game, hardly speaking but united in spirit. Or they would take turns reading aloud or reciting from memory, his father's well-trained, resonant preacher's voice providing a model for young Paul to follow.

At the age of sixty-two, encouraged by friends, Paul's father returned to preaching, moving to Westfield, New Jersey, with Paul, and later to Somerville, New Jersey, where he became pastor of the Downing Street African Methodist Episcopal Zion Church, a post he held until his death in 1918 at the age of seventy-three.

Paul attended Somerville High School, where he sang in the Glee Club under the skillful direction of Miss Vosseller, the music teacher, who took particular interest in Paul and helped in the training of his voice. He also played football and other sports, wrote for the school magazine, the *Valkyrie*, and, with the instruction and advice of his English teacher, Miss Anna Miller, became a skillful debater and a pretty good actor. As a matter of fact, it was Miss Miller who first selected Paul for a part that was later to bring him fame on Broadway and throughout the world—Othello, which he did in his senior year at Somerville when the class presented excerpts from several of Shakespeare's plays.

The Reverend Robeson had kept a close eye on Paul's studies during his high school years, reading Virgil and Homer with him and admonishing him not to be content with a mark of 95 when 100 was possible. Knowing Paul's ability, he urged him, in the spring of 1915, to take a statewide scholarship examination for Rutgers College, then a small private college on the banks of the Raritan River in New Brunswick. His father's confidence had not been misplaced. Paul won a four-year scholarship to Rutgers College, where his achievements both in scholarship and athletics were outstanding.

On the athletic field Paul won letters in track, basketball, baseball, and football. He was star catcher on the Rutgers baseball team in the spring and defensive quarterback on the gridiron in the fall. Football was really his game, however, and he led the Rutgers eleven to a string of victories, winning national fame as "Robeson of Rutgers" and nomination to the All American Football Team. In fact, his father, who enjoyed coming from nearby Somerville on Saturday afternoons to watch Paul play ball, felt compelled to remind his son that he had come to college "to study, not to play." But the reminder was unnecessary, for despite a busy athletic schedule, Paul mastered his studies easily, winning election to Phi Beta Kappa, the academic honor society, in his junior year. At commencement, in 1919, he was named to Cap and Skull, Rutgers' highest scholastic honor.

In those days, when professional football was still a sport rather than the industry it has since become, it was possible to combine football with other career activities. That is exactly what Paul Robeson did after graduating from Rutgers, playing with the Akron Indians and later with the Milwaukee Badgers of the National Football League on weekends and attending Columbia Law School during the week. While he was at Columbia, he met Essie Goode, who was completing a degree in chemistry at Teachers College and working as a pathologist at Columbia Presbyterian Hospital. They were married in August 1921.

But Essie had other interests besides chemistry and medicine. For one thing, she liked the theater, and she soon reignited Paul's interest, more or less dormant since high school days. Soon he was taking small parts in amateur Harlem productions. Then one day in Greenwich Village in the early spring of 1924, Paul met Eugene O'Neill, the brooding genius whose plays were revitalizing the American theater. A dedicated group of theater people had given O'Neill's plays life on a wharf in Provincetown, Massachusetts, and now, in a converted stable on MacDougal Street in Greenwich Village, the Provincetown Players were making dramatic history, challenging the dominance of Broadway with its prejudices and commercialism. Already, Charles Gilpin, a black actor starring in *The Emperor Jones*, had had a notable triumph. Now Paul Robeson was prevailed upon to duplicate Gilpin's role as the tragic black emperor and also to take the role of Jim Harris, the anguished young lawyer in a new play by O'Neill, *All God's Chillun Got Wings*.

The results were profoundly stirring. Writing of Paul's work in a review in *The American Mercury*, George Jean Nathan, the critic, said: "Robeson, with relatively little experience and with no training to speak of, is one of the most thoroughly eloquent, impressive, and convincing actors that I have looked at and listened to in almost twenty years of professional theatre-going." His comments were typical. A major event had occurred in the American theater. There could be no turning back now to a career in law. Urging Paul to join the Provincetown Players, O'Neill had said, "You'll have a universal language all men will understand."

Shortly thereafter Paul went to London to take part in a British production of *The Emperor Jones.* Before going abroad, however, he sang in a recital in Greenwich Village organized by the Provincetown Players. Accompanied by Lawrence Brown at the piano, Paul sang spirituals to a sold-out house that wouldn't stop applauding when he finished the program and demanded so many encores that he exhausted his repertory. Upon his return from London, he decided to undertake a concert tour, starting at Town Hall in New York on January 5, 1926, and taking in Philadelphia, Baltimore, Chicago, and Boston.

The following year he was asked to return to London to do a play called *Taboo* with the outstanding English actress Mrs. Pat Campbell. This time Essie could not accompany Paul abroad as she had done before. She was expecting a baby. So Paul sailed for London by himself. And Paul, Jr., was born on November 2, 1927, while his father was being acclaimed in London.

In 1928, however, the whole family returned to London. They took a large house in Hampstead, a London suburb, converting the top floor into a nursery for little Pauli. And Paul, Sr., took the role of Joe in Oscar Hammerstein's *Show Boat*, with music by Jerome Kern. The role was a small one, too small, in fact, for an actor of Paul's stature, and for this reason the producers had hesitated to offer it to him. But Jerome Kern wanted Robeson, so Paul took the part. And "Ol' Man River," which he sang in the show, became the hit of London. Ever since the song has been Robeson's "Ol' Man River" as much as Kern's.

Fully in command of his great voice now, Paul gave Sunday

evening concerts of spirituals, accompanied by his friend and fellow artist Larry Brown at the piano. When *Show Boat* ended its successful run, Paul returned to America for a triumphal concert tour, followed by a tour of central Europe, with engagements in Paris, Cologne, Düsseldorf, Dresden, Prague, Warsaw, Bucharest, Budapest, and Vienna.

Other triumphs followed, including an appearance in the great Max Reinhardt's production of *The Emperor Jones* in Berlin in 1930. That same year a concert tour took him to Ireland, where he sang in Dublin and Belfast. But the greatest triumph of all, he felt, would be to appear in London—the city of Shakespeare's great triumphs—in one of Shakespeare's greatest plays: *Othello.* And that, too, came to pass. The production was Maurice Browne's, at the Savoy Theatre, with Peggy Ashcroft as Desdemona, Sybil Thorndike as Emilia, and Browne himself playing Iago. Commenting on Robeson's performance following opening night, on May 19, 1930, the *London Morning Post* pronounced it "noble" and said, "There has been no Othello on our stage, certainly for forty years, to compare with his dignity, simplicity, and true passion. . . ."

There was yet another career for Paul Robeson in motion pictures, with starring roles in the film version of *The Emperor Jones*, in *The Song of Freedom*, and *King Solomon's Mines*, among other films. There was a revival of *Show Boat* in New York. There was more O'Neill, including a superb London production of *The Hairy Ape*, with Paul as Yank. There were concert tours, with Paul expanding his repertory to include many songs of the ordinary people of the lands he visited— French, Russian, African, and Scandinavian work songs, sea chanteys, love songs, soldiers' marching songs.

Having found "the universal language all men will understand" to be song, Paul Robeson turned from the concert halls and the fancy West End theaters of the rich to the music halls and the trade union halls of the workers in the slums of

London, Liverpool, Glasgow, Birmingham, and Manchester, bringing joy and beauty to the downtrodden and oppressed. As his social awareness grew, Paul's sympathies broadened. He joined the Unity Theatre of the Labor and Trade Union Movement and gave free performances in St. Pancras, a poor section of London. At the suggestion of his friend the Dean of Canterbury, he visited Russia and was enthralled by the apparent success of the country's gigantic economic and social experiment.

In the summer of 1939 Paul Robeson returned to America. He had been away, except for brief visits, for ten years. But he was welcomed back with applause, even when the play he was in was *John Henry*, a not-very-good musical that he did in New York. He was offered a motion-picture contract. There were radio broadcasts and recordings. On one occasion Paul sang "Ballad for Americans" over the Columbia Broadcasting System, and congratulatory telephone calls tied up the switchboard for more than an hour.

More important than any of this, however, was Robeson's appearance in the American Theatre Guild production of *Othello*. Thirteen years had elapsed since he had played the part of the noble Moor. At forty-five, he was mature and fully experienced for the demanding role, and he gave it everything he had, creating an Othello of brooding power and great dignity. It was the high point of his career and a high-water mark in the American theater. Opening on October 19, 1943, the play ran until July 1, 1944, packing the Shubert Theatre for 296 consecutive performances, a record run for Shakespeare in New York.

The years following World War II were years of tribulation for Paul Robeson. His beliefs in human equality, his sympathetic feelings for the people of the Soviet Union, his outspoken criticism of colonialism, war, and racism, brought down upon his head the wrath of the U.S. House of Representatives'

Committee on Un-American Activities, which was investigating political subversion. These were trying times in America, and Paul Robeson, like many Americans with strong convictions and the courage to speak out for them, was penalized for his unwillingness to remain silent. Having publicly criticized the American government for its treatment of black people, Robeson was haled before the House committee and questioned on his political affiliations. It was alleged that he was part of an international conspiracy to overthrow the government. Although he was neither tried for nor convicted of any crime, his passport was revoked, preventing him from giving concerts or acting abroad. At home he was blacklisted and thus denied employment.

In 1958 Robeson published *Here I Stand*, a book outlining his position as an American and a citizen of the world and correcting the distortions that had been spread concerning his political affiliations. Finally, in July 1958 Robeson's passport was returned, and he resumed his stage and concert career abroad at the age of sixty, after eight long years of enforced inactivity. But in 1961 in London he was stricken with a circulatory illness that was to force his retirement from public life.

In 1963 Paul Robeson returned to America again, settling in Harlem with his wife, Essie, who had had a distinguished career as an anthropologist and writer, having published *Paul Robeson, Negro* (1930), a biography of her famous husband, and *African Journey* (1945), a journal of an anthropological trip to Africa.

In 1965 Essie died. Alone and ill, Paul Robeson lived on, seemingly forgotten by his countrymen to whom he had once given so much joy. But he had not been forgotten. In 1973, on the occasion of his seventy-fifth birthday, he was feted at a tribute in Carnegie Hall, attended by a host of well-wishers. Living in Philadelphia now, in impaired health, Paul was too ill to attend the celebration. But a recording of his mighty voice filled the auditorium, to the delight of the audience, who were happy to know that

> *Ol' Man River . . .*
> *He keeps on rollin' along.*

KATHERINE DUNHAM

For three days and nights she lay on the dirt floor of a back-country compound, crowded in with eight other initiates, sweating in the tropical heat, her bones aching, her hair a tangled mass of cornmeal, eggs, feathers, and herbs. Finally, blinking in the bright sunshine and hungry from fasting, the group was herded out of the compound for a feast of celebration, preceded by a wild dance in which a young dancer, possessed by the serpent god Damballa, bit into the neck of a live chicken and drank its blood.

This was Katherine Dunham's initiation into the rites of voodoo, which she had come to Haiti to study. It was a long way from Glen Ellyn, Illinois, where she had been born on June 22, 1909. And life was very different in Haiti from the restricted life in the apartment over her father's cleaning establishment in Joliet, forty miles from Chicago, where she had grown up. There she had been a drudge, helping her stepmother care for the apartment or tagging clothes in her father's shop, a hostage, like the other members of the family, to her father's driving ambition to make the shop a financial success.

It had not always been thus. Katherine remembered freer times, when she sat on her father's knee to hear stories, rode in the family carriage to Sunday afternoon picnics, and listened from her crib in the evenings to her parents making music in the next room. Mostly she remembered the music: her mother,

John Launois/Black Star

Katherine Dunham

Fanny, with her pale, fair face and dark hair piled high, seated at the parlor organ or bending close to her harp, weaving sweet sounds from its strings, her husband accompanying her on the guitar. But the music had not lasted. Katherine's mother, who was much older than Albert Dunham, her second husband, had died before Katherine was three. Albert, brokenhearted, had left his work as a tailor and gone on the road as a traveling salesman, leaving Katherine and Albert, Jr., who was four years older than she, in charge of his sister Lulu, a Chicago beautician.

Her brother was in school by this time, but Katherine spent long listless hours in the back room of the downtown beauty parlor where her aunt gave shampoos and manicures while Katherine stuffed herself with day-old pastry and tried to play quiet games that wouldn't disturb the patrons. At night she would doze on the long train ride back to the single room in the South Side tenement district where her aunt lived and where, after a hasty meal of hot tamales from the street vendor, Katherine and her brother and her aunt would all pile into the room's one bed for the night.

Later, when Aunt Lulu lost her beauty parlor lease and started going to customers' homes to set hair, Katherine had her first taste of the theater. A stage-struck second cousin, with whom she stayed during the day, often took her to the old Grand or to the Monogram Theater on State Street. There she heard Bessie Smith, Ida Cox, Ethel Waters, and other singers and comedy teams like Cole and Johnson and Buck and Bubbles. To be sure, the acquaintance was made at the cost of an empty stomach and chilblains, for the cousin in question pinched the money for the theater tickets from the amount Aunt Lulu left for lunches and for fuel to heat the room.

Then one day while Aunt Lulu was out working, Fanny June Weir, one of the haughty, light-skinned daughters of their mother's first marriage, swept into the room where Katherine and Albert were sniffling with colds, huddled under blankets, alone before a dying coal stove fire. She brought them home to her own family's comfortable apartment. Fanny June's intentions were good, and the removal was later supported by a court order giving her responsibility for the children. But Katherine and Albert were unhappy. They loved Aunt Lulu, and they couldn't get used to the Weir family's gibes about the impoverished Dunhams or to their snobbery about their own light skin color.

Katherine was five years old, her brother nine, when they were returned to their father's custody. He had married Annette Poindexter, a former schoolteacher from Iowa, and had saved up enough money to buy a dry-cleaning shop in Joliet, Illinois. Annette, a small, slim brown woman, was kind to them, treating them as if they were her own children. But their father had changed. Preoccupied with enlarging his business, with getting ahead, he had no time for fun, stories, music. Nor would he allow the time to his family. They all worked at the shop, his wife at the sewing machine, making repairs and alterations; Katherine sorting and tagging clothes for cleaning; Albert making deliveries and tending to the horse.

Albert suffered most. The older of the two children, he was expected to work harder. Moreover, he was a brilliant student, and he required time for reading and study, time that his father resented giving him, feeling that he should be content to work in the shop, learning the business with a view to following in his father's footsteps. However, Albert detested the shop, and he soon came to hate his father, a feeling that Katherine shared as her brother's punishments increased.

Worse than the punishment, however, was one of his duties. It involved servicing the dust wheel, a huge contraption his father installed above the shop, with an eye to expanding his business. Bought secondhand to beat the dust out of carpets, the machine frequently broke down. Then his father propped the jaws of the monster device open with a plank, called Albert, and sent him into the bowels of the machine, in thick blackness and dust, to splice a broken strap, repair a gear, or do whatever was necessary to set the giant carpet thumper in motion again. Albert was terrified of the machine. So were his stepmother and sister. They all hated the constant din and the dust that filtered through the apartment when it was in motion. But when the noise stopped, their hearts stopped, too, resuming only when Albert, red-eyed, trembling, and choked with dust, returned with his mission accomplished.

Escaping from the dust and din, the anger and the fear of her home, Katherine frequently climbed the steep hill behind the shop to visit Mrs. Jameson, an old woman who lived in a crumbling mansion atop the cliff. Surrounded by costumes, old pictures, newspaper clippings, fans, jewelry, and other mementos of the past, the old lady would give Katherine tea and talk to her about her early life on the stage. Back in her own room, Katherine dreamed of a career in the theater.

A measure of prosperity came to the family, but it brought small joy with it. The shop delivery wagon was replaced by a truck—in fact, a whole series of trucks, for Mr. Dunham was always making "deals" in secondhand vans, which generally broke down. In addition, the family acquired a touring car, and there were vacation trips to St. Louis, Missouri, and to Delavan, Wisconsin, where Annette had relatives. But Albert Dunham was too busy with his shop to go along. Katherine had dancing and piano lessons, but her practice of the instrument was so rigidly supervised by her father, who beat with a stick on the ceiling of the shop to remind her to practice her scales, that the piano became a trial.

Finally, things came to a climax. Albert, who had been awarded a scholarship at the University of Chicago, left the house in a rage after a battle with his father, promising never to come back. Soon thereafter Annette left, too, taking her stepdaughter with her. Katherine and her stepmother found an apartment in another part of town. Both continued to work in the shop, and after a time Annette invited her husband to their place for visits and an occasional meal. But family life, as Katherine had known it in the apartment over the dry-cleaning establishment, was at an end.

Freed from her father's close supervision, Katherine joined the Terpsichorean Club, named after the Greek muse of the dance, in high school. She also played center on the girls' basketball team and was elected president of the Girls' Athletic Association. Upon graduating, she enrolled in the junior college at Joliet.

After completing junior college, Katherine went to Chicago, where she got a part-time job working in a library near Hamilton Park, and enrolled at the university. Rooming with Frances Taylor, a friend of her brother's and later his wife, she quickly became one of his circle of friends, attending discussions at the Dill Pickle Club and becoming a member of the Cube Theater, which Albert had helped found. It was on the stage of the Cube Theater that Katherine played her first acting role, in a dramatization of F. Scott Fitzgerald's *The Man Who Died at Twelve O'clock*.

But Katherine's main interest was the dance. She took ballet lessons from Ludmila Speranzeva, a White Russian dancer who had come to America with the Chauve Souris Company, which stressed the story line and acting in the dance, elements that would become important in Katherine's work, too. Before long, with the aid of two other dancers, Ruth Page and Mark Turbyfill, Katherine had established her own school, emphasizing African-inspired dances, and developed a dance group named Ballet Nègre—it was later renamed the Negro Dance Group—which gave its first major public performance, *Negro Rhapsody*, at the Chicago Beaux Arts Ball in 1931.

About this time Katherine married a fellow dancer named Jordis McCoo. It was the period of the great depression, however, and Jordis had to take a night job at the post office, leaving him small time for dancing—or for Katherine. Katherine's dancers, too, though they won applause, attracted few new recruits in these hard times. Happily, her work at the university went well. There, in Dr. Robert Redfield's ethnology class, she studied various social and ethnic groups—their origins, distribution, and cultures—and she began to see how dance could reveal to people of African descent something of the strength and beauty of their culture. Moreover, she had her first big success as a dancer, at the Chicago Opera House, in the lead role of *La Guiablesse*, a ballet based on Martinique folklore composed by her friend Ruth Page to music by William Grant Still.

Now things began to come together for Katherine. In 1933 she was chosen to select and train one hundred and fifty young black people for a dance program at the upcoming Chicago Century of Progress Exposition. In 1935 she was granted a $2,400 Julius Rosenwald Foundation travel fellowship to visit the Caribbean for a year in order to study West Indian dances.

Katherine Dunham was twenty-five years old when she left for the West Indies to investigate the survival and transformation of African dances in the Caribbean. The first leg of her journey took her to Accompong, a remote hill village in the mountainous northeastern portion of Jamaica, where she lived for several months with the Maroons, descendants of the warlike Koromantee tribe from the West Coast of Africa. Later Miss Dunham would write a book, *Journey to Accompong*, published in 1946, about her life in this community where, isolated from the white man's civilization, many African folkways had been preserved.

Miss Dunham visited Martinique next, where she saw the fighting dance called "Ag' Ya," which she afterward incorporated into a folk ballet, *L'Ag' Ya*, presented for the first time at Chicago's Great Northern Theater on January 27, 1938.

Trinidad was the next stop on her anthropological journey of discovery, and there the journey almost ended when a knife-wielding Shango priest heard the whirr of her motion-picture camera as she tried to film a secret religious ceremony. A native friend's intercession saved her from harm, but she decided to forgo the use of the camera thereafter.

Haiti was the island on which Miss Dunham made her longest stay and probed most deeply into the life and culture of the people, whom she got to know well, defying caste and class barriers to penetrate into every level of society, from the highest official to the poorest peasant. Her study of Vaudin, the voodoo religious practice, which she describes in her book *Island Possessed* (1969), involved her own initiation into the cult. In fact, so deep was her attachment to the country that she later bought a home there, to which she returned periodically from her world travels.

Katherine Dunham's research in the Caribbean won her a bachelor's degree in social anthropology from the University of Chicago and the promise of a Rockefeller Foundation grant for additional research toward a master's degree. However, Miss Dunham was troubled, torn between a feeling of commitment to scholarship and a desire for a career as a dancer. A talk with Dr. Redfield determined her course. Recognizing Katherine's profound affinity for the theater, her former teacher inquired, simply, "What's wrong with being a dancer?"

Her doubts were resolved. Soon her career was launched with a job as dance director of the Federal Theater Project of Chicago, which produced the successful *Ballet Fedre* in 1938, featuring Miss Dunham's highly regarded *L'Ag' Ya*. The following year Miss Dunham was invited to New York as dance director of a musical about the garment industry, *Pins and Needles*. Then, adding singing and acting to her accomplishments as a dancer, she opened at the Martin Beck Theater in New York, in September 1940, for a long run as Georgia Brown in the all-black musical *Cabin in the Sky*.

Meanwhile, Miss Dunham, whose first marriage had ended in divorce in 1939, had married a talented young white stage designer named John Pratt. She had also formed her own company, the Dunham Dance Company. Together with her husband, who designed the colorful sets and brilliant costumes, she staged, over the next two decades, a series of highly successful reviews, including *Tropics and Le Jazz Hot* (1940), *Tropical Review* (1943), *Bal Nègre* (1946), *Caribbean Rhapsody* (1950), and *Bamboche* (1962), among others.

Touring with her dance company took Miss Dunham all over America and Canada. She also traveled extensively with her troupe in South America and the Caribbean as well as in Europe, which she visited frequently, and the Far and Near East. In short, she was responsible for popularizing the art of black, African-derived dance throughout the world. More than that, the Katherine Dunham School of Dance, founded in New York in 1945, not only provided the touring company with replacements for dancers who left, but trained a generation of dancers in the age-old dances that Miss Dunham discovered in the Caribbean and in Africa.

Miss Dunham and her company have appeared in several motion pictures, including *Carnival of Rhythm, Star Spangled Rhythm, Pardon My Sarong, Stormy Weather, Mambo,* and *Cakewalk.* In addition, Miss Dunham did the choreography for *Green Mansions* when it was made into a motion picture in 1958, and in 1963 she choreographed Verdi's *Aïda* at the Metropolitan Opera House in New York.

In 1965 Katherine Dunham was invited to Africa to help train the Senegalese National Ballet and to serve as technical cultural adviser to Senegal's President Léopold Senghor at the World Festival of Negro Arts at Dakar in 1965 and 1966. More recently, she has been serving as cultural affairs consultant and director of the Performing Arts Training Center at Southern Illinois University.

In 1968 when *Dance Magazine* gave one of its annual awards to Katherine Dunham for her service to the dance, her friend Erich Fromm, the noted psychiatrist, in presenting the award, said of her: "She had the courage and curiosity to walk into little known worlds, uncover a vast segment of her people's heritage, and thereby enrich us all."

Miss Dunham's dancing days are over, but she continues to enrich us all. Her books, in addition to those mentioned above, include an authoritative study of Haitian dance, *Les Danses d'Haiti* (1950), and *A Touch of Innocence* (1959), the story of her early life. As a teacher, she is training dancers for the enrichment of the dance theater of tomorrow. And, of course, her work as a choreographer continues to enrich audiences of today with work like "Missa Luba," a Catholic Mass set to folk tunes of the Congo, performed in St. Louis, Missouri, in February 1972, and *Treemonisha*, an opera by black composer Scott Joplin performed with Katherine Dunham's dances at the Carbondale campus of Southern Illinois University late in 1972.

DICK GREGORY

Nigger is what he calls his autobiography. Track star, topflight entertainer, author, candidate for the Presidency of the United States in 1968, civil rights leader, and probably one of the most widely known black men in America—Dick Gregory, "nigger."

The word is an ugly racial slur, and Gregory's use of it as the title of his book indicates his determination to make that ugliness public. It is also a key to his humor, a humor often based on the morbid and the absurd. For if it is morbid or unwholesome to use a demeaning label like "nigger," it is comically absurd for Gregory to apply it to himself. In fact, his use of it turns the label around so that a slur becomes a badge: I am what *you* call a nigger, Gregory is saying. How absurd to think that the label damages or diminishes me or anyone else.

Dick Gregory owes his sense of humor to his mother, who, he says in his autobiography, was always smiling. "When there was no fatback to go with the beans, no socks to go with the shoes, no hope to go with tomorrow, she'd smile and say: 'We ain't poor, we're just broke.'" Gregory explains that "poor is a state of mind you never grow out of, but being broke is just a temporary condition."

For Lucille Gregory, abandoned by her husband to raise six children on welfare, the "temporary condition" lasted most of her forty-eight years. Suffering from diabetes and high blood pressure that caused her legs and feet to swell, she worked seven

Dick Gregory

days a week to keep her family together. Often she would work until after midnight as a domestic in a white St. Louis suburb for $2 and carfare, then return to her flat on North Taylor Street with the orange-crate chairs and secondhand lamps, where the lights had been turned off for months because she couldn't pay the electric bill, where the pipes were frozen and the wind came in through the cracks in winter. "She'd have to make deals with the rats," says Gregory, "leave some food out for them so they wouldn't gnaw on the doors or bite the babies. The roaches, they were just like part of the family."

Harassed by welfare agents who considered her work as a domestic "cheating" on welfare, evicted from her flat for not paying her rent, humiliated by her neighbors who looked down upon her raggedy children, overworked, underpaid, frequently ill, generally in debt, "Mama" Gregory maintained that you had to smile twenty-four hours a day. "If you walk through life showing the aggravation you've gone through," she said, "people will feel sorry for you, and they'll never respect you."

From his earliest years in St. Louis, where he was born on Columbus Day 1932, Dick Gregory worked. With his friend "Boo" Simmons and his older brother Presley, he shined shoes, cleaned windows, shoveled snow, hauled groceries, sold wood and coal, washed automobiles.

On Saturdays they would get up before daylight. "After working the white neighborhoods," he says in his autobiography, "we'd come back to the Negro neighborhood and haul groceries from about two o'clock to about four o'clock. After that we'd get our shoeshine boxes and while we were walking around looking for customers we'd sell wood and coal. . . . That night we'd work the white taverns shining shoes, and then sell the Sunday papers until about three o'clock in the morning. Come home, get up at six o'clock to deliver more papers until about 9:30."

Working like that on a diet consisting largely of beans and baloney sandwiches—and often there was no bread for the baloney, or no baloney for the bread—it is small wonder that Dick Gregory was the skinniest kid on the block. He was frequently so hungry that he ate paste from the paste pot in school to kill the hunger pangs and sometimes stole sandwiches from other kids' lunches in the closet. Small wonder, too, that he didn't pay attention in school and was often placed in the "idiot's seat," a seat in the back of the room with a chalk circle drawn around it, marking the troublemaker.

In the streets he was a natural victim. Skinny, poor, fatherless, he was a favorite target of bullies. Older kids would gang up on him and make fun of his poverty until he cried or ran. Then they would beat him up. Soon, however, he learned a response.

Badgered about rats in his house, he'd retort: "Other night I crawled through one of them ratholes in the kitchen, would you believe it, them rats were sleeping six to a bed just like us."

In the winter he might say: "We don't worry about knocking the snow off our shoes before we go into my house. So cold in there, no snow's going to melt on the floor anyway."

And when an especially big kid started to rough him up, Gregory would freeze, roll his eyes down at the tough's feet, and say: "Baby, you better kill me quick. If you don't, I'm gonna steal those cool shoes you wearin'."

When Richard started at Sumner High School, a segregated high school with the finest black track team in the state, he turned to track not because he particularly fancied running, but because he had heard that members of the track team got to take showers every evening after practice. The track roster was full at the time, but the coach let him shower with the team anyway, on condition that he not get in the way of their practices.

Dick showed up every afternoon after school. Starting at three, he would run until six o'clock without taking a break, circling the block in which the school was located so as not to interfere with the team practicing on the school track. After his shower, he would go to White's Eat Shop and wash dishes in return for dinner.

Gregory ran by himself all that fall and through the winter, sometimes in snow, building up his speed and endurance. The next spring he made the team, and under the guidance of Warren St. James, a new track coach, he was soon winning races. In 1951 he did the mile in 4 minutes 28 seconds, one of the best high school times of the year, capturing the black Missouri State Meet for his school with the win. He was elected captain of the track and cross-country teams at Sumner. When track meets were finally integrated in Missouri, during Gregory's years at Sumner, he beat the best white and black runners in the state in everything from the half mile up. In the big all-state cross-country meet at Forest Park, running against the fastest distance runners—black and white—in Missouri, he captured first place. He was state champion.

Dick Gregory had his picture in every newspaper in the state. Fellow students and townspeople treated him with deference. He was a celebrity. But more important than the victories or the praise was the change in him as a person. Running gave Gregory a goal and an identity, a desire to be somebody and the means to achieve it. "I don't think I ever would have finished high school without running," he says. "It was something that kept me going from day to day."

As a drummer in the high school band, he traveled to nearby states—West Virginia, Illinois, Kansas. He learned something of Beethoven, and Bach, and Mozart—"cats I never even heard of," as he says in his life story. He made new friends, took a cooking class so that he might learn etiquette, and was elected president of his senior class.

At the University of Southern Illinois, at Carbondale, Dick continued his track career under the guidance of coach Leland P. Lingle. "Doc" Lingle was a fine coach and, more important, a fine man. Gregory describes him as "the first white man to stretch out his hand to me." He helped Gregory to improve his running, so that he eventually brought the half-mile record down to 1 minute 54.1 seconds. He also laughed at Gregory's jokes. In fact, recognizing his talent, "Doc" suggested to the young track star that he might one day become an entertainer. And he urged the comedian-to-be to take speech, music, and drama courses in addition to the business subjects in which he majored.

Dick Gregory became the fastest half-miler in the eighty-four-year history of the University of Southern Illinois. And in 1953 he was named Outstanding Athlete for the year at the university. The honor didn't follow the accomplishment automatically, however. In fact, Gregory might well not have been named had he not spoken up. One day he noticed that despite the many photographs of black athletes along the walls of the Athletic Department, the top row, reserved for the pictures of Outstanding Athlete of the Year, was lily white. Gregory walked into the office and threatened to quit if he wasn't named Outstanding Athlete. He was on an athletic scholarship, he was captain of both the track and the cross-country teams, and he was the fastest runner the school had ever had. He got the award. Moreover, the following year another black athlete, Leo Wilson, won it. The lily-white tradition had been broken by Gregory's threat.

Yet, for all his triumphs, life was far from sweet. Southern Illinois University was integrated, but Gregory could not eat in a Carbondale restaurant with his white teammates when they went downtown. In the local movie house he was expected to sit in the balcony. Gregory didn't know that at first. He had always preferred the balcony, and back in St. Louis had often tipped the usher to find him a place there. In fact, when the white usher in the Carbondale movie had shown him to the balcony without a tip, he thought he was being given preferential treatment because of his fame as a track star.

He soon learned the truth. One night, having stood up a girl to take out another, he sought seats in the orchestra section, anxious to avoid the balcony, where he thought the first girl was sitting. The "friendly" white usher, with a hard edge to his voice now, asked him to step into the manager's office. In his autobiography Gregory recounts the episode:

I told the girl I'd be right back, never knowing I was leaving her down there with all that hell, the white folks downstairs turning and hissing and grumbling, and the Negroes upstairs cheering, yelling, "Go, baby, go, you give it to 'em, Greg." Until I got into the manager's office, I thought the balcony was cheering me for last week's race.

"I'm sorry, Mister Gregory, but you know you can't sit in the orchestra."

"Why not?"

"Because colored seating is in the balcony."

My St. Louis dream died that night, my dream about always being able to afford the balcony. In Carbondale, the balcony was my place. I stood there, so confused, wondering if the usher back home in St. Louis had been cheating me all those years, or if this man was trying to destroy something I had.

Threatened with the police, Gregory got his date, who was in tears, and left. When the manager offered to refund his money, Gregory responded, "Keep it. I'll be back." He did return—alone. And he sat downstairs in the orchestra. Later he brought some black friends, and they sat downstairs. Dick Gregory had lost his preference for the balcony. And he had beaten a restrictive practice in one Carbondale establishment.

In 1953 Lucille Gregory died. Dick was so numb with despair and guilt that he couldn't even cry at the funeral. He was thinking about her sacrifices and wishing that he had not gone to college but to work so that he might have made Mama's life a little easier during her last years. His triumphs seemed very small indeed in the light of his great loss.

For several years after his mother's death, Dick Gregory's life seemed to him to have neither meaning nor direction. He was drafted into the army and served two years. When he got out, in the spring of 1956, he returned to Southern Illinois University. But he still had not found himself. Life seemed meaningless, college even more so. The following fall he left the university, taking the Greyhound bus to Chicago, where his brother Presley was working.

He didn't find his brother, and since he was completely broke, he had to take any job he could find. He worked briefly as a postal clerk. Then an army friend, Jim Ellis, got him a job on the production line in the Ford Aircraft factory, which lasted about a year.

One Saturday night in late January 1958, after many months without either money or a job, Dick wandered into a South Side neighborhood bar. The place was packed, and a show was in progress. It was pretty bad, with the master of ceremonies, who was also the comic, doing a routine of moldy old jokes. But somehow Dick found himself laughing along with the rest of the customers. His mood of depression lifted. After the first show, he went backstage to talk to the MC. During the conversation Gregory mentioned the fact that he had been in Special Services in the army and had entertained troops as a comedian. The MC seemed impressed and hinted that for a $5 tip he might let Gregory try his stuff in the second show that night. Dick planked down the five and the die was cast. He was on his way to a career in show business that would net him hundreds of thousands of dollars and bring laughter and a new awareness of the human condition to millions of people all across America.

In April 1958 Dick started to work in the Esquire Show Lounge, another South Side neighborhood bar with weekend entertainment. Serving as master of ceremonies and comedian, he worked Friday, Saturday, and Sunday nights, with an afternoon show on Sunday, for $30 a week. Buying new clothes to help establish an image as a successful entertainer and books and magazines in which he found material for his act just about exhausted his salary. And all of his spare time was spent working up new routines, trying them on friends, attempting to discover what makes people laugh, what they think about, how their experiences could be illuminated through humor. And, as he says in his autobiography, ". . . I was selling a talent that wasn't really mine yet, and I had to develop it from every angle. I was hung up in something, and I had to find out how it worked."

Dick Gregory's first break in the world of big-time entertainment came on January 13, 1961, when he was asked to replace another comedian, who was too ill to perform, at the Playboy Club in Chicago. Dick was so good that he was signed to a three-year contract, starting at $250 a week. Then came appearances on national television on the Jack Paar Show and later with David Susskind. Shortly afterward, Colpix Records offered him a $25,000 advance for a two-record comedy album. Thereafter a steady succession of engagements in the biggest night spots and supper clubs, on television and in concert performances from San Francisco and Los Angeles to Las Vegas, Chicago, and New York made Gregory's name a household word. His fees were among the highest in the entertainment business. More important, he achieved his success without compromising his effort to make comedy a way to expose injustice and racial inequality.

Using subjects like discrimination, which comedians had generally avoided heretofore, he gives social point to his routines. Commenting on an early experience in a segregated restaurant, for example, Gregory recalls a waitress coming up to him as he sat at a table and saying, "We don't serve colored people here." His reply: "That's all right, I don't eat them."

Or he recalls another time, in the South. He had ordered chicken and was just about to cut off a leg and start eating when three Ku Klux Klanners approached his table. "Boy," one of them said, "anything you do to that chicken, we're gonna do to you." So he picked up the chicken and kissed it.

Reflecting on his harassment by the police in the Deep South, Gregory says, "That's the only place where I've given out more fingerprints than autographs."

Of course, the harassment of black people is not confined to the South, though it takes different forms up North, as Gregory's satirical observation suggests. "Like in my hometown, Chicago," he says. "When black folks are concentrated in a large ghetto area and it begins to look like we might control the vote, the cats in City Hall don't say anything nasty or threatening to us—they have a slum clearance."

"Personally," the comedian says, "I've never seen much difference between the South and the North. Down South white folks don't care how close I get as long as I don't get too big. Up North white folks don't care how big I get as long as I don't get too close."

It was during the 1960s that Dick Gregory achieved national recognition as a comedian. This was also the period when civil rights leaders—Roy Wilkins, Whitney Young, James Farmer, Martin Luther King, Jr., Medgar Evers—and such organizations as the NAACP, the Southern Christian Leadership Conference, and the Student Nonviolent Coordinating Committee were campaigning strenuously in the battle against racism in the South. Thousands upon thousands of black people were risking their lives and going to jail for the cause of freedom, and Gregory could not remain apart from the struggle.

He joined voter registration drives in Mississippi, participated in sit-ins in segregated institutions throughout the South, spoke at civil rights rallies all over the country, and demonstrated for a wide variety of causes, ranging from demands for the restoration of Indian fishing rights in Olympia, Washington, to the massive protest against the neglect of America's ill-clothed, ill-housed, and ill-fed at Resurrection City in Washington, D.C. He undertook at least five public fasts for various causes as well. One of the most widely publicized began at a peace rally in San Francisco on April 24, 1971, when he vowed that he would eat no solid food until the United States withdrew all of its troops from Vietnam. Subsisting on about a gallon of water or fruit juice a day, Gregory lost about eighty pounds.

He has been beaten and jailed on numerous occasions in his role as "Lone Ranger of the Civil Rights Movement," as he has been called. Attempting to restore order during the Watts riots in 1965, he was wounded in the leg by a stray bullet. Sacrificing concert dates and other engagements to take part in a broad range of civic activities, he has suffered income losses in the neighborhood of $2 million and was at one time in debt to the tune of $200,000. He has been the subject of government surveillance and harassment for his involvement in unpopular causes, and with characteristic humor, he maintains that his telephone has so many bugs that his wife and he have to put roach powder on it each night.

In 1966 Gregory ran for the office of mayor of Chicago. In 1968, with Mark Lane as his running mate, he was a write-in candidate for the Presidency of the United States. His lectures to college audiences, for which he receives a minimum fee of $1,500, run to a half dozen a week, and he has appeared at as many as fourteen schools in a single week, crisscrossing the country and putting in more time in the air than many airline crews. Recently, he has returned to the cabaret circuit as well, convulsing audiences with material drawn from the headlines of what he calls the "funny papers" and providing what one commentator described as "catharsis for political and social insanity."

Experience has taught Gregory the need for constant exposure of bigotry and prejudice as a means to getting rid of them. Hence, in addition to his other activities, he has published many articles and a number of books on the subjects, including, *From the Back of the Bus, No More Lies, Dick Gregory's Political Primer,* and *Write Me In!* Experience has also taught him that progress in race relations is more often boasted of than achieved. Summarizing his feelings, he observed ironically, "The biggest breakthrough for black folks in the history of America took place a couple of years ago in the South—in the state of Texas. We got our first colored hurricane—Beulah. Now that's *progress.*"

Art

It was not until the opening decades of the twentieth century that Americans and Europeans began to recognize that the peoples of Africa had produced a great art. The fact is, however, that an important tradition dates back for centuries among the major African tribes. Moreover, as has been demonstrated by major exhibitions of African art, such as the African Art and Motion Exhibition at the National Gallery of Art in Washington, D.C., during the summer of 1974, African art is as rich, complex, and varied as the art of the West. Slavery, of course, prevented the black American from keeping in touch with this rich heritage. But even in the early days in America, when he was cut off from the artistic tradition of his people and denied the opportunity for full participation in a new culture, the artistic impulse of the black American manifested itself anonymously in skilled craftwork. "Negro craftsmen," as Dr. Alain Locke has pointed out, "were well-known as cabinet makers, marquetry setters, wood carvers and ironsmiths as the workmanship of many colonial mansions in Charleston, New Orleans and other colonial centers of wealth and luxury will attest."

It was not until after the Civil War that individual black artists began to be recognized in America. Edward M. Bannister, a landscape painter and founder of the Providence Art Club in Rhode Island, was a pioneer in the field. Contemporary with him was the woman sculptor Edmonia Lewis, who won favorable notice with her exhibition of portrait busts at the Philadelphia Centennial in 1876. Robert Duncanson, another pioneer of the same period, won fame through his artistic versatility as an outstanding landscapist, a good figure painter, a portrait artist, and a painter of murals. His historical paintings illustrating life in the American West are among his best-known works.

Between the pioneers and the period of the great flowering of black art in America stands the career of the master painter Henry O. Tanner. Born in Pittsburgh in 1859, the son of a bishop in the African Methodist Church, Tanner sailed for Rome in 1891 to study art, despite the opposition of his family. Most of his productive career was spent in Europe, where he painted the great biblical series upon which his fame rests. "Daniel in the Lion's Den," "Resurrection of Lazarus," "Christ on the Road to Bethany," and "The Annunciation" are among the finest of his paintings, which are now owned by many prominent European and American museums.

A number of factors contributed to the great outpouring of black art that our century has witnessed, but among the most important was the encouragement black artists received and the sense of community they felt in seeing their work exhibited. The special exhibits of the work of black artists instituted in 1920 at the 135th Street branch of the New York Public Library helped to promote a sense of accomplishment. The stimulating series of prizes for achievement in art sponsored by the Harmon Foundation in 1926 and the influential exhibits begun in the following year served the same end. Perhaps most important of all was the incentive provided by the WPA Federal Arts Project, beginning in the early thirties. In addition to providing support for artists without regard to color, the WPA fostered community cultural centers and encouraged the teaching of art. The Harlem Art Workshop and the Harlem Community Art Center employed such artists as Charles Alston, Henry Bannarn, and Gwendolyn Bennett as teachers. Among their students were such black artists of the future as Norman Lewis, Romare Bearden, Robert Crichlow, and Jacob Lawrence.

Today black artists representing all schools—from the most traditional to the extreme modernists—are among the outstanding names in American art. Typical of the more traditional painters are Laura Wheeler Waring, Palmer C. Hayden, and Aaron Douglass. Hale Woodruff, Archibald Motley, Malvin Gray Johnson, and Lesesne Wells are representative of the host of black painters who have, to a greater or lesser degree, broken with the tradition of the academic painters. Among sculptors, two women, Augusta Savage and Elizabeth Prophet, and two men, Sargent Johnson and Richmond Barthé, have won fame for their work.

Let us turn to two artists, a sculptor and a painter, as examples of the black creative spirit.

RICHMOND BARTHÉ

"For years the genuineness of Barthé's sculptural talent has been recognized. . . . It may be said without the slightest hesitation that he now ranks among the very best of our contemporary sculptors." So wrote a distinguished art critic of Richmond Barthé, the extent and variety of whose work is as great as its quality is fine. Barthé has executed everything from small clay heads to monumental figure groups and friezes. His sculpture includes studies of such varied types as burly stevedores, delicate children, African warriors, Hindu temple dancers, coy adolescents, and work-worn peasants. His portrait heads and busts have given immortality to a great number of theatrical personalities, ranging from Katharine Cornell, John Gielgud, Maurice Evans, and Rose McClendon to "Garbage" Rogers, the comedian, and Gypsy Rose Lee.

He has undertaken historical subjects, like the head of Lincoln, and religious ones: John the Baptist, Mary, and Christ, among others. He has been commissioned to do equestrian statues of national heroes, like the one of General Dessalines at the request of the Haitian government; portrait busts, like the one which Dr. Hans N. Gebhard, former Metropolitan Opera director, took back to Germany with him; commemorative plaques—Arthur Brisbane in Manhattan's Central Park; and architectural embellishments of the sort he contributed to the Harlem River Housing Project. He has worked in clay, brass,

Richmond Barthé

marble, terra-cotta, wood, and stone. Yet he was not trained as a sculptor and never wanted to be one. Indeed, it was quite by accident that he turned to that form of art after having studied another.

This great sculptor-by-chance, Richmond Barthé, was born in the Bayou section of Bay St. Louis, Mississippi, on January 28, 1901, of black, French, and Indian ancestry. His father, who was also named Richmond, died when the boy was a mere infant. His mother, Marie Clementine (Roboteau) Barthé, brought young Richmond up, supporting him through her skill as a seamstress until she remarried, when the boy was six years old. Then her second husband helped to provide for her son. It is, as a matter of fact, to his mother that Richmond attributes his stamina and his dexterity. A remarkable woman, she was extremely capable despite her small size, and thought nothing of chopping wood for fuel, returning from her exertions to execute delicate designs in lace and embroidery.

It was his mother, too, who discovered and encouraged Richmond's artistic ability. Claiming that he could draw before he could walk, she remembered that she could keep him occupied while she was absent from home for long periods of time searching for work merely by supplying him with a pencil and some paper. Upon her return she would find Richmond in the very same position he had taken when she left, his papers now filled with drawings of everything under the sun—and some things of more doubtful location.

By the time Mrs. Barthé remarried, Richmond was ready for school. Since his mother and stepfather were devout Roman Catholics, he was enrolled at the St. Rose de Lima Parochial School. Later he attended the Valena Jones High School for a time, quitting it for a job at the age of fourteen. He held several different jobs during the next few years, office boy, helper on an ice truck, and busboy. But he had acquired the habit of reading and he did not give it up just because he had left school. The local stationery store had a lending library, and Richmond borrowed books from it at every opportunity. He got to know Miss Josie Welch, the woman who operated the lending library, and from her he heard stories about great and famous black men, men like Booker T. Washington and Paul Laurence Dunbar, whom he would one day portray in stone and in metal. From Miss Welch, too, came his interest in "the spiritual side of the Negro," an interest later to find expression in works like "The Negro Looks Ahead," a handsome sculptured head expressive of the aspirations of the race.

At seventeen Richmond went to work as butler to Mr. Harry Pond. He was fortunate in his employer, for the Ponds treated him as a member of the family rather than as a servant. They spent the winter in their New Orleans town house, and took Richmond along each year, treating him to the theater and other entertainments that they enjoyed in the city. It was at this time that young Barthé developed his interest in and love for the theater, an interest and an affection that were to have important consequences for his later work. That work was furthered more directly by Richmond's job, for the Ponds had a fine collection of paintings. He began to make drawings and sketches of some of the paintings. The Ponds, observing his skill, gave him his first set of oils, and it was while he was in their employ that he executed his first painting.

Soon, too, Richmond made friends in New Orleans, among them Miss Leslie Ducrows, an author who was writing for the New Orleans *Times-Picayune*. It was she who encouraged him to try water color, providing him with his first set of such colors. She also introduced him to Lyle Saxon of her paper, a man with some knowledge of art. Saxon was immediately impressed with the quality of Barthé's untrained talent, and he brought young Richmond to the attention of people who were in a position to further his career. Saxon even went so far as to write a laudatory essay on Barthé's work, but his paper refused to accept the article because Barthé was black. However, when the young artist had established himself and his reputation began to grow, the paper was happy to accept reviews of his work from all sources.

Richmond Barthé was twenty-three years old and still working for the Ponds when his first picture was sold. The artist got no money for his painting, for he had contributed it to the Blessed Sacrament Church in New Orleans for sale at its May Charity Bazaar. But the occasion was an important one for Barthé. His work was scrutinized by the Reverend Harry F. Kane, a Jesuit priest with an interest in art and a willingness to help young artists. Father Kane was enthusiastic about the young butler's painting and he tried to get him into a New Orleans art school. But not even the power of the church was sufficient to overcome the force of bigotry, and Father Kane was unsuccessful. He was not, however, a man to accept defeat without a struggle. Finding his protégé shut out of the world of art in New Orleans, he collected a small purse among his friends and sent Barthé off to Chicago to study.

The four years that followed (1924–28) were devoted to the study of painting and drawing. To support himself and pay for his lessons, Barthé took a job as a waiter in a restaurant called Le Petit Gourmet on Chicago's North Side. But his real work was accomplished at the Chicago Art Institute, where he enrolled for courses in painting, and in the studio of Charles S. Schroeder, with whom he studied figure construction and anatomy. Barthé made real progress with his painting in Chicago, and he never would have thought of abandoning his canvas and his palette for clay and modeling tools if it had not been for a certain slant of light that glanced off the bony structure and carved deep, shadowy hollows in the face of a fellow student in the studio with him one afternoon in 1928. The sun-splashed face bore a striking resemblance to certain of the anatomical plaster casts of heads that hung upon the studio walls. Barthé, marveling at the sun's work, returned home and, taking some clay, began to construct a head. His friend posed for him, and in time he succeeded in modeling the face. His new career had begun.

Barthé had completed another piece of sculpture when, later in the year, the Chicago Women's Club decided to hold an exhibition of the work of black artists. The club had a plentiful supply of paintings from which to draw, but no sculpture. Hearing of the women's plight, a lawyer friend suggested that Barthé submit his new work. He did, and it was not only shown, but praised as well. Encouraged by his success, Barthé decided to work more seriously at sculpture. As a matter of fact, while attending the exhibit at which his work was shown he studied the heads of some black singers who participated in the program, thinking that they might make an interesting group sculpture. On the way home, his thoughts centered on the group's soloist, and ultimately "The Jubilee Singer" was created, an impressive piece of work, though it was but the third effort of an untrained man working, without benefit of a model, from memory.

"The Jubilee Singer" brought Barthé some attention and resulted in an invitation to do a head of Toussaint L'Ouverture for the Lake City Children's Home in Gary, Indiana. It was his first commission. And with his next piece, "Tortured Negro," he won his first prize, an honorable mention in a Harmon Foundation show. Both commissions and prizes have been awarded Barthé with astonishing regularity ever since. He has won the Eames McVeigh Prize of the Chicago Art League, two Rosenwald fellowships, two Guggenheims, a $1,000 grant from the American Academy of Arts and Letters, the Audubon Artists' gold medal, and a $500 award from the Metropolitan Museum of Art. The commissions have been too numerous even to begin to recount, but two at least must be mentioned. One was for the bronze group called "The Birth of the Spirituals," placed at the 110th Street entrance to Central Park in Manhattan. Drawing its inspiration from James Weldon

Johnson's famous poem beginning, "O Black and unknown bards . . . ," the group was to be a memorial to the poet. Unfortunately, funds for its completion were never made available. The other noteworthy commission was for a bust of Booker T. Washington, which was installed in the Hall of Fame. Both subject and sculptor were the first black men to be so honored.

After Barthé had won his first Rosenwald fellowship, he went to New York, where he studied at the Art Students League for a year. There he met Jo Davidson, the noted sculptor, who advised him to be his own teacher and form his own style. He took the older man's advice, and returned to Chicago to put it to work. Then, in 1931, Barthé went back to New York and stayed there until 1934, when he visited Europe. Upon his return to America he made his home in New York. Broadway helped him to renew his early interest in the theater, and to this period belong his well-known portrait busts of theatrical personalities. Moreover, in 1936 when he was selected to execute the bas-reliefs for the Harlem River Housing Project, he recalled "the best thing done by Negro actors" and put two scenes from Marc Connelly's *The Green Pastures* into the monumental friezes that adorn the project. The two forty-foot panels, though they were his first attempt at bas-relief, are among the best things that Barthé has done. Among his other great works are the wonderfully sensitive head of a small boy, "Julius"; a fine "Blackberry Woman"; two African figures, "Benga" and "African Boy Dancing"; a dramatic group study of a lynching scene, called "The Mother"; and a head suggested by the Bible and called "Lot's Wife."

With his sculpture in fine museums, public buildings, and private collections throughout the country and with works in such widely separated portions of the globe as Austria, Canada, Africa, England, Germany, and Haiti, Richmond Barthé has decided to let the future take care of his reputation as a sculptor. He has retired to a small, tree-covered estate in

Jamaica, the British West Indies, and hopes to live out his remaining years in modest comfort, devoting himself to his long-neglected painting. Perhaps from his seclusion will come forth a series of paintings as significant as his sculptures. On the other hand, he may eventually decide to return to his modeling tools and his chisels. Whatever the outcome, his reputation is secure in the hands of the future because his own hands have already wrought it so well.

JACOB LAWRENCE

Jacob Lawrence is a painter. As a matter of fact, he has been called "the nation's (and probably the world's) foremost Negro painter." His work has been compared to that of Picasso, Orozco, Daumier, Hogarth, and other great artists. Like Hogarth, Lawrence is a storyteller as well as a painter. He paints not single pictures but a series of them—sometimes as many as sixty on a single subject—giving thereby the history of a man, an epoch, or a place or describing an institution, an experience, or an event. But he is no mere illustrator. Each of his paintings stands up as a self-sufficient work of art, complete in itself. In this, again, he is like Hogarth.

To accomplish his end—telling much in little through his pictorial story—Lawrence reduces the complex details of the story to a few simple elements. His method has been described in the catalogue notes of one of his exhibitions as follows:

. . . Lawrence . . . uses large flat forms, height and width only, no depth and no details; pure colors—three reds, three yellows, two blues, two greens, brown, black and white—in tempera or gouache; steep perspective. Each picture has also an accompanying title and all titles together make a story's running script. The method is the same—brevity, facts, few adjectives, a skeleton of economy.

The *John Brown* series, for example, is a history, based on extensive research, of John Brown's efforts to overthrow slavery

Terry Dintenfass, Inc.

Jacob Lawrence

in America prior to the Civil War. One of the pictures in the series bears the following legend:

In spite of a price on his head, John Brown in 1859 liberated twelve Negroes from a Missouri plantation.

The liberation is shown only as footprints on a road and the leg and foot of one hurrying man. Another painting in the series depicts the climax of John Brown's activities, the raid on Harpers Ferry. The caption is starkly factual:

Sunday, October 16, 1859, John Brown with a company of twenty-one men, white and black, marched on Harpers Ferry.

And the dramatic action is suggested by twenty-one bayonet points held high on guns, the marching men concealed by a hill.

Lawrence, who has produced almost a dozen series of paintings, in addition to many separate works, book illustrations, posters, and sequences of paintings on such themes as civil rights, was born in Atlantic City, New Jersey, on September 7, 1917. When he was only two years old, he moved with his parents, Jacob and Rosealee (Armstead) Lawrence, to Easton, Pennsylvania, where his father abandoned them. Shortly after young Jacob started school, his mother moved the family to Philadelphia and then, when Jacob was twelve, to New York City.

In New York, Jacob attended Frederick Douglass Junior High School and later, for two years, the High School of Commerce. But it was in the Utopia House classes that he went to after school, while his mother worked, that Lawrence first developed an active interest in art and, as a result of the encouragement he got there, began to think of becoming a painter.

From Utopia House Jacob progressed to the College Art Association classes, where, at the age of fifteen he began to study under the great black painter Charles Alston. After two years with Alston, young Jacob enrolled under another fine black artist-teacher, Henry Bannarn, in WPA-sponsored art classes at a studio on 141st Street.

Except for a period of about six months, when he worked in the Civilian Conservation Corps at a camp near Middletown, New York, Jacob participated in the activities of the studio on 141st Street for three years. Speaking, afterward, of the WPA Workshop, Lawrence said:

It was my education. I met people like Saroyan before he got famous. They all used to talk about what was going on in the world. Not only about art, but everything.

The importance to Lawrence of learning ". . . what was going on in the world" during those depression years cannot be overestimated. His great series of paintings, . . . *and the Migrants Kept Coming*, depicting the black migration from the South between World Wars I and II, and his equally famous series, called *Harlem*, devoted to aspects of Harlem life, are both enriched by an awareness of social change that developed in him while he was at the workshop. Similarly, his belief that "the human subject is the most important thing" in a painting is an outgrowth of ideas generated in conversations with workshop friends during those years when so many human beings became the hapless victims of unregulated economic forces.

Lawrence made rapid progress as an artist and in 1937 he was awarded a full tuition scholarship to the American Artists School. Mornings he worked there under such instructors as Refregier, Sol Wilson, and Eugene Morley. Afternoons he spent in the 135th Street branch of the New York Public Library, where the famous Schomberg Collection of books by and about black people is housed. In the course of his reading, Lawrence came upon several books about Toussaint L'Ouverture, the liberator of Haiti. He was fascinated by the events of L'Ouverture's career and decided to depict some of the more outstanding of them in paint. As he worked at his sketches the project grew, and before the year of his scholarship had ended he had completed a series of forty-one paintings outlining the history of the colorful general.

Research in the Schomberg Collection also provided Lawrence with material for a pictorial biography of Frederick Douglass, the great black orator and reformer. This project, consisting of thirty paintings, was completed in 1938. Immediately, Lawrence set to work upon another series, also of thirty paintings, setting forth the career of Harriet Tubman, the heroic woman who, prior to the Civil War, had so much to do with making the Underground Railroad for runaway slaves a success.

At the age of twenty-one Lawrence had held his first one-man exhibition at the Harlem Y.M.C.A. The following year he joined the WPA Federal Arts Project, in which he worked for about eighteen months. In 1940 he was granted a Rosenwald Fellowship to do research for a series of paintings depicting the population shift that brought more than a million black migrants from impoverished southern farms to the industrial North during and after World War I. The exodus, or migration as Lawrence calls it, was not wholly advantageous to the black man. For if he escaped oppression when he left the South, he faced segregation and discrimination in the North. He was considered, often, a sort of second-class citizen, whose rights were strictly circumscribed. With the drop in production and the increase in the labor force that took place after the war, unemployment increased. And the black laborer, hired during an emergency when labor was scarce, was either fired by his boss or persecuted by white workers fearful of their own jobs.

There were other difficulties, too, and Lawrence illustrates them in his series of sixty paintings. One of those paintings, for instance, bears the following caption:

Cramped into urban life, they [the migrants] contracted a great deal of tuberculosis. The death rate was very high.

The picture shows a cheap coffin borne aloft by three pallbearers, whose stiff, black pyramid-like coats intersect the horizon in jagged, threatening lines.

Another title from the series runs as follows:

The vast number of migrants made housing difficult. They were overcrowded in dilapidated tenement houses.

A dingy room is depicted, its interior partially obscured by a grill of bars. The bars form the head and footboards of the many beds crowded into the room. They evoke the atmosphere of a prison and thus provide a grim comment on the scene.

When Lawrence had finished his *Migration* series it was purchased by the Museum of Modern Art and the Phillips Memorial Gallery, each organization taking thirty of the paintings. *Fortune* magazine reproduced a selection of pictures from the series, commenting on the artist's "extraordinary force" and asserting that his talent promised to earn for him "the same high recognition" accorded to other outstanding members of his race. Some of that recognition came immediately, for the Rosenwald Foundation renewed its grant to Lawrence in 1941 and again in 1942. On one of these grants he completed his research for the *Life of John Brown*. When the twenty-two paintings of the series were finished he traveled through the South, storing up impressions for future use. Upon his return in 1942 he plunged into work on a new group of paintings. Fresh from the rural South, Lawrence saw the metropolitan black community with new eyes. The *Harlem* series is a record of that vision, and so striking a record is it that it too received nationwide circulation when it was reproduced in *Vogue* magazine.

In 1941 Lawrence had married Gwendolyn Knight. Shortly thereafter, World War II began, and with Nazi and Japanese submarines playing havoc with American shipping, Lawrence decided to join the Coast Guard. He was inducted into that service on November 3, 1943, and served his country well for two years. Though he was on active duty aboard a troopship in the European Theater of Operations much of the time, he managed, nevertheless, to paint a fine series of pictures depicting the activities of the Coast Guard. He painted everything: troops departing, ships returning, air-raid alerts, gun drill, men in their bunks, shore leave, even cooks in their galleys. Commenting on his subject matter, Lawrence has observed, "The cooks might not like my paintings, but they appreciated that I was painting a cook." Whatever the attitude of the cooks may have been, most people liked the paintings enormously, and they are now in the United States Coast Guard Archives, where they constitute a permanent record of the role played by the Coast Guard in World War II.

Soon after his release from active service, on December 6, 1945, Lawrence was granted a Guggenheim Fellowship. He spent a year recalling his wartime experiences and putting them on canvas. Describing his method, Lawrence said, "I work long on the *idea* for a painting. I want the idea to strike right away." The actual painting occupied much less time than that spent in figuring out how to express the fevered state preceding the plunge into battle or the exhaustion following its termination, the boredom of the serviceman or the loneliness of the woman reading a letter from overseas. But working regularly ("Good painters are never flighty," Lawrence says), he turned out *War*, a series of fourteen paintings that *Time* described in December 1947 when they were exhibited as "by far his best work."

The vitality of his work was now bringing many commissions to Lawrence. He did a series of illustrations for such widely different magazines as *The New Republic, Fortune*, and *New Masses*. In the summer of 1946 he was employed to teach painting at Black Mountain College in North Carolina, the first of a series of collegiate appointments that, over the years, were to take him to Pratt Institute, Brandeis University, the New

School for Social Research, California State College, and the University of Washington, where he was made full professor of art in 1971.

In 1947, *Fortune* magazine commissioned him to travel through the Deep South and record his impressions. The result of this trip was the ten-painting series called *In the Heart of the Black River.* Examining black life in the South, he saw and recorded everything, from the cotton choppers piling into trucks after their day in the fields to the hard-pressed business-men, sharing with the professional people and the church in the job of leading their people. One of the most impressive paintings in the group is one depicting life in Gee's Bend, an all-black community on the Alabama River. Rehabilitated with government assistance after it went bankrupt during the depression, it became a flourishing agricultural community.

Under the pressure of work and the emotional excitement of his painting, Lawrence succumbed to a nervous disorder and entered New York's Hillside Hospital for treatment in July 1949. Discharged in August 1950, he immediately went to work on a series of paintings depicting hospital life. As a matter of fact, as his condition had improved, he had gradually resumed his work while in the hospital. Bearing such titles as "Psychiat-ric Therapy," "Sedation," "Depression," and "Occupational Therapy," the paintings bring into vivid focus the dark underside of man's emotional life as it is revealed under clinical conditions.

Restored to normalcy and working at a slower pace, Lawrence took time out to renew his acquaintance with the theater. The result is one of his most bizarre and engaging series of paintings, *Performance.* The twelve paintings in the group are concerned with various aspects of the theater, from "Mario-nettes" to "Tragedy and Comedy." Lawrence looks backstage and gives us "Make Up." He joins the audience for "Curtain" and retires behind the scenes again "After the Show." He presents us with entertainments ranging from the "Ventriloquist" to "A Christmas Pageant." He looks with the casual passerby at the "Billboard" and permits us to share with the tired trouper the agony of going on "Night After Night." Giving us much in little, Lawrence seems to show us that "all the world's a stage."

But the world is something more than a stage, too, as Lawrence came to realize during the McCarthy era, when private citizens were being harassed by powerful government agencies concerned with the orthodoxy of their beliefs. In the *Struggle* series (1955–56), Lawrence turned to the revolutionary history of the American people, reasserting through paintings of marked social realism the need for the artist to be concerned with the world in which he lives.

That world erupted in violence during the sixties as black people, in their effort to claim long-deferred rights, met opposition, first in the South and later in the big cities of the North. Lawrence responded with indignation in a group of angry paintings on the general theme of civil rights that is an indictment of racial injustice and bigotry.

Then, in 1964, Lawrence and his wife traveled to Africa. It was a symbolic homecoming and a liberation, and the *Nigeria* sequence that he painted, based on his stay in that country, is filled with panoramic vistas that convey a lively sense of joy and renewal. Freer, and using fewer contorted shapes and less intense color than earlier work, the paintings have an almost decorative, lyrical quality.

Some of these qualities carry over into Lawrence's later work, particularly those sequences called *Library* and *Builder*. As the catalogue of his big exhibition at the Whitney Museum in New York in May 1974 points out, Lawrence seems to suggest that the future of the black "lies in education and constructive, creative labor, and along with whites," for in the *Builder* sequence black people and white work together. As Lawrence himself pointed out in a two-part interview with Carroll Greene on October 25 and November 26, 1969, he has always considered the struggle of his people to be part of a larger "struggle of man always to better his conditions and to move forward . . . in a social sense."

Again in the *George Washington Bush* series, completed in 1973, where Lawrence returns for subject to the early history of our country, black and white men struggle together against the magnitude of nature and rejoice as one in the difficulties overcome. The last painting in the series bears the caption:

"Thank God All Mighty, home at last!"—The settlers erect shelter at Bush Prairie near what is now Olympia, Washington, November, 1845.

The painting is an affirmation of the inextricable oneness of black and white in the building of America. Painted by a realist who has seen—and painted—the evils of which men and women are capable and the suffering his people have borne, the work is no statement of sentimental hope but an open-eyed recognition of a fact that must be accepted and lived with if we are to survive as a nation.

Literature

Black literature in America had its beginnings during the years of slavery. Jupiter Hammon, a slave who lived in what is now Queens Village, New York, was the first known black poet in America. His first collection of poems was published in 1761, but most of his verse has been lost.

At about the same time, a very talented black woman poet, Phillis Wheatley, born in Africa and shipped to Boston in chains, was writing. Her *Poems on Various Subjects, Religious and Moral* was published in 1773.

More important than these and the other identifiable black poets who flourished during the period of slavery, however, were the "black and unknown bards" of whom James Weldon Johnson speaks in one of his poems, the unknown creators of a great body of black folk literature—work songs, ballads, rhymes, tales, and, above all, the spiritual. This was the literature that reflected black experience and sustained black hope "way down in Egyptland."

The folk tradition continued after slave days into the period of the Industrial Revolution and beyond. "John Henry," for example, makes a poetry out of the sound of a "hammah suckin' wind" that compares favorably with anything in the great ballad tradition. And "Good Morning Blues," like other great blues, captures a characteristic bittersweet quality of modern urban life.

In the nineteenth century Paul Laurence Dunbar was the first black American poet of distinction to use the black folk experience and idiom for conscious literary expression. Writing around the turn of the century, Charles W. Chestnutt did for prose, in the short stories of *The Conjure Woman*, published in 1899, what Dunbar had done in verse.

A transitional figure, James Weldon Johnson was both a collector and preserver of the best poetry (and the great spirituals) from the black man's past and a poet who, in his book *God's Trombones: Some Negro Sermons in Verse*, introduced new forms and pointed a way to the creative use of the past.

Dr. Carter G. Woodson, who brought out the first issue of the *Journal of Negro History* in 1916, was a historian who provided the black man with a firm historical foundation for his pride. He has been followed by such men as Alain Locke, the first black Rhodes scholar, and Jay Saunders Redding, whose books include *To Make a Poet Black*, *They Came in Chains*, and *The Lonesome Road*.

Centering in New York City, the "Harlem Renaissance" of the 1920s reflected the aesthetic ferment of literary modernism in the verse of Claude McKay and Countee Cullen and the poetry and prose of Langston Hughes.

Richard Wright is, of course, the most widely known of modern black authors. His novel *Native Son*, published in 1940, gave expression to the bitterness, despair, and rebellion of the urban black, trapped in our cities' destructive ghettos. His work influenced a generation of black writers, including the prolific novelist and essayist James Baldwin, the sardonic Chester Himes, Ann Petry, who has written for both adults and young people, and Ralph Ellison, whose *Invisible Man* has been called one of the best novels about the black American ever published.

In *Report From Part One* (1973) Gwendolyn Brooks, who won the Pulitzer Prize for poetry in 1949, says of her earlier work: "I wrote. . . . But it was white writing. . . . Today I am conscious of the fact that my people are black people: it is to them that I appeal for understanding." Her new consciousness is a consciousness shared by numerous black writers today, including, for example, Imamu Baraka, the militant poet and dramatist, Ishmael Reed, the satirist, and Maya Angelou, poet and novelist.

Finally, no survey of black writing, no matter how brief, would be complete without reference to the marvelous flowering of dramatic literature. Beginning with William Wells Brown's *The Escape*, or *A Leap to Freedom*, in 1858, there has been a steady outpouring of black plays, including Louis Peterson's *Take a Giant Step*, William Branch's *In Splendid Error*, and Alice Childress' *Trouble in Mind*, among others. More recently, Lorraine Hansberry, whose *A Raisin in the Sun* has been called "one of the most perfectly structured plays ever to appear on Broadway," contributed to the outpouring until her untimely death at the age of thirty-four. And the flow continues with the work of Imamu Baraka, who is a poet as well as a dramatist, James Baldwin, better known as one of America's fine contemporary novelists, Ed Bullins, Charles Gordone, and others.

JAMES WELDON JOHNSON

In his autobiography, *Along This Way*, James Weldon Johnson has this to say of his activities in New York at the beginning of his career:

I wrote and jotted down ideas for new work; and I read a great deal; I went to the theatre as part of my job; nearly every Saturday night, because it was popular price night, I went to the opera, and in that way heard the whole Metropolitan repertory, but even so, I found time on my hands. It was then that I discovered an explanation as good as any of whatever success that has come my way: I discovered my abhorrence of "spare time." I thereupon cast about to find a means of using up all I had of it in some worthwhile manner.

Among the means were his various occupations: teacher, high school principal, poet, lawyer, songwriter, anthologist, diplomat, politician, editor, translator, librettist, organizer, professor, and administrator.

In addition, Johnson managed to participate in a number of important events and activities. He helped to fight the spectacular fire which razed his birthplace, Jacksonville, Florida, at the beginning of the century. As United States Consul at Corinto, Nicaragua, he assisted in the squelching of the rebellion of 1912. His observations on conditions in Haiti, after the American occupation of 1915, helped check American imperi-

James Weldon Johnson

alism and promoted the welfare of the people of Haiti. Joining the National Association for the Advancement of Colored People as field secretary in 1916, Johnson spread the ideas of that organization among the black people of the South, thereby laying the groundwork for the association's "Southern Empire." And through his books Johnson called attention to the contributions the black man had made and was making to American culture; thus he became the unofficial spokesman for the black American and spurred him on to new creative efforts. Considering all this activity, one wonders how Johnson ever discovered that he loathed "spare time."

This energetic man, who later in life came to love New York so well, might have been born in that city, for his father and mother met there shortly before the Civil War. But with the outbreak of the war, Helen Louise Dillet's mother took her back to Nassau, in the Bahamas, where she had been born. James Johnson, the poet's father, smitten with Helen Louise's beauty, followed the girl to the British colony and, after securing a job as headwaiter at the Royal Victoria Hotel, married her there on April 22, 1864.

With war money plentiful in Nassau, the Johnsons prospered. Soon they were blessed with a baby girl, whom they called Marie Louise. But with the end of the war in America the boom collapsed and James Johnson decided to move to Jacksonville, Florida. There James Weldon Johnson was born on June 17, 1871. His arrival, however, was shadowed by tragedy. Marie Louise, the Johnson's firstborn, had sickened and died during the first year in the new home.

There were other reasons for misery in the Johnson home. The house was a poor one in bad repair. Funds were low. And by comparison with beautiful Nassau, with its glistening white streets and pretty houses, Jacksonville was an ugly place.

With the opening of the fashionable St. James Hotel, things began to look up in Jacksonville, though, and in the Johnson home in particular. Mr. Johnson was hired as headwaiter of the hotel, a position he held for twelve or thirteen years. Some of young James's earliest recollections were connected with his father's job. He remembered, for instance, the small gifts—an orange and some raisins and nuts—that were deposited under his pillow after a banquet at the St. James. And he remembered his first visit to the hotel, a gorgeous place full of white napery, gleaming silver, sparkling crystal, and smartly uniformed waiters who hopped at his father's command.

James Johnson, as his son remembered him, was a quiet, unpretentious man, naturally conservative, cautious, and full of common sense. Although he had no formal education, he read Shakespeare and Plutarch for pleasure. He knew Spanish as well as English, having learned the former language, characteristically, to increase his value as a hotel employee. Late in life Johnson's father became a preacher and was made pastor of "a very small church made up of very poor people." His adaptation of the tenets of his faith to his daily life was so moving that it made, said his son, "a deeper impression on me than all the formal religious training I had been given."

Johnson's mother was artistic and, unlike his father, "more or less impractical." According to her husband, she had "absolutely no sense about money," but she did supplement the family income by teaching school until, in middle life, increasing lameness prevented her from carrying on her duties. She also sang in the church choir, having "a splendid voice." She had a talent for drawing, too. And once she revealed to her son that she had written verse and displayed to him "a thin sheaf of poems copied out in her almost perfect handwriting."

The characteristics of James Weldon Johnson's mother and father blended in him in almost equal proportions, as he himself recognized. In his autobiography he points out, in simple and touching language, the importance of that dual heritage.

The years as they pass keep revealing how the impressions made upon me as a child by my parents are constantly strengthen-

ing controls over my forms of habit, behavior, and conduct as a man. It appeared to me, starting into manhood, that I was to grow into something different from them; into something on a so much larger plan, a so much grander scale. As life tapers off I can see that in the deeper and fundamental qualities I am each day more and more like them.

There were, of course, other influences in young Johnson's life. There was his grandmother, who came with the family from Nassau and who wanted her grandson to be a preacher; and there was her second husband, John Barton, who was partial to James and once bought him a goat. "Pa John" died, however, before he could finish building the goat cart he had promised the boy. James's younger brother, J. Rosamond, was his constant companion in childhood, and the intimacy of the two continued into later life, when they became collaborators on a number of popular song hits. Other members of the household during Johnson's youth included Agnes Marion Edwards, a girl adopted by the Johnsons, whom James came to know and love as a sister, and Ricardo Rodriguez Ponce, a Spanish-speaking Cuban boy who came to live with the family in order to learn English before continuing his education in the United States. Ricardo learned enough English to enable him to enter Atlanta University with James, but not before the Johnson boys had thoroughly mastered conversational Spanish.

Johnson's college days at Atlanta University passed smoothly enough, though he lost a year when a yellow-fever epidemic broke out in Jacksonville during his first summer vacation and quarantine prevented him from returning to Atlanta in the fall. Ensuing summers were spent in various sections of Georgia, teaching rural black children their ABC's. He was paid only about a nickel a day for each child taught, but his salary defrayed the nominal cost of tuition at Atlanta University. And his experience as a rural schoolmaster helped equip him for the job of principal of Stanton School—which he had attended as a boy in Jacksonville—when he was graduated from Atlanta in 1894. His summer jobs also taught him, he said, "to know the masses of my people." He was thereafter always to feel "that the forces behind the slow but persistent movement forward of the race lie, ultimately, in them; that when the vanguard of the movement must fall back, it must fall back on them."

Despite his youth and his relatively limited experience, Johnson made a good grade-school principal. But he did not remain one for long. At a time when there were but three high schools for blacks in the entire South, James Weldon Johnson had the imagination and the courage to make Stanton into a high school. At the same time, he managed to start *The Daily American*, the first black daily ever published in America. And while managing these very different affairs, he studied law, becoming, before he left Jacksonville, the first black lawyer admitted to the Florida bar.

Meanwhile, James W. Johnson had been writing verse. When Rosamond Johnson returned to Jacksonville after completing his musical education, he examined some of his brother's work and grew excited about it. James was stirred by his brother's praise, and the two thereupon decided to collaborate on some songs, James supplying the words and Rosamond the music. One of their earliest efforts was a song written in 1900 for the Stanton School's exercises in honor of Lincoln's birthday. The song, "Lift Every Voice and Sing," was soon widely acclaimed and came to be popularly known as the Negro National Hymn.

For several years James Johnson spent each summer in New York, working with his brother and another talented young black musician, Bob Cole. The three made their headquarters in the Marshall Hotel on Fifty-third Street, a place that soon became the mecca of an industrious group of black artists and entertainers. Each fall James would return to Jacksonville to resume his duties as principal at Stanton while his brother and

Bob Cole went on tour with various musical comedy and concert groups. After the Jacksonville fire had razed Stanton, James extended his stay in New York, awaiting the reconstruction of the school. Ultimately, he gave up his job as principal to devote his time to song writing. From about 1901 to 1906, he and his brother and Bob Cole constituted a team that was top-notch among composers of American popular music. From their pens came the hit tunes for the singing stars of the day, among them "The Maiden with the Dreamy Eyes," for Anna Held; "My Castle on the Nile," for Bert Williams; "Oh! Didn't He Ramble," for George Primrose; "The Maid of Timbuctoo," for Lillian Russell; and "Congo Love Song," for Mary Cahill. The latter song alone netted $13,000 in royalties for its creators.

The song-writing trio eventually disbanded when James W. Johnson, who had become active in politics, supporting Theodore Roosevelt for President, was offered the post of United States Consul at Puerto Cabello, Venezuela. Johnson accepted the appointment, but he did not abandon his writing while in Central America. However, he did turn to more serious forms of literature, and his work appeared in *The Century Magazine* and *The Independent*. Among the poems which he wrote at this time were his famous apostrophe to the anonymous creators of the black spiritual, "O Black and Unknown Bards," and his well-known sonnet "Mother Night." He also began to use prose as a creative medium for the first time, starting *The Autobiography of an Ex-Colored Man*. This work, published anonymously in 1912, was designed as a human document, depicting the life of a colored man who had married a white woman. It was *not* the story of Johnson's life, but it was so widely interpreted as his autobiography that the author later decided to tell the real story of his life in *Along This Way*.

In the spring of 1909 Johnson was transferred by the State Department to Corinto, Nicaragua. Before taking up his duties as consul he returned to the United States for a vacation, and while there he renewed his acquaintance with Grace Nail, a beautiful girl whom he had known for a number of years. On his next leave they were married and Grace went back to Corinto with him. But Nicaragua was in the throes of a revolution and Johnson's new wife soon had to return to the United States. Her departure was well-timed, for new outbreaks of violence occurred shortly thereafter. Johnson tried to arrange a truce between the contending parties, but his efforts were in vain. A fleet of American warships anchored in Corinto harbor intervened, bombarding the coast of Nicaragua and landing marines to protect American interests in the country and to safeguard the right of the United States to what was then considered the best route for an interocean canal across Central America.

Johnson left the consular service in 1914 and became editorialist for *The New York Age*, one of the oldest black newspapers in New York. He continued writing verse and undertook some translations of Spanish works. In 1915 his translation of Granados' grand opera *Goyescas* was produced at the Metropolitan Opera House in New York. But it was his work for the National Association for the Advancement of Colored People that occupied most of his time during the next several years. His work as organizer, investigator, lecturer, pamphleteer, and lobbyist for that organization was extremely successful. And though he did not succeed in his efforts to have the Dyer Anti-Lynching Bill enacted into law, he did alert the American public to the horrors committed by lynch-mad mobs.

Johnson also made many Americans aware of the evils of the imperialistic course upon which our country had recently embarked. While American intervention in Nicaragua had been justified, perhaps, by the fact that it had been undertaken in accordance with the wishes of the government in power and with the object of sustaining that government, the seizure of Haiti in 1915 could not be so justified. After an extensive investigation of conditions in Haiti, Johnson reported in a series of four articles for *The Nation* on the oppressive and corrupt measures of the American forces of occupation and on the patriotic spirit of native Haitians. This material was later incorporated in Johnson's book *Self-Determining Haiti*, published in 1920. The book fostered interest in the island and spurred a movement for the restoration of its independence from the United States.

In 1917 Johnson had published a volume of his verse, *Fifty Years and Other Poems*. Realizing that the work of other black poets was little known in America, he then decided to compile an anthology of black verse. *The Book of American Negro Poetry*, published in 1922, was the result. It contained representative selections of black poetry from Phillis Wheatley to Paul Laurence Dunbar and Claude McKay and was prefaced by an introductory essay in which Johnson "called attention to the American Negro as a folk artist, and pointed out his vital contributions, as such, to our national culture."

Johnson's interest in black folk art soon led him to other work. In 1925, together with his brother Rosamond, who made the piano arrangements, he published *The Book of American Negro Spirituals*. The book, consisting of sixty-one spirituals and prefaced by a brief history of the form, was so successful that, in 1926, the brothers published *The Second Book of Negro Spirituals*.

Johnson's interest in black folk art had important consequences for his own creative work. As a youth in Jacksonville, he had been dragged to church by his grandmother to hear every visiting clergyman who came to town, for she wished to fire him with religious enthusiasm. He remembered the old-time black preacher as an actor and an orator who "preached a personal and anthropomorphic God, a sure-enough heaven and a red-hot hell." Now, with his interest in the phenomena renewed, he turned some of the sermons he had heard into verse, producing, in *God's Trombones: Some Negro Sermons in Verse*, some of his best creative work.

Other books followed, among them *St. Peter Relates an*

Incident of the Resurrection Day (1930), *Black Manhattan* (1930), *Along This Way* (1933), and *Negro America What Now?* (1934). In 1930 Fisk University made Johnson professor of creative literature, and in 1934 New York University made him visiting professor in the same subject. He was awarded the Spingarn Medal, "the most distinguished badge of merit that an American Negro may wear," and he won the Harmon Award. The degree of Litt.D. was conferred upon him by Talledega College and by Howard University. And still he sought uses for his "spare time," uses that benefited his race, his country, and his fellow man. But on June 26, 1938,

> . . . *God sat back on his throne,*
> *And he commanded that tall, bright angel standing at his*
>   *right hand:*
> *Call me Death!*
> *And that tall, bright angel cried in a voice*
> *That broke like a clap of thunder:*
> *Call Death! — Call Death!*
> *And the echo sounded down the streets of heaven*
> *Till it reached away back to that shadowy place,*
> *Where Death waits with his pale, white horses.*
> *And Death heard the summons,*
> *And he leaped on his fastest horse,*
> *Pale as a sheet in the moonlight.*
> *Up the golden street Death galloped,*
> *And the hoofs of his horse struck fire from the gold,*
> *But they didn't make no sound.*
> *Up Death rode to the Great White Throne,*
> *And waited for God's command.*
>
> *And God said: Go down, Death, Go down,*
> . . .

James Weldon Johnson was killed in an accident when a railroad train struck his car at a grade crossing near his summer home at Dark Harbor, Maine, on June 26, 1938. But his work lives on—the work of author, poet, educator, public servant, writer of popular songs, scholar, and crusader for civil rights; the work of a man whose only rest was to be that last long one which no man escapes.

LANGSTON HUGHES

"That night your grandfather seemed nervous. Not fearful of anything—just terribly anxious. It seemed there was something he wanted to do. Something important."

Mary Langston was talking about her first husband, Lewis Sheridan Leary, who had done something important. He had been one of five black men who had joined the abolitionist John Brown in his attack on the federal arsenal at Harpers Ferry, Virginia, in the cause of freedom.

Seventy years old now, his widow, a remarkable woman who had been the first black woman to attend Oberlin College in Ohio, told her seven-year-old grandson how her husband had left, promising to return soon. All that had come back had been his old shawl, returned to her several weeks later, full of bullet holes.

Her grandson was Langston Hughes, born to her daughter Carrie in Joplin, Missouri, on February 1, 1902. Shortly after Langston's birth, Carrie's husband, James Hughes, had left his wife and child and fled to Mexico, embittered by being denied the right to take the bar examinations, as a black man, after years of studying law.

Carrie was an unusual woman, too. She had studied at the University of Kansas, and after being abandoned by her husband, she went to Topeka, Kansas, where she found work as a stenographer to a black lawyer. A reader, she introduced

Henri Cartier-Bresson/Magnum

Langston Hughes

young Langston to books. And when it was time for him to go to school, she took him to the Harrison Street School, the nearest school to her one-room apartment in a downtown business block. It turned out to be all white, and Langston was rejected. However, his mother persisted, taking her case to the school board.

Eventually Carrie Hughes won her fight. Langston was admitted to the Harrison Street School. Except for one teacher, everything would have been all right. But she was mean. She ridiculed him in class and encouraged the students to persecute him. Many of them did so. But he had his defenders, too, as he recalls in the autobiography of his early years, *The Big Sea*, published in 1940.

When Carrie lost her job and had to search for another, she left her son with her mother, in Lawrence, Kansas. It was his grandmother who told young Langston about John Brown, Frederick Douglass, David Walker, Nat Turner, and Harriet Tubman—early heroes in the fight for freedom. It was in her house, too, that he read the Topeka *Plain Dealer* and W. E. B. Du Bois's *The Crisis*, learning from the black weekly newspaper of the racist horrors committed against his people and discovering in Dr. Du Bois's magazine the accomplishments of black people and a sense of pride in being black.

When Langston was twelve years old his grandmother died, and for two years he lived with "Auntie and Uncle Reed," as he called the friends of his grandmother who took him in. The Reeds had a large garden and kept chickens and a few cows, so food was fresh and plentiful, which had not been the case in his grandmother's poor home. Langston helped with the garden, did chores, delivered papers, and later worked in a seedy Lawrence hotel after school, sweeping up and cleaning and polishing the big brass spittoons in the lobby.

By this time the boy's mother had remarried and was living in Lincoln, Illinois, with her new husband, Homer Clarke, an amiable man whom Langston liked at once. Soon after

Langston joined them, however, the family moved to Cleveland, Ohio, where his stepfather found work in a steel mill. Here Langston attended Central High School and participated in the activities of Karamu House, a community center with a well-developed arts program operated by Russell and Rowena Jellife.

At Central High Langston came under the influence of Helen M. Chestnutt, daughter of the black writer Charles W. Chestnutt and the only black teacher at the school, and, particularly, Ethel Weimer, who taught him Shakespeare and encouraged him to write for the school paper. It was Miss Weimer, too, who introduced him to modern poetry, especially the work of Carl Sandburg, who was to have a profound influence on his own work.

In the spring of his junior year, Langston received a letter from his father, inviting him to spend the summer in Toluca, Mexico, where he had established a lucrative business in law, real estate, mortgages, and loans. He found his father, whom he had not seen in almost eleven years, preoccupied with making money and with little time for companionship. He was, by turns, harsh and demanding, nagging the boy to learn bookkeeping, for which he had little aptitude, or indifferent and uncommunicative.

The following summer, lured by a hint from his father that he might send him to college in the fall, Langston returned to Mexico. On the train ride down, as he crossed the Mississippi, an impulse seized him and he scrawled these lines on the back of an envelope he had in his pocket:

I've known rivers:
I've known rivers ancient as the world and older
  than the flow of human blood in human veins.

My soul has grown deep like the rivers.

Completing the poem before his journey ended, he called it "The Negro Speaks of Rivers" and sent it off to *The Crisis*, where it was published in June 1921. It was to become one of his best-known poems.

The summer of 1921 was an uncomfortable one for Langston, despite the publication of his poem and several other pieces in *The Crisis*. He wanted to be a writer. His father had decided he would be a mining engineer. He wanted to go to Columbia University, mainly because it was in New York City and he was anxious to see and experience Harlem. His father wanted to send him to Europe to study. In the end, he went to Columbia, but it was a mistake. He found the university cold and indifferent. Required subjects like physics and mathematics did not interest him. Except for the time he spent in Harlem, he was lonely and dissatisfied. But he continued to write, putting his feelings in the language of the people and the rhythms of the Harlem streets that he got to know and love—

> *I got the Weary Blues*
> *And I can't be satisfied.*
> *Got the Weary Blues*
> *And can't be satisfied—*
> *I ain't happy no mo'*
> *And I wish that I had died.*

Getting nowhere at Columbia, he dropped out and, after drifting for a bit, shipped as a steward on the S.S. *Malone*, a freighter bound for Africa. It was the first leg of a lifetime of travel that would take him right around the world. Between voyages he worked—as a doorman in a Montmarte nightclub, as a laundry sorter, a journalist, a dishwasher, a member of a film production company, a lecturer, a translator. And he continued to write poetry—

> *Goin' down de road, Lawd,*
> *Goin' down de road.*
> *Down de road, Lawd,*
> *Way, way down de road.*

> *Got to find somebody*
> *To help me carry dis load.*

One day, while Langston was working as a busboy in a Washington, D.C., hotel, Vachel Lindsay, the poet, came into the restaurant. Too shy to introduce himself, Langston dropped three of his poems at Lindsay's table when he picked up the dishes. That night Lindsay, who was giving a reading of his own work, read the poems to his audience, praising them highly. The next day Langston Hughes was famous, his picture, as busboy poet, in newspapers everywhere. But Vachel Lindsay, who had gone all over the United States reciting his poems for a living, gave Langston something more than instant notoriety. He gave him an idea. He, Langston, could sing for his supper, too. And he did, organizing reading tours that took him all over the country reciting his verse for fees varying from a few dollars to considerable sums.

During the 1920s Langston Hughes, whose work had appeared in *The Crisis* and *Opportunity* and other magazines, began to be more widely published. Along with other new black writers, his work was included in Alain Locke's anthology *The New Negro*, which heralded what has been variously described as the "Harlem Renaissance" or the "Black Renaissance." This flowering of black artistic expression, in the work of such writers as Claude McKay, Countee Cullen, and Jean Toomer, abandoned the attempt of many in earlier generations of black writers to imitate the cultural expression of whites. Instead, it gave voice to the hopes, aspirations, fears, and joys of ordinary black people, whose perspectives had been changed by the migration of millions to the cities during the years of World War I and after. Hughes expressed the attitude of these new young writers when he said, in a essay in *The Nation*:

To my mind, it is the duty of the younger Negro artist . . . to change through the force of his art that old whispering "I want to be white," hidden in the aspirations of his people, to "Why should I want to be white? I am a Negro—and beautiful!"

In *Weary Blues* (1926) and *Fine Clothes to the Jew* (1927), Hughes's principal contributions to the Harlem Renaissance, he wrote of porters, elevator boys, prostitutes, and bad men, trying, as he said, "to express our individual dark-skinned selves without fear or shame." And when the Renaissance petered out in the hard times brought on by the depression, Langston Hughes continued. Writing often in dialect in rhythms based on the blues or jazz, he turned out volume after volume of poetry over the years, expressive of "our dark-skinned selves," becoming in the process the laureate of his people. The volumes include *Dear Lovely Death* (1931), *The Dream Keeper* (1932), *Shakespeare in Harlem* (1942), *Fields of Wonder* (1947), *One-Way Ticket* (1949), *Montage of a Dream Deferred* (1951), and *Ask Your Mama: 12 Moods for Jazz* (1961).

Hughes took time off from his travels to return to college for his degree, this time attending Lincoln University, an all-black school near Philadelphia from which he graduated in 1929. Even while attending college, he continued to write. In fact, his novel *Not Without Laughter*, published in 1930, was written during his senior year at Lincoln.

In the 1930s Langston turned to the short story, a genre in which he was almost as prolific as in verse. *The Ways of White Folks* (1934), *Laughing to Keep from Crying* (1952), and *Something in Common and Other Stories* (1963) are three of his books of collected stories.

In 1937 the Baltimore *Afro-American* sent Hughes to Spain as a war correspondent to report on the black Americans fighting against fascism in the International Brigade. For six months Hughes lived in the bombed cities and on the battle lines of the Spanish Civil War, sending back reports to his paper and turning his observations into the verses of *Letters from Spain*.

Shortly after graduating from Lincoln University, Langston had spent some time at the nearby Hedgerow Theater, where he had written his first play, *Mulatto*. The play was not staged then, but it was produced six years later in New York, where it ran for a year on Broadway. Hughes had also written several plays which the Karamu House in Cleveland had put on. Back from Spain, Hughes returned to the theater, helping to establish the Harlem Suitcase Theater in the loft of an old building on 125th Street. There his new play, *Don't You Want to Be Free*, opened on April 21, 1938. Soon thereafter, he was off again, this time to California, where he formed the New Negro Theater in Los Angeles.

Much of Hughes's work for the theater was hastily done and sketchy, little more than a framework to be filled in by the director and cast during production. However, the best of his theater pieces have been collected in *Five Plays by Langston Hughes*. These include *Mulatto*, *Soul Gone Home*, *Little Ham*, *Tambourines to Glory*, adapted from his novel of that name published in 1959, and *Simply Heavenly*, based on his Simple stories.

The Simple stories, growing out of a weekly newspaper column that Hughes wrote for the Chicago *Defender*, deserve separate mention, for they are among the most delightful things that the writer ever did, inviting comparison with the comic creations of Mark Twain. In fact, the Simple stories, like their central character Jesse B. Semple, nicknamed "Simple" but far from it, are anything but simple. A man of little formal education but much common sense and wry, ironic humor, Simple, a hardworking Harlemite up from Virginia, has had his troubles, but he has endured—not barely, nor gloomily, nor bitterly, but, through his humor, triumphantly.

I have had so many hardships in this life [he says] that it is a wonder I'll live until I die. I was born young, black, voteless, poor, and hungry, in a state where white folks did not even put Negroes on the census.

In fact, he continues,

My mama should have named me Job instead of Jesse . . . I have been underfed, underpaid, undernourished, and everything but undertaken—yet I am still here.

Still here and always talking, about everything on earth from sex to segregation, brotherhood to betrayal, destitution to the military draft, Simple demonstrates the wisdom of everyman in the victory of common sense and good humor over almost every form of adversity, pretense, hypocrisy, bigotry, and fear. His stories are collected in *Simple Speaks His Mind* (1950), *Simple Takes a Wife* (1953), *Simple Stakes a Claim* (1957), *The Best of Simple* (1961), and *Simple's Uncle Sam* (1965).

Hughes recognized the value of humor. In 1966 he edited *The Book of Negro Humor*, including in it jive, jokes, nonsense verse, folktales, songs, gags, and other inducements to laughter. "Humor," he said in an introductory note, "is your own unconscious therapy. Like a welcome summer rain, humor may suddenly cleanse and cool the earth, the air, and you."

"Humor is a weapon, too," he realized, "of no mean value against one's foes." Sometimes, however, the weapon fails. Then anger, militancy, defiance are required. And these qualities, too, are in Langston Hughes. As a matter of fact, his last book, *The Panther and the Lash*, published posthumously in 1967, contains them in good measure, reflecting the militant spirit of the times in which they were published.

Langston Hughes died on May 22, 1967, at the age of sixty-five. At his funeral, in Harlem, his poem "Wake," from *Shakespeare in Harlem*, was read. In the poem he urges those who mourn for him to "mourn in red"—

> *Cause there ain't no sense*
> *In my bein' dead.*

—and a jazz trio played, as he had requested, "Do Nothing Till You Hear from Me."

The song was a kind of private, parting joke for his friends. It was appropriate for a man to whom humor had been so large a part of life to exit with a joke. Moreover, it is likely that we shall be hearing from Hughes for a long time to come. For in addition to the poetry and short stories that he produced in such quantity, he had written in almost every form—plays, novels, autobiography, history, books for children, anthologies, translations, even the text for a book of photographs called *The Sweet Flypaper of Life.* He had received many prizes and awards during his life, including honorary doctorates, Guggenheim and Rosenwald fellowships, the Spingarn Medal, election to membership in the American Academy of Arts and Letters, and other marks of recognition. But he had written of, and for, the ordinary man in the street, particularly the black man, using his idiom and the rhythms of his speech, song, and laughter. Touching so many so closely, it is unlikely that he will be let go—

> *Cause there ain't no sense*
> *In [his] bein' dead.*

RICHARD WRIGHT

"Fire! Fire! Fire!"

The words rang with panic as clouds of black smoke issued from the frame house and flames crackled and jumped over dry boards.

"Richard! Richard! Where are you, Richard? Richard, come here, the house is on fire!"

But three-year-old Richard knew. He had set the fire. Bored by the restrictions placed upon him because of his grandmother's illness, he held broom straws tipped with blue flame from the fireplace to the fluffy white curtains hanging at the window and watched the flame leap and run. When the fire began to billow in yellow globes and the heat beat on his face, Richard ran to his hiding place beneath the house.

Young Richard was found before the flames reached him and was dragged from beneath the house to a punishment that almost proved fatal to him. He was beaten until he was unconscious and for weeks he lingered, delirious, between life and death. Then, slowly, the dark balance fell and he began to recover.

The episode, which took place in 1911, is stage one in a boyhood marked by repression, rebellion, violence and awful retribution.

Ten years later, in October 1921, in Jackson, Mississippi, Richard and a friend stopped to talk after school one day. The

Richard Wright

conversation, as reported by Wright in his autobiography, *Black Boy*, went something like this:

> *"You can't sit in school all day and not eat," he said.*
> *"What am I going to eat?" I asked.*
> *"Why don't you do like me?"*
> *"What do you do?"*
> *"I sell papers."*
> *"I tried to get a paper route, but they're all full," I said. "I'd like to sell papers because I could read them. I can't find things to read."*
> *"You too?" he asked, laughing.*
> *"What do you mean?" I asked.*
> *"That's why I sell papers. I like to read 'em and that's the only way I can get hold of 'em," he explained.*

And so thirteen-year-old Richard followed his friend's advice and sent to Chicago for newspapers to sell. He devoured the magazine supplement because it contained stories like Zane Grey's *Riders of the Purple Sage*, full of the color and adventure his own life lacked. But the newspaper itself went unread, except by the boy's customers. It provided him with another form of nourishment, however: boxes of vanilla wafers which he could now afford to buy and wolf down. The wafers were not very substantial, but they did stop the gnawing hunger pangs, particularly when they were followed by quantities of water rushing full force from the tap straight into his stomach, stretching it tight.

Then one day a hint from one of his subscribers awakened him to the fact that the paper he was distributing was anti-black. Sponsored by Ku Klux Klan sympathizers, the paper was filled with the lynch passion of that extremist group. Once aware of the nature of the publication, he could not, of course, continue to sell it. So there were no more papers for him to read.

The episode is the second stage in Wright's life: a youth marked by hunger, physical and spiritual.

Several years later, in the summer of 1924, he found a job in an optical company. The boss was a fair-minded man from the North, and Richard was to learn the trade, but his fellow workers, Pease and Reynolds, were jealous of his opportunity. One day they trapped him behind a workbench. Pease, at one end of the bench, accused:

"Did you call me 'Pease,' nigger? Reynolds says you called me 'Pease.' "

At the other end, Reynolds, swinging a steel bar, edged up the bench.

The episode is the third stage in Wright's life: a young manhood marked by fear.

The thread of events connecting these stages is a twisted one, woven from strands of poverty, prejudice, ignorance, and religious fanaticism. For Richard Wright this thread first began to unwind on a cotton plantation in Natchez, Mississippi, where he was born in 1908. Before Richard and his younger brother were of school age, however, the family moved to Memphis. Young Richard was excited about the move, for they were to sail up the Mississippi on the *Kate Adams*, a boat that loomed, in his childish imagination, as big as a mountain and snowy white on the mud-brown river. And despite his disappointment when he saw "a tiny, dirty boat that was not at all like the boat I had imagined," the trip was much more attractive than the destination was to be. For after the plantation, "the stone buildings and the concrete pavements looked bleak and hostile" and "the absence of green, growing things made the city seem dead." Moreover, living quarters for the family of four were two small rooms in a one-story brick tenement.

Soon, though, there were only three in the family. Richard's father, who worked as a night porter in a Beale Street drugstore and who was "always a stranger" to the boy, "alien and remote," abandoned his wife and their two children shortly after they got to Memphis. Unfortunately, an uninvited guest came to sit in the father's empty chair at the table—Hunger!

Eventually Richard's mother got a job as a cook. Starvation was averted for the time. But another problem arose. Working all day, she had to leave her two sons unsupervised. Inevitably, they were claimed by the unwholesome streets of Memphis. And when she fell ill the specter of hunger returned to haunt the household. Then, when the rent on the dingy flat could no longer be paid, the boys were put into an orphan home, where they were inadequately fed and set to senseless tasks. Richard tried to run away but was caught and returned to the institution. Finally, when his mother had accumulated enough money to pay the train fare, she took her sons to live with her mother in Jackson, Mississippi.

Once again there were green fields to play in and there was enough food to eat. And for young Richard there was something even more important—stories to excite the imagination and set the heart racing. But the stories were not to last. One day Richard's grandmother heard Ella, the young schoolteacher who boarded with her, telling Richard the story of Bluebeard. Flaring into a rage, she snatched the child from the girl's knees.

"You stop that, you evil gal!" she shouted. "I want none of that Devil stuff in my house!"

And when Richard protested, saying that he had enjoyed the story and that Ella had not finished, his grandmother slapped him across the face with all her might, shouting that such things were "the Devil's work" and telling the boy that he was going "to burn in hell."

Granny's religious fervor burned very hot. And there were no more stories.

There was, however, plenty of "Devil's work" in the small southern towns in which Richard Wright was brought up. One particularly disastrous sample of it was provided young Richard and his family when they went to live with Aunt Maggie and Uncle Hoskins. Uncle Hoskins was an affable man who owned a profitable tavern in Elaine, Arkansas. Since it was profitable, some greedy white people wanted it. One night shortly after his wife's relatives had come to stay with him, Uncle Hoskins went to his tavern as usual. He never came back. Those who coveted his property shot him dead. And the community ignored the episode. As Richard Wright describes the event:

There was no funeral. There was no music. There was no period of mourning. There were no flowers. There was only silence, quiet weeping, whispers, and fear. I did not know when or where Uncle Hoskins was buried. Aunt Maggie was not even allowed to see his body nor was she able to claim any of his assets. Uncle Hoskins had simply been plucked from our midst and we, figuratively, had fallen on our faces to avoid looking into that white-hot face of terror that we knew loomed somewhere above us.

The Wrights fled to West Helena in 1916, settling in a flat near the small town's railroad yards. There, terror struck again. Richard's mother suffered a paralytic stroke. Taken back to her mother's home in Jackson, "she remained abed ten years, gradually growing better, but never completely recovering, relapsing periodically into her paralytic state." Since Granny could not bear the financial burden of caring for her ailing daughter and her two sons, a family council was called. It was decided that the boys would be taken by other members of the family, Richard's brother going to live with Aunt Maggie in Detroit and Richard himself going to Uncle Clark in nearby

Greenwood. Soon, however, Richard returned to Jackson, where the suffering of his mother and the poverty of his surroundings—five years of "painful, baffling, hunger-ridden days and hours"—fixed his character.

A somberness of spirit that I was never to lose settled over me during the slow years of my mother's unrelieved suffering [says Wright], a somberness that was to make me stand apart and look upon excessive joy with suspicion. . . .

Richard's somberness was lit by one ray of bright hope, however. He wanted to be a writer. It was a foolish and dangerous aspiration for a black boy living in the Deep South to nourish. And in his grandmother's home it was considered a sinful ambition as well. But Richard held fast to his aim. Having had but one year's schooling in his first twelve years, he settled down to equip himself for his job. And he did remarkably well on his indigestible two-meal-a-day diet of mush and cooked greens. He even managed to have a story he wrote in the eighth grade published in the local newspaper, to the amazement and chagrin of his grandmother and his pious Aunt Addy.

Paying his own way by working at odd jobs after classes and during the summer, Richard Wright graduated from school and, at seventeen, left the poverty-stricken and repressive Jackson home of his grandmother to meet life on his own. He went to Memphis, where he found a job which paid $10 a week. After work, while consuming his supper—a can of beans heated under the hot water tap in his room—he read. And far into the night he would read, borrowing books from the Memphis library on the card of a friendly white man. (The privilege of drawing books from the public library was denied to black people in Memphis.) H. L. Mencken's *A Book of Prefaces* was one of the first volumes Richard drew and, though he was shocked by the author's bitter, ironic style and by his caustic comments on American institutions, Wright was aroused by Mencken to a new conception of the function of letters. After reading the book, Richard commented to himself,

Yes, this man was fighting, fighting with words. He was using words as a weapon, using them as one would use a club. Could words be weapons? Well, yes, for here they were. Then, maybe, perhaps, I could use them as a weapon?

Richard Wright was to use words as weapons, weapons in the fight against the bigotry, poverty, and hatred in which he had grown up. He had already struggled free of the toils of ignorance and superstition that had bound him in his grandmother's home. He had broken the bonds of provincial Jackson. Now he fought to free himself of the chains imposed by prejudice in the South, saving money to go north, to Chicago and freedom. The battle was a tough one, for he had not only to free himself, but also to reach back a helping hand for his invalid mother, still subject to the harassment of Granny Wilson. With the aid of his brother, he succeeded in bringing his mother to Memphis. Then, after two years of struggling and saving, the family left for Chicago with high hope for a new way of life.

The new way of life proved disappointing, for though prejudice took somewhat different forms in the North, its existence was everywhere apparent. And with the coming of the great depression in the thirties, the family, like thousands of others, was reduced to direst poverty. Now, however, Wright began to realize that prejudice and hate and fear, like the ignorance and superstition that had plagued him all his life, were but the bitter fruit whose poisoned root was poverty. And he sharpened his weapons to hack at the root. The stories in *Uncle Tom's Children* (1938), the critical analysis of *Twelve Million Black Voices* (1941), the portrait of Bigger Thomas in *Native Son* (1940), and the record of childhood and youth provided in *Black Boy* (1945) reveal those weapons at work, laying bare, in their different ways, the ugly root of the evils Richard Wright had known so well.

Native Son, a realistic novel of great dramatic intensity, was particularly successful in its exposure of the plight of black immigrants in the northern urban ghetto. Told from the point of view of Bigger Thomas, driven by oppression and fear into hatred and crime and then hunted, caught like a rat in a trap, and executed, the story is a vehement denunciation of racism seen through the eyes of the black man who is its victim. So powerful was the novel that it sold two hundred thousand copies in less than three weeks, breaking all sales records for its publisher and making Wright the first black author of a best seller.

The autobiographical *Black Boy* was almost as successful as *Native Son*. Exposing the narrowness and deprivation of black life in the South, it destroyed the myth of the "happy Negro," manufactured by whites to disguise the consequences of their oppression. A bleakly pessimistic book, sensational in its revelation of the details of stunted, thwarted lives, it is an anguished cry for rebellion against a system geared to thwart any such effort.

Wright was to know another bitter fruit of poverty during those years in Chicago and later in New York, and to know it well, though failing to recognize its poisonous qualities at first. During the depression he joined the Communist Party. The Communists were fighting poverty too; or so they said. And they seemed to offer minority groups a chance for the full participation in life which had everywhere been denied them. But the offer was misleading, as Wright discovered. Time and time again he saw his race, his class, and his humanity betrayed in the interest of the party. In 1944 he withdrew from the Communist organization, and later he told the story of his ten-year delusion in the chapter he contributed to *The God That Failed* (1949).

In 1946 Richard Wright moved to Paris with his second

wife, Ellen, and their daughter, Julia. (His first marriage to
Dhimah Rose Meadman ended in divorce.) Except for several
visits to America and travel that took him to Spain, Africa,
Indonesia, England, and Scandinavia, Paris was to be his home
thereafter, and his second daughter, Rachel, was born there in
1949.

Never a facile writer, Richard Wright was to take a long
time on his next novel, *The Outsider*, which was not published
until 1953. Generally accounted a failure, the book has been
said to deal more in symbols than in recognizable human
beings. In 1958 he published *The Long Dream*, recounting the
initiation of Fishbelly, a black youth from Mississippi, into
manhood through racism. Other works of fiction include *Eight
Men* (1961), a collection including the fine story "The Man
Who Lived Underground," and *Lawd Today*, published posthumously in 1963.

In his later years Wright turned increasingly to nonfiction as
a vehicle for the expression of his ideas and feelings. He
published many articles and essays in newspapers and magazines. *White Man, Listen!* (1957) collects some of his essays.
Pagan Spain (1956) is an extended travel journal. Perhaps the
best-known works produced during Wright's years in Europe,
though, are *Black Power* (1954) and *The Color Curtain* (1956).

The latter book, a report on the Bandung Conference of
Asians and Africans held on the island of Java in 1955, has
been called "a vivid and illuminating job." Documenting a
historic event, Wright depicts the black, and yellow, and
brown-skinned peoples of the world "getting a new sense of
themselves, getting used to new roles and new identities," as
they see "men of their color, race and nationality arrayed [for
the first time] in . . . aspects of power."

Black Power is a book of observations on life in the Gold
Coast, an African colony aspiring to independent national life.
A curious book, *Black Power* is confused, often prejudiced,
sketchy, yet important. It is important because Wright, a

product of oppression like the people about whom he writes, observes a new Africa emerging to challenge the West. He fears that Western man, in Africa as in his own case, "will make no meaningful concessions to the sense of justice and freedom which he himself helped to instill in men's hearts." The result might be a capitulation, like Wright's, to the tyranny of communism. And he feels there might be no chance for the reversal which he experienced.

Richard Wright died in Paris on November 28, 1960. He had been living in France for fourteen years, and his reputation among the French, who saw him as the greatest of Afro-American writers, was that of a major literary figure, comparable to William Faulkner, Ernest Hemingway, or John Steinbeck. In his own country, however, his early reputation had evaporated, and he was largely ignored. It was not until the violence of the mid-sixties recalled the bitterness and despair of Wright's earlier work that that work was reexamined. Then the accuracy of Wright's observations and the sharpness of his insights were reaffirmed. There would be no easy resolution of the racial strife in America. Wright had foreseen that in looking deeper than any of his contemporaries into the frustration and pain that black men had suffered. *Native Son* is a terrible monument to his penetrating vision. And *Black Boy* is another. Those books have influenced a new generation of black American writers, thereby refuting the saying that a prophet is without honor in his own country.

ANN PETRY

Ann Petry, who was born in Old Saybrook, Connecticut, on October 12, 1911, loves its old houses and traditions. One tradition that has played a very important part in her life is the family tradition of pharmacy. Her grandfather was a chemist who worked for a drug manufacturing concern. He helped to make some of the old reliable salves and ointments that were popular as remedies in his day and are still in use today. Ann's father, Peter C. Lane, was a druggist. Indeed, the Lane drugstore is an Old Saybrook landmark. The building dates back to colonial days. It was in this building that Ann and her sister were born, for her father and her mother, Bertha (James) Lane, lived above the drugstore. "When I was growing up," Mrs. Petry says, "a drugstore was a drugstore. It has since become a sort of combination restaurant and supermarket, selling everything from hot dogs to sofa pillows." But the Lane drugstore was a pharmacy in the traditional sense. And so was the drugstore in the neighboring town of Old Lyme, which was owned by Ann's Uncle Fritz and Aunt Louise, both of whom were pharmacists.

While in high school Ann began to write for her own amusement. She wrote a number of short stories and a few essays. On finishing high school, however, she knew that she would have to put this pleasant hobby aside, at least for the time, and devote her efforts to her college work. After

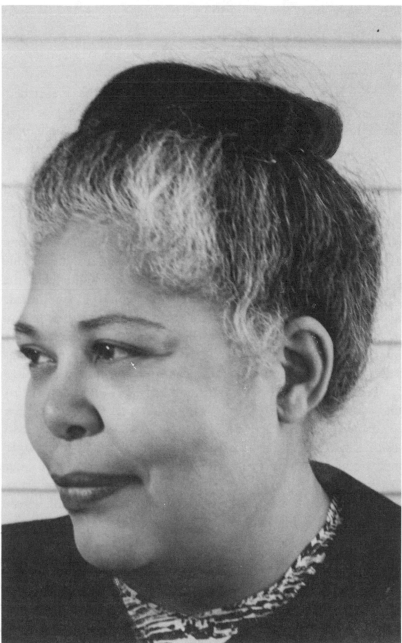

Hilda Bijur

Ann Petry

graduating from Old Saybrook High School in 1929, she enrolled in the College of Pharmacy at the University of Connecticut, then located in New Haven.

Ann was a good student. She completed the prescribed course of studies, and in 1934 she was granted the degree that made her a graduate pharmacist. The coveted diploma was hung on the wall beside the yellowing certificate of her father, and Ann went to work in the family stores, helping her father or her uncle as occasion demanded.

For three years Ann mixed cough medicine, removed cinders from inflamed eyes, recommended remedies for constipation, eczema, sunburn, poison ivy, and toothache. Occasionally she was called upon in an emergency to administer first aid. Invariably she was called upon to listen sympathetically to stories of affliction, accounts of accidents, recitals of symptoms. Soon she knew a great deal about the private lives of her fellow townsmen. Stories began to form in the young pharmacist's mind. And once again, in her spare time, she turned to writing, jotting down incidents, sketching characters, outlining plots.

The year 1936 was a turning point in her life. For it was in that year, on a visit to Hartford, that she met George Petry, a handsome bespectacled young New Yorker who was also visiting in Hartford. During the next months the young couple met frequently and their friendship ripened into love. On Washington's Birthday 1938 they were married in Old Saybrook. After the wedding they moved to Manhattan, where George worked, and there, on 129th Street in Harlem, they made their home.

Now a new life began in earnest for the girl from the country drugstore. To develop her writing talent, Ann got a job with the *Amsterdam News*, a Harlem newspaper. She began her newspaper career in 1939, writing advertising copy and selling advertising space. By 1941 she had joined a rival paper, *The People's Voice*, where she covered general news stories and edited the women's page. Looking with fresh eyes upon New

York's black community, she saw beyond the headlines she wrote while covering fires, accidents, murders, and other assignments. As she climbed rickety tenement stairs in search of news for her paper, she saw families of ten or more crowded into two or three dingy rooms. She saw the bad housing and bad food of poverty, the misery of illness, the dangers that exploitation brought, the recklessness bred by despair.

Unemployment was an ever-present threat to the people who lived in those streets, and Ann Petry saw its shadow fall on the faces of many of those whom she interviewed. The menial jobs available to most black people were drudgery, offering no incentive to effort, no reward for ability. Shiftlessness, illiteracy, vice, and crime grew. There was neither stability nor security in the cellars and the cell-like rooms in which many Harlem residents lived.

Mrs. Petry was particularly appalled by the plight of the children, many of whom roamed the streets unsupervised while their parents worked. So in the summer of 1944 she accepted a position with the New York Foundation, which was engaged in an experimental educational program in the New York City grade schools. Mrs. Petry worked with so-called problem children in P.S. 10 at St. Nicholas Avenue and 116th Street. Helping to plan a wholesome recreational program for these children, Mrs. Petry got to know them and their environment well. Her work at the school helped to focus her attention on 116th Street, with its poverty, its broken homes, its crime and delinquency. One Hundred and Sixteenth Street became, for her, The Street—Harlem in miniature—with important consequences for her literary career.

That career received new impetus from her work with the children of Harlem. Mrs. Petry resumed her writing, turning for the first time to the drama. She wrote children's plays to interest the youngsters with whom she worked. She joined the now famous American Negro Theatre group and began acting in amateur productions. Then she turned again to short stories.

And this time her work met with success. She had a story published in *Phylon*, an Atlanta University magazine. *The Crisis*, a monthly organ of the National Association for the Advancement of Colored People, accepted three of her stories for publication, among them one called "On Saturday the Siren Sounds at Noon."

It was this story that started Mrs. Petry on the road to fame. An enterprising editor at Houghton Mifflin, the book publishers, saw the story in the November 1943 issue of *The Crisis* and, impressed with its quality, wrote to ask Mrs. Petry if she were at work on a novel. She was not. But the editor's query started her thinking. Why not write a novel based on her knowledge of 116th Street? The seed had been planted for her first book, *The Street*.

Within a year Mrs. Petry had outlined her novel and written five chapters. She submitted the chapters and a synopsis of the rest of the book to Houghton Mifflin, hoping to get some valuable criticism. Much to her surprise, she won the publishing company's $2,400 literary fellowship for 1945. Ten months later she finished the novel and in 1946 it was published.

Drawing upon her firsthand knowledge of Harlem, Mrs. Petry presented an accurate picture of that city within a city. "There are," as she says, "no statistics in *The Street*, though they are present in the background, not as columns of figures but in terms of what life is like for people who live in overcrowded tenements." Yet the story moves swiftly, holding the attention of the reader. When he reviewed *The Street* in *The New York Times*, Charles Poore called it "a skillfully written first novel." And he added, "You won't forget that Harlem Street."

The publication of *The Street* brought fame to Ann Petry. Indeed, she soon found that demands upon her time were so great that she had little opportunity for writing. And she was anxious to get to work on another novel. So when her husband returned from his tour of duty with the army, he and Ann started looking for a place in the country. Their notions of country living were somewhat grandiose at first. They scanned the Houses for Sale columns, looking for a place with 150 acres of ground. When Ann's father, Mr. Lane, heard this, he laughed. "One man can take care of exactly one half acre of land in his spare time," he said. "That's old-fashioned advice, but it's good advice." His daughter and son-in-law came to agree and gave up the idea of becoming gentlemen farmers. Instead they purchased the house they live in today, an eighteenth-century house with green shutters and a wide lawn not far from the family drugstore in Old Saybrook. And Ann settled down to work on her second book.

Country Place, which draws upon Old Saybrook for its background, was published in 1947.

While living in New York, Ann had been an active member and at one time executive secretary of Negro Women, Inc., an organization which encouraged active participation in politics. And in Old Saybrook she was even more active in civic affairs. She was a member of the League of Women Voters and was on the board of directors of that organization for three years. She also served on the board of the regional library and on her local Board of Education.

It was the birth of her daughter that increased Mrs. Petry's interest in school problems. Elisabeth was born in Old Saybrook shortly after Mrs. Petry returned there to live. When she started school Mrs. Petry began to remember her own school days. Like her daughter, she was one of a few black children in a predominantly white school. Though her school years were pleasant enough, she still remembers the painful week in high school when the subject of slavery was discussed in history class. The slaves were depicted as passive and content with their lot, enjoying the protection of kindly masters, hardly aware of the fact that they were not free. After the first lesson on the subject, Ann was so embarrassed and ashamed that she stayed home from school for the rest of the week.

Since then, Ann Petry has learned that the slaves in the South before the Civil War lived under quite a different set of conditions from those described in many history books. In *Harriet Tubman: Conductor on the Underground Railroad*, a book for young people published in 1955, Mrs. Petry did much to correct these false impressions.

The book is a biography of the stalwart woman who came to be known as "the Moses of her people" for the part she played in leading more than three hundred slaves out of bondage. In describing Harriet's life Mrs. Petry gives a detailed picture of the times. She pictures the one-room, windowless, dirt-floored, sway-back cabins huddled together in the "quarter," "out of sight of the Big House, but not quite out of hearing." She shows us the children, "clothed in one-piece garments made of coarse material like burlap, reaching to the knees, . . . fed in a haphazard fashion, a bit of corn bread here, a scrap of pork there." She tells us about the work—Harriet, not yet eight, cleaning house all day and rocking the mistress's baby half the night—and the punishment—Harriet whipped so often with a rawhide whip that her back was covered with scars, "crisscrossed with scars so deep that they would be visible for the rest of her life." This was what slavery was like.

Nor were the slaves passive. Despite awful punishment, enforced ignorance, fear of the unknown and of the cold North where safety lay, thousands of them fled northward to Canada and freedom. They were given courage by black people like Denmark Vesey, the Bible-reading carpenter who felt that all men should be free, and Nat Turner, the Prophet, who led a revolt against the masters in Southampton County, Virginia. Most of all, they were inspired by Harriet Tubman, the woman who knew more than anyone else about the secret routes to the North and the places along the way where fugitive slaves would be safe.

Mrs. Petry dedicated *Harriet Tubman* to her daughter, in the hope that the book will help Elisabeth and her friends to understand better the dark period in our country's history when slavery existed.

Harriet Tubman was not Mrs. Petry's first book for young people. In 1949 she wrote a book for her young niece. It is called *The Drugstore Cat* and it tells the story of Buzzie, a kitten with a temper as short as his tail. Buzzie has a wonderful time in a drugstore very much like the Lane pharmacy in Old Saybrook. Before the story ends, Buzzie has grown so fond of the place that he manages to curb his temper so that he will be allowed to remain. *Tituba of Salem Village*, published in 1964, is another book for young people. It is a story of fear and hysteria, having as its background the witch hunts of American colonial days.

In 1953 Mrs. Petry published another adult novel, *The Narrows*, and in 1971, gathering some of the stories she had written over the years, including "Like a Winding Sheet," which was named the best American short story for 1946, she published a collection called *Miss Muriel and Other Stories*. Her most recent book for young people, *Legends of the Saints*, appeared in 1970.

Writing for both children and adults, Mrs. Petry appeals to all ages. Drawing upon her knowledge of country and city, early history and the present day, she writes with an accuracy sharpened by her scientific training and made vivid and dramatic by the ability of a skillful journalist who looks beneath the surface of events she describes to discover where and how those events touch the human heart.

JAMES BALDWIN

James Baldwin was born on August 2, 1924, in Harlem Hospital in New York City. He never knew his true father. But his stepfather, David Baldwin, a preacher whom his mother married in 1927, he knew all too well. He knew David Baldwin's authority certainly, for it was dictatorial. He knew his anger, for it was frequent and extreme. He knew his harsh tongue and his hard hand, for he felt the force of both of them often. He knew, finally, his stepfather's hatred, for it filled the man almost completely, leaving small room for anything else. And young Jimmy responded to the hatred in kind.

It was not until long afterward, after he had escaped into the dangers of the world from the more immediate dangers of confrontation with his stepfather, after his stepfather's paranoic rage at the world had driven him to his death in the madhouse, that Jimmy came to know David Baldwin more fully. By then Jimmy was himself a man, struggling for his own identity in a white-dominated America that seemed to deny that possibility. He came to know that the rage bottled up in his stepfather and vented terribly, and inadequately, against his own family was the same rage that exploded in shattered glass and flying masonry in the Harlem riots of 1943. In fact, James Baldwin came to know in his own psyche the madness that drove his stepfather to destruction. Writing in *No Name in the Street* (1972) of a period a few years after David Baldwin's death,

James Baldwin

when his own inner turmoil drove him to Paris to try to become a writer, Baldwin says: "I was mad, as mad as my dead father. If I had not gone mad, I could not have left." Happily, his own madness drove him not to death but to an environment where he could put his rage and madness into perspective, directing it outward against bigotry and prejudice instead of bottling it up within as his stepfather had done.

James Baldwin's most vivid memories of his mother during his childhood were of her regular visits to the hospital, where she was always "having another baby." So frequently did the babies come that Baldwin remembers the year as a crowded calendar of birthdays: "I, James, in August. George, in January. Barbara, in August. Wilmer, in October. David, in December. Gloria, Ruth, Elizabeth, and . . . Paula Maria, . . . all in the summertime."

A full calendar! And so was the Harlem tenement flat full. For in addition to the children, David's mother, Barbara, lived with the family and, for a time, David's son by an earlier marriage, Sam.

However, by the time Sam was seventeen he had left home, swearing to return only to bury his puritanically strict father. His leaving grieved David. In fact, James says the departure broke his father's heart, destroyed his will, and drove him mad.

In this crowded, tension-filled household then, James Baldwin grew up. Commenting on his early years in *Notes of a Native Son*, published in 1955, Baldwin recalls his mother's "exasperating and mysterious habit of having babies" and reflects on his own role in helping to raise them:

As they were born, I took them over with one hand and held a book with the other. . . . in this way I read Uncle Tom's Cabin *and* A Tale of Two Cities *over and over and over again; in this way, in fact, I read just about everything I could get my hands on.*

The mystery of the recurring births and his own early responsibility for the care of the babies quickened James's sense of the miracle of life, of its infinite variety, and of its fragile vulnerability.

At the age of seventeen, James Baldwin left home. By that time his capacity to love and care for the messy, demanding, joyous miracle of human life had expanded enormously, in spite of the apparently unpromising circumstance of a joyless, repressive stepfather and a threatening, life-denying environment.

By that time, too, young James had discovered the world of literature and had made some early efforts to become a part of that world. His mother recalls that as a small, rather frail child, he "lived in books." Starting with the copy of *Uncle Tom's Cabin* that he balanced in one hand, while juggling a baby with the other, and that, together with *A Tale of Two Cities*, he read again and again, he soon progressed to the library on 135th Street, which he visited three or four times a week, reading "everything there."

At Frederick Douglass Junior High School, where he was editor of *The Douglass Pilot*, James Baldwin had sympathetic understanding from his teachers, particularly from two of them, Countee Cullen and Herman W. Porter, and, as he had in elementary school, torment from most of his contemporaries. Small and scrawny with enormous luminous eyes, Baldwin was dubbed "Froggy" and "Popeyes," teased as a teacher's pet, and bullied as a sissy. But everyone recognized him as the best writer in the school. And Countee Cullen, who was renowned already as a poet, provided an example of what a black man could achieve in literature. Cullen, who had spent several years in France, also made James and the other writers in the literary club that he directed aware of the possibilities in the large world outside of the Harlem ghetto, which most of them saw as the apparently inflexible boundary of their lives. Closer to home, Mr. Porter, who served as adviser to *The Pilot*, introduced Baldwin to scholarly research, taking him to the 42nd Street library to do an article for the newspaper on "Harlem—Then and Now." The article, which Baldwin wrote when he was in the ninth grade, was a thoroughly professional job, as Mr. Porter, a janitor's son and a Harvard graduate, had confidently anticipated.

Troubled during adolescence by the changes taking place in his body, numbed by his preacher stepfather's stern lectures on sinfulness, overwhelmed by the violence of the Harlem streets, young James found a friendly atmosphere in the home of his schoolmate Arthur Moore, where he became almost a part of the family. There "Baldy," as they called him, relaxed as he couldn't at home and talked about himself, his hopes and his fears. It was Art Moore, too, who took Baldy with him, when he was fourteen, to meet Mother Horn, the pastor of the Mount Calvary of the Pentecostal Church.

Mother Horn, a powerful and successful preacher, had the authority of James's stepfather without his bitterness. And she gave James the warmth and sympathy that his mother could not, for his mother was always either bearing children, working to help support them, or intervening between her irritable husband and her rebellious son.

Like the Moores, Mother Horn provided a refuge for young James. Moreover, her fiery sermons and "shoutin'" congregation provided an alternative to the violence of the streets and an outlet and a direction for the passionate turmoil in the fourteen-year-old Baldwin's heart. He was converted—"saved" in the language of the church—and a short time later he became a young preacher himself, channeling his developing creative talents into emotional sermons in an effort to "save" others.

Baldwin remained a preacher for about three years, gradually losing fervor as he grew older and more skeptical. Later, looking back on the period of his refuge in the church, he came to see that refuge as a delusion, an escape from the world and the flesh which should have been confronted and dealt with rather than consigned to the devil and avoided. He came to feel that it was not the much-acclaimed principles of faith, hope, and charity that brought men to the church, but rather that blindness, loneliness, and terror drove them there, as they had driven him.

However, within the church there existed a real sense of community and an excitement that continued to stir Baldwin long after he had abandoned the pulpit. A sense of communal involvement and redemptive purpose informs his work. The preacher's scorching invective is there also. And the music: shout and spiritual, resonant biblical phrase, chant of exhortation and hymn of praise. Finally, his work is pervaded by a dramatic force born of the church. But it is a drama laced with irony, an irony growing out of his rational assumption that one is saved, if at all, for the world, not from it.

At DeWitt Clinton High School in the Bronx, he began to read widely again, resuming a habit that his preaching had temporarily interrupted. There, too, he met youngsters from a variety of racial, ethnic, and religious backgrounds, an experience damaging to the concept of special election embraced by Baldwin's church, that is, that one is "saved" while all others outside of one's own small group are eternally damned. As it happened, two of Baldwin's best friends at high school, Emile Capouya and Richard Avedon, were Jews. In *The Fire Next Time* Baldwin tells how, when he brought one of them to his house, his religious conviction received one of its strongest shocks.

. . . *afterward [Baldwin says, describing Capouya's visit] my father asked, as he asked about everyone, "Is he a Christian?"—by which he meant "Is he saved?" I really do not know whether my answer came out of innocence or venom, but I said coldly, "No. He's Jewish." My father slammed me across the face with his great palm, and in that moment everything flooded back—all the hatred and all the fear . . . —and I knew that all those sermons and tears and all that repentance and rejoicing had changed nothing. I wondered if I was expected to be glad that a friend of mine, or anyone, was to be tormented forever in Hell. . . . I told my father, "He's a better Christian than you are," and walked out of the house.*

At DeWitt Clinton, he and Avedon served in turn as editor-in-chief of the literary magazine, *The Magpie.* (Avedon was later to become a celebrated photographer, and in 1964 Baldwin and he collaborated on a book of pictures and prose giving their impressions of life in America, *Nothing Personal.*) Other members of the staff, including Capouya, would gather to plan the next issue of the magazine and talk about books and writing, themselves and their worlds. It was another refuge for Baldwin. But it was outside the ghetto, and it permitted wider intellectual scope than any of the refuges he had thus far known.

Then, in 1943, he moved to Greenwich Village, where he spent five years working at a variety of jobs to keep alive and teaching himself to write. He worked in the shipyards, then in a wartime factory manufacturing rifles. He was copyboy on the newspaper *PM* for a while. And for eighteen months he was busboy-dishwasher-waiter at the Calypso, a Village restaurant operated by a large, affable black woman named Connie, who was to figure as Hilda in Baldwin's 1968 novel *Tell Me How Long the Train's Been Gone.*

After work, at whatever job he happened to have, Baldwin turned to his real work—writing. Subsisting on two or three hours' sleep a night, he learned his craft by practicing it, writing and rewriting. Speaking of his method, he says, "I'm not a writer. I'm a re-writer." Eventually some of his pieces sold to magazines—to *The Nation, The New Leader, Commentary.* The piece that he did for *Commentary,* on "The Harlem Ghetto," represented a real breakthrough. For one thing, its success made it easier for him to sell his work to other publications, like *Partisan Review* and *The Reporter.* More important, during the six months that he struggled over the essay he worked closely with the late Robert Warshow, a man whom Baldwin described emphatically as "the *greatest* editor I ever *had.*" Warshow made Baldwin realize that writing "was not simply the act of writing—that it was something else, something much harder. Which is to tell the truth."

The cost of seeking the truth was high, as Baldwin was to learn from his relationship with another great man whom he met during his apprenticeship in Greenwich Village: Richard Wright. It was Wright, in fact, who helped Baldwin to his first tangible reward as a writer: a Eugene F. Saxton Memorial Trust Award. The purpose of the award was to enable Baldwin to finish his first novel, a sixty-page segment of which he had shown Wright shortly after they met. But burdened with his gratitude to Wright, his idolatry of the man who had published *Native Son* when Baldwin was in high school, and his effort to establish his own identity as a writer, Baldwin couldn't finish the novel. Written and rewritten and rewritten again, what had begun as *Crying Holy* became *In My Father's House* and was eventually abandoned, only to be resumed in Paris, finally completed at an isolated chalet in the Swiss Alps, and published, ten years after Baldwin had begun it, as *Go Tell It on the Mountain* in 1952. But by then Baldwin had become another man.

Meanwhile, frustrated and humiliated at what he thought was a betrayal of Wright, Baldwin turned to other work, including a documentary, with photographer Theodore Pelatowski, on Harlem's storefront churches. The documentary was not published, but it did win Baldwin a fellowship from the Rosenwald Foundation which enabled him to go to Paris. Actually, he had not betrayed Wright, nor was he to do so subsequently, although many people, including Wright himself, thought that he did. The truth of the matter was that he was not at all like Wright, whom he admired greatly. The temptation to become like Wright was great, for Wright was not only

Baldwin's benefactor, he was also a literary success, providing a ready model for imitation. But Baldwin resisted the temptation to imitate.

In order to resist effectively, he had to know himself, always a continuing effort for a writer—and no easy task. He also had to assess Wright as an artist. It was this latter effort that led to accusations that he had betrayed Wright. For in analyzing Wright's work, Baldwin found it to be in the mainstream of the protest novel, like *Uncle Tom's Cabin*, which he had devoured uncritically as a child but had come to recognize as a "very bad novel." In fact, commenting on Wright's main character in *Native Son*, Baldwin says, "Bigger is Uncle Tom's descendant, flesh of his flesh. . . ." Indeed, he saw *Native Son* and *Uncle Tom's Cabin* as the violent and sentimental counterparts of one another. And in his essay "Everybody's Protest Novel," assessing this type of work, he accurately sees that its failure lies "in its rejection of life, the human being, the denial of his beauty, dread, power, and its insistence that it is his categorization alone which is real and which cannot be transcended."

Pointing to the oversights and evasions of the Stowe-Wright school in "Everybody's Protest Novel," Baldwin warned:

In overlooking, denying, evading man's complexity—which is nothing more than the disquieting complexity of ourselves—we are diminished and we perish; only within this web of ambiguity, paradox, this hunger, danger, darkness, can we find at once ourselves and the power that will free us from ourselves. It is this power of revelation which is the business of the novelist. . . .

Baldwin spent nine years in Europe, most of the time in Paris, interrupted by a couple of visits home. There he rewrote *Go Tell It on the Mountain*, the book that he had begun in Greenwich Village, an autobiographical novel reflecting his troubled relations with his stepfather and his early experience in the church. However, *Go Tell It on the Mountain* was finished not in Paris but in Loeche-les-Bains, a small village high in the

Swiss Alps that he memorializes in "Stranger in the Village," included in his first collection of essays, *Notes of a Native Son* (1955). Another essay in that volume, "Equal in Paris," describes his trials and tribulations as a young writer in Paris, which he, unlike many American expatriates, did not romanticize. In fact, though Paris was for him a haven from racial persecution, he recognized that it was so only because he was an American. His Algerian friends found no such haven in the city, where they were persecuted as enemies of French colonial power for daring to seek freedom from French control.

Giovanni's Room (1956), Baldwin's personal favorite among his novels, was written, almost entirely, during a two-year period at Les Quatre Chemins, near Cannes, on the French Riviera. A poetically evocative love story that ends in betrayal and violence, *Giovanni's Room* takes place mainly in Paris, which Baldwin recalled and depicted with the careful eye of a painter.

When Baldwin returned to America in the summer of 1957, it was to an America on the brink of revolution, as black people, particularly those in the South, vigorously sought their long-denied rights in a series of encounters that shook the country to its foundations. Baldwin heard warning rumblings in Europe and decided to come home and join the fray. He did so, traveling to the South to observe what was happening and reporting on what he saw in *Partisan Review*, *Harper's*, and other magazines. Later his reports, along with observations on a variety of other subjects, including some tart ones on liberal ineptitude, middle-class blacks, and *de facto* segregation in the North, were published in his second collection of essays, *Nobody Knows My Name* (1961), which soon became a best seller, bringing Baldwin popularity and affluence and thereby providing him with the opportunity to be a greater force in the civil rights struggle.

Another Country, also published in 1961, is a novel expressing Baldwin's anguish over the human condition, made harsher

by race, as reflected in the tragically tangled personal relation-
ships of a young black drummer and his sister in the literary
and theater world of New York.

Two later books of essays, *The Fire Next Time* (1963) and
No Name in the Street (1972), grew out of Baldwin's effort to
give expression to what he might ironically have called "The
White Problem," the problem of America's terrible—and
unforgivable—innocence, its lack of comprehension and unwillingness to grasp the significance of what its destructive
power had done to the world and to itself. The former book,
especially, is an Isaiah-like challenge to white America to wake
up and turn the country around before the coming of the
holocaust that will surely destroy us all. Originally published in
the November 17, 1962, issue of *The New Yorker* as "Letter
From a Region of My Mind," it skyrocketed him to fame.

Later novels by Baldwin include *Tell Me How Long the
Train's Been Gone* (1968) and *If Beale Street Could Talk* (1974).
The former book covers a variety of experiences in places
ranging from a slum brothel in New York to a penthouse
apartment overlooking San Francisco Bay, as Leo Proudham-
mer, recovering from a heart attack suffered at the peak of his
career, reflects on his rise to eminence as a black actor. *If Beale
Street Could Talk* is about Tish Rivers and Fonny Hunt, a black
Romeo and Juliet, whose love sustains them when Fonny is
falsely accused and imprisoned for a crime he did not commit.

In addition to novels and essays, Baldwin has written short
stories, a collection of which was published in 1965 under the
title *Going to Meet the Man*. He has also published two
transcribed conversations, one with Margaret Mead, the anthropologist, called *A Rap on Race* (1971) and the other, *A
Dialogue* (1973), with the young black poet Nikki Giovanni.
And he has been active in the theater. In the spring of 1955
Howard University produced *The Amen Corner*, Baldwin's play
about Harlem's storefront churches, based on his adolescent
experience of conversion with Mother Horn, who appears in the

play as Sister Margaret Alexander. The play is about Sister Margaret's rejection by her congregation because of her rediscovery, through her estranged husband and her rebellious son, of human values she had once rejected in her pursuit of power in the church. Since it deals with the hypocrisy of the church, *The Amen Corner* took ten years to reach Broadway. That fact, as Baldwin is probably correct in asserting, "says a great deal more about the American theater than it does about this author." *Blues for Mister Charlie*, produced at the ANTA Theater in New York on April 23, 1964, is roughly based on the Emmet Till case, that is, it tells the story of Till's murder by a white man who was later acquitted of the crime by a Mississippi jury.

Baldwin's indictment of white America in *No Name in the Street* and particularly in *The Fire Next Time*, delivered with the passionate intensity of an Old Testament prophet, is an accurate and necessary comment on racism and economic exploitation. But in his later novels and plays, where, as he says, "the disquieting complexity of ourselves" should be explored, Baldwin seems to have sacrificed the subtle immediacy of exploration of the self for more general truths about race and society. Perhaps, in view of the seriousness of the questions Baldwin raises, it is, in his words, "a sign of frivolity so intense as to approach decadence to suggest that these books [and plays] are . . . badly written. . . ." But one has the feeling that, however serious the questions and however accurate Baldwin's answers to them are, neither questions nor answers are adequately served in novels like *Tell Me How Long the Train's Been Gone* or plays like *Blues for Mister Charlie*. Commenting on such matters in "Everybody's Protest Novel," Baldwin had this to say:

Whatever unsettling questions are raised are evanescent, titillating; remote, for this has nothing to do with us, it is safely ensconced in the social arena, where, indeed, it has nothing to do with anyone, so that finally we receive a very definite thrill of virtue from the fact that we are reading such a book at all. This report from the pit reassures us of its reality and its darkness and of our salvation.

Since, as Baldwin's essays so vigorously and accurately demonstrate, we are, as a nation, far from any sort of salvation, the works in question are, to say the least, somewhat misleading in their effect.

However, no one who has read much of Baldwin can, in fact, be so misled. And if he occasionally misses the high mark he has set for himself, in fiction or in the drama, the body of his work, rich, full, and various, attests to his power as a critic and his sensitivity as an artist. Subtle, passionate, proudly black and deeply human, he is a poet in prose, tormented by the evil he sees but affirming the values of human life and celebrating its joys in tense, dynamic language as vivid as the world he encounters in sorrow and delight.

Education and
Public Affairs

Though in many areas and for long periods of time they were denied the right to participate fully in the affairs of our country, black Americans have compiled an impressive record of leadership in education and in widely varied civic activities. Frederick Douglass, a powerful orator, was one of the earliest of black statesmen. A marshal of the District of Columbia and a minister of Haiti, he was, in addition, founder and editor of the *North Star*, a paper which advocated emancipation.

Immediately after the Civil War, suffrage was extended to all black men on the same basis as white men. The Freedmen's Bureau established schools for the former slaves. The newly freed Americans took full advantage of their opportunities and wisely used their political privileges during the hectic days of Reconstruction.

When federal troops were withdrawn from the South, however, the Ku Klux Klan rode and a reign of terror began. That era is known to all the world as the most shameful period of American history. The constitutional rights of the black man were denied him by law and through intimidation. Lynchings were the order of the day.

Of course, a great degree of freedom and security continued to exist for blacks in the North. But as the black worker moved away from the bigotry and poverty of the decaying South in increasing numbers, he began to be feared as a rival in the highly competitive labor markets of the North. Pressures were brought to bear upon him. He was segregated, denied admission to labor unions, discriminated against in hundreds of ways. Such behavior reached its low point during periods of depression, when the black man became a scapegoat upon whom was visited all the troubles of the distressed masses.

Under these circumstances, it was inevitable that black talent would be drawn into certain fields. Bigotry and prejudice had to be fought before the black man could hope to come into his own. The National Association for the Advancement of Colored People has been an effective instrument in this fight, battling lynch law with court law, fighting oppression and segregation with organized opposition, and helping to give blacks a sense of identity and accomplishment through the work of W. E. B. Du Bois and other men and women of stature.

Furthermore, some measure of economic security had to be achieved if the black man was not to be a pawn, pushed about by forces beyond his control. The work of men like A. Philip Randolph helped to provide some black workers with the means whereby they could achieve this security.

Men like Dr. Ralph Bunche, working for world peace at the United Nations, helped to open up new horizons for the black man in international affairs. Women like Mary McLeod Bethune overcame poverty and prejudice to extend educational opportunity for poor blacks in the South.

But progress was maddeningly slow. Then, on May 17, 1954, the United States Supreme Court ruled that separate but equal facilities for blacks and whites in schools were not, in fact, equitable. Hope rose, only to be crushed, for the following year the Court, in what was described as an effort to "implement" its decision, ruled that integration should proceed "with all deliberate speed." The catch was in the word "deliberate," for it gave racists the signal they were seeking: an opportunity for endless delay.

This equivocation set off a revolution in black America, nonviolent and integrationist at first, under the general leadership of Dr. Martin Luther King, Jr., but increasingly militant as the peaceful demonstrations were met with shocking brutality and the demands for civil rights went largely unheeded. Spokesmen for this later phase of the struggle were such remarkable men as Eldridge Cleaver and Malcolm X, born in the ghettos and self-educated in the prisons where a heedless and wasteful society had thrown them.

The struggle continues, with uncertain results. Violence has taken its toll, inflicting heaviest damage on black neighborhoods. However, in the struggle a new spirit has been forged among black people of all political convictions, and some gains have been made, especially in the South. There integration has begun in the schools, and many public facilities have been desegregated. Moreover, massive black voter registration has resulted in the election of a significant number of black public officials throughout the South.

In the North, bussing schoolchildren out of the districts in which they live to overcome *de facto* segregation has met strenuous opposition and has had, thus far, questionable results. A moderate increase in economic opportunities for blacks in certain areas of employment has been offset by inflation and continuing high unemployment rates. And while general awareness of the plight of urban blacks has increased, concrete steps to improve their condition have been few.

W. E. B. DU BOIS

"I was born by a golden river and in the shadow of two great hills, five years after the Emancipation Proclamation." So says William Edward Burghardt Du Bois in an essay, "The Shadow of Years," published fifty years after his birth, which took place on February 23, 1868. The river was the Housatonic. The hills were part of the Berkshire Mountains, which flanked the town of Great Barrington, Massachusetts, "a beautiful place," as Du Bois recalls it, "a little New England town nestled shyly in its valley with something of Dutch cleanliness and English reticence." Despite the Dutch cleanliness, however, it was the paper mills of the town that turned the river golden—with pollutants. And there was no reticence, no restraint, in the name some townspeople used to describe the Irish immigrants who worked in the mills, lived in the slums near the river, and swelled Great Barrington's population to five thousand. They were scum—dirty foreign scum. By comparison, the town's twenty-five to fifty black inhabitants—some of them property owners, most with ancestries dating back to the Revolutionary War—were well regarded. In fact, Du Bois himself grew up, as he tells us in his autobiographical *Dusk of Dawn* (1940), participating fully

in the ordinary social affairs of the village—the Sunday school with its picnics and festivals; the temporary skating rink in the town

W. E. B. Du Bois

hall; the coasting in crowds on all the hills—in all of these, I took part with no thought of discrimination on the part of my fellows, for that I would have been the first to notice.

Indeed, Du Bois's own ancestry in America went back, on his mother's side, some two hundred years to an African slave boy named Tom, who won his freedom from his Dutch captor, Coenraet Borghardt, through active service in the Revolutionary War. For a hundred years the black Burghardts had lived in western Massachusetts. In Du Bois's boyhood they were represented by three farming brothers, Uncle Ira, Uncle Harlow, and "Uncle Tallow," as his grandfather Othello Burghardt was called. In fact, the first home that William remembered, the "delectable place" that he recalls nostalgically in "The House of the Black Burghardts," was his grandfather's house with its great stone fireplace, big flagged kitchen, and yard with a brook running through it and a mighty elm towering over the house.

William never had the companionship and guidance of his father, Alfred Du Bois, whom he described as "a dreamer, romantic, indolent, kindly, unreliable." In short, he was quite unlike the deep-rooted, hardworking Burghardt farmers. And soon after Alfred's marriage to Mary Burghardt and the birth of their son, he began his "restless wandering." He was, apparently, a barber in New Milford for a while. Later he became a traveling preacher and drifted out of the lives of his wife and son altogether. No doubt he was put off by the Burghardt clan, who saw this pale-faced, handsome wanderer as an interloper and, according to report, discouraged Mary from traipsing off after him to New Milford. In any case, Mary and her son went back to the ancestral home, the House of the Black Burghardts. After a time, she and William moved to Great Barrington, where she supported herself and the child by day work and through boarding William's uncle, who was the barber of a neighboring town.

Du Bois attended school in Great Barrington and helped to eke out his mother's meager income by doing various jobs: "splitting kindling, mowing lawns, doing chores." His contact with the world beyond the town was through Johnny Morgan's news shop, which occupied the front end of the post office. Later, in high school, he was to become, through the good offices of Mr. Morgan, the local correspondent of the Springfield *Republican*, the area's chief newspaper. In high school itself, his principal suggested, quite as a matter of course, since he was intellectually capable, that he take the college preparatory course, which he did, setting his mind on Harvard and studying algebra, geometry, Latin, and Greek. Books, which were expensive beyond the family's means, were provided by a schoolmate's mother, the wife of one of the local millowners.

Du Bois was graduated from high school in 1884, the sole black graduate in a class of thirteen. In the fall of that year his mother died and he went to live with an aunt, putting off, temporarily, thoughts of college. Instead, he went to work, receiving the "fabulous wage" of a dollar a day as timekeeper on a construction project in Great Barrington. The following year, offered a scholarship designed to insure educated leadership for southern blacks during the difficult period of Reconstruction, Du Bois enrolled as a sophomore at Fisk University in Nashville, Tennessee. There, in addition to gaining an insight into natural science, he edited the *Fisk Herald* and developed his powers as an orator. During the summers he taught school in a little valley near Alexandria, in east Tennessee, where there had been a public school for black children for but one short period since the Civil War.

Du Bois graduated from Fisk in 1888. His dream of attending Harvard still unrealized, he applied for and won a Price Greenleaf Award. With one bachelor's degree already obtained, he enrolled at Harvard as a junior to study under some of America's profoundest thinkers and best teachers. He "sat in an upper room and read Kant's Critique" with George

Santayana. He was a member of the Philosophical Club and talked with Josiah Royce and George Herbert Palmer. He was frequently a guest in the house of the great William James, whom he described as "my friend and guide to clear thinking." It was James, in fact, who turned Du Bois from philosophy to the study of American history and social problems, pointing out that "it is hard to earn a living with philosophy." Thus it was that Du Bois came under the influence of A. B. Hart, the eminent historian. He became one of Hart's favorite pupils and was guided by him through his graduate course. Later, in Germany, he studied for two years on scholarships from the Slater Fund. In 1895 he was awarded a doctorate at Harvard, the first Ph.D. achieved there by a black man. His thesis, on *The Suppression of the African Slave Trade to the United States*, was published as the first volume of the new Harvard Historical Series.

For the next sixteen years, Du Bois was a teacher, beginning his career at Wilberforce University in Ohio, where he taught Latin, Greek, German, and English. It was while he was at Wilberforce that he met the "slender, quiet and dark-eyed" Nina Gomer, whom he married in May 1896. Then the couple moved to Philadelphia, where Du Bois taught at the University of Pennsylvania and, living in a black seventh ward slum, researched and wrote *The Philadelphia Negro*, the first systematic sociological study of the black man in America. As a result of his ground-breaking study, Du Bois was invited in 1897 to take charge of the program in sociology at Atlanta University in Georgia, where he taught until 1910, and to direct the Atlanta University Studies.

These studies of black life, which had been started in 1896, took on, under Du Bois's direction, new depth and scope. Within a historical framework describing the modification of African culture by American experience, the studies focused each year on a new area, from health, education, and family life to crime, morality, business, and the church. As Du Bois pointed out later, at the time of the publication of this work, between 1896 and 1914, "Atlanta University was the only institution in the world carrying on a systematic study of the Negro and his development, and putting the result in a form available for the scholars of the world." Widely used by others, the work was accomplished by Du Bois on an annual budget of $5,000, often much less.

Meanwhile, the condition of the black man in America was deteriorating badly from the hopeful days following the Civil War. Between 1884, the year in which Du Bois had graduated from high school, and 1900, some twenty-five hundred black people were lynched in America. In 1895 the Plessy v. Ferguson case decision resulted in legalized segregation of schools. By 1909 all of the southern states had passed laws depriving blacks of the right to vote. Poverty increased. Crime grew. In the face of this worsening situation, dominant black leadership, as represented by Booker T. Washington, head of Tuskegee Institute in Alabama, made every effort to pacify southern white public opinion, urging black submissiveness. Political power, civil rights, higher education, were not to be sought. Instead, industrial training, of the sort available at Tuskegee, was to provide the basis for economic advancement for the black man and—eventually—the improvement of his hard lot.

Naturally enough, Washington's attitude won wide support in the white world of the Gilded Age, a post-Civil War period characterized by wide-scale corruption and financial growth at the expense of human and civic values. Honors rained upon Mr. Washington. He was consulted by Presidents Theodore Roosevelt and William H. Taft on any action involving black citizens, including federal appointments. The "Tuskegee Machine," as Du Bois began to call it, flourished, attracting funds and exercising, through Booker T. Washington, control over scholarly work at places like Atlanta University and other institutions where the prevailing philosophy differed from his own.

Du Bois's philosophy differed markedly from Washington's. Recognizing that if Washington's educational practices prevailed "the Negro would have to accept white leadership, and that such leadership could not always be trusted to guide this group into self-realization and to its highest cultural possibilities," Du Bois advocated "the higher education of a talented tenth" of the black population to provide leadership. In 1903 Du Bois published "Of Mr. Booker T. Washington," an essay pointing out the damaging effects of Washington's program and insisting upon the importance, to the black man and to the nation, of upholding three main principles: "1. the right to vote, 2. civic equality, and 3. the education of youth according to ability." The essay became part of a book, *The Souls of Black Folk*, which, because it challenged Washington's humble, subservient stand, gave new heart and hope to blacks. *The Souls of Black Folk* soon rivaled Washington's *Up From Slavery* in popularity and has since become a classic of black literature.

As part of his effort to counter the effect of the Tuskegee Machine, in 1905 Du Bois organized the Niagara Movement. Named for the place of its first meeting, near Niagara Falls in Ontario, Canada, the Niagara Movement strove by "unceasing agitation" to assert the black American's demand for "full manhood rights." It has been called the first black protest movement of the twentieth century. Short-lived though it was, functioning effectively between 1905 and 1910, the movement raised a voice of dissent at a time when the struggle for equality seemed all but forgotten.

The opening decades of the twentieth century saw social reformers like Lincoln Steffens, Ida Tarbell, and Upton Sinclair attacking the materialism and corruption of the Gilded Age with a vigor and effectiveness that gave a name—"the Progressive Era"—as well as a new moral tone to the period. But the progressives were slow to take up the plight of the black man. In fact, during the early years of this period racist violence increased in the North, with riots in a number of cities. It was against this background that the National Association for the Advancement of Colored People was formed, a coalition of whites and blacks working together for the first time since the abolitionist period. The goal of the organization, which was founded in New York City on May 12, 1910, was to secure black rights under the law. Dr. Du Bois, a founding member and at first its only black national officer, became director of publications and research and through *The Crisis*, the magazine that he initiated, wrote for, and edited for twenty-four years, the chief public voice of the NAACP.

Created without a penny of capital, *The Crisis* was soon self-supporting, increasing from an initial circulation of one thousand copies in November 1910 to a peak of more than one hundred thousand copies. Moreover, Du Bois built circulation without compromising his demands for progressive social action, often battling timid NAACP leadership in order to maintain his independence as an aggressive spokesman in the cause of social justice. In fact, it was just such a battle that led to his resignation as editor of *The Crisis* on June 26, 1934, after the NAACP executive board ruled that no paid official could criticize the association in *The Crisis* without prior approval of the board. This was censorship, and it demonstrated to Du Bois the spiritual poverty of the board. So he quit, returning to Atlanta University as head of the Sociology Department, where he remained until his involuntary retirement at the age of seventy-six.

Serving as the vigorous conscience of his race and "single-handedly educating and arousing thousands of people" as editor of *The Crisis* for twenty-four years had come nowhere near exhausting Du Bois's energies. He had also published widely in a variety of fields, including fiction, the personal and reflective essay, biography—his study of *John Brown* (1909) is a standard work on the abolitionist leader—and such historical studies as *The Negro* (1915), *Black Reconstruction* (1939), and *Black Folk Then and Now* (1940). After he returned to Atlanta, he also edited *Phylon*, a black journal.

Writing, however, was but one of Du Bois's outlets. He lectured widely and traveled much, particularly in Africa, Europe, and the Soviet Union. He was active in the theater, too, having produced a pageant history of the black people, *The Star of Ethiopia*, which was staged in various parts of the country. He also organized the Krigwa Players, the most successful theater company of the Harlem Renaissance. Perhaps Du Bois's greatest single nonliterary activity was his participation in a series of conferences sponsored by the black peoples of the world in the interest of their cooperative self-development. For his role in these conferences from 1900 on, Dr. Du Bois has been called "the father of Pan-Africanism."

In 1950 Du Bois's wife of fifty-three years died. The following year, Shirley Graham, who had been a friend for many years, "persuaded herself that," as Du Bois put it, "I needed her help and companionship, as I certainly did. . . ." At the age of eighty-three, Du Bois was married for the second time on February 14, 1951. He and his wife took up residence thereafter at 31 Grace Court, Brooklyn.

During Du Bois's final years he was as active as ever: serving on the Council of African Affairs at Paul Robeson's behest; opposing the nuclear arms race and America's role in the cold war with Russia; defending Julius and Ethel Rosenberg, who were convicted of supplying information on nuclear arms to the Russians and executed; and running for senator from New York on the American Labor Party ticket. He was also indicted for "failure to register as agent for a foreign principal" for his involvement in the Peace Information Center in 1950, during the Korean War. The charges were eventually dropped, but his opposition to the war, his sympathy for Russia, and his support of Marxist ideology brought him under increasing surveillance and restriction. Invited by Kwame Nkrumah in 1957 to attend Ghana's independence day celebration, he was refused a passport by the U.S. government, a serious blow to the "father of Pan-Africanism." Finally, at ninety-three, embittered by his treatment by the country he had served so long, suspicious of that country's role in world affairs, and more and more attracted by communist doctrine, Du Bois joined the Communist Party.

In 1961, too, Kwame Nkrumah invited Du Bois to come to Ghana to complete his work on the *Encyclopedia Africana*, a project Du Bois had initiated in 1909 and worked at intermittently over the years. Du Bois decided to accept the invitation.

Although Dr. Du Bois spent his last two years in Africa, where in 1963 he died a citizen of Ghana, his long, productive life was lived in America, where he made significant contributions to our culture. He helped to establish sociology as an important branch of knowledge, developing its methodology in a scientific way and applying its techniques to the first comprehensive examination of a number of important aspects of black life. As a reforming educator, he exposed the limitations of a strictly technological training for black people and helped to develop intellectual leadership for black Americans. As a journalist, he made *The Crisis* an immensely important reflector of black life and an organ for the expression of black points of view at a time when there were few avenues for such expression. His contribution to the struggle to obtain full civil rights for the black man through his role in the establishment and development of the NAACP was considerable. His books, particularly *The Souls of Black Folk*, constitute a substantive part of that American culture which black and white people share as their precious heritage. Perhaps most important of all, through his forthrightness and independence, Dr. Du Bois provided a model of aggressive black leadership in an era when it was sorely needed and left a high standard of accomplishment for generations to come.

MARY McLEOD BETHUNE

Her great-grandmother was the daughter of an African chief. Her parents, Sam and Patsy, were born in slavery on the neighboring McLeod and Wilson plantations, about five miles from the village of Mayesville in Sumter County, South Carolina. Hired out by McLeod to a lumber mill so that he could earn enough to buy Patsy from the Wilsons, Sam had hauled logs fourteen hours a day. At the end of two years Patsy became a McLeod slave, and Sam was able to marry her and go back to work in the McLeod cotton fields. Mary herself was born free, on July 19, 1875, twelve years after the signing of the Emancipation Proclamation.

By then her father had acquired the deed to a five-acre patch of the Wilson plantation that had gone uncultivated for years. Having been all his life "McLeod's Sam," he became, with freedom and the purchase of his farm, Sam McLeod, taking his surname from his former master. The land was planted in cotton, and Sam built a three-room cabin on it.

There was not much furniture in the cabin: a homemade table and some rough benches before the fireplace, which served for cooking as well as heating; a one-armed rocker where Patsy's mother, Sophia, smoked her corncob pipe in the evening; a shelf for the kerosine lamp and the Bible, which no one could read but all revered. For bedding there were

Mary McLeod Bethune

straw-filled pallets spread on the floor, which was of wood, unlike the packed-earth floors of the slave cabins.

Outside were the big iron washpots in which Patsy did the laundry that white folks brought her and that she and the children delivered in big wicker baskets. Behind the cabin Mary's mother had a small garden where she raised vegetables. And beyond that, stretching to the swamp on one side and down to the dirt road that ran in to Mayesville on the other, cotton grew, row after row. In those rows the family labored from dawn to dusk, planting in the spring, chopping weeds and tending the growing plants in the hot summer, and picking the bolls to bring to the gin in the fall.

Mary was the fifteenth of seventeen children born to Sam and Patsy McLeod. So there were plenty of hands to tend the cotton. And all were needed, even Grandma Sophia and Patsy, who hoed or picked with the others right up until her babies were due and was back in the fields—when she wasn't sweating over the laundry pots or tending the garden—within a week after each child was born.

Mary worked in the cotton fields from the age of five. By the time she was eight or nine years old she could pick two hundred and fifty pounds of cotton a day. And when Ole Bush, their mule, died one spring when Mary was about fourteen, she quit school to take his place, hitched to the plow to pull it through the earth.

Mary did not start school until she was eleven. The reason for the delay was simple: There were no schools for black people in Mayesville. During the days of slavery the owners had prevented slaves from learning to read, fearing that knowledge would make them dissatisfied with their hard lot and encourage rebellion. Black men had fingers cut off—and worse—for possessing a Bible. During the Civil War, northern soldiers set up tent schools for freed slaves, and later, during Reconstruction, the Freedmen's Bureau and various charitable and religious organizations established some schools for black people in the South. But none had come to Mayesville, which was a backwater where the old attitudes prevailed. In fact, while Mary was still a little girl, she had felt the force of this bigotry. Taken by her mother to help deliver some laundry to the Wilsons, she had lingered in the yard with the two Wilson girls, who were playing with dolls and were delighted to show off their new blue dollhouse with real glass windows. Mary was enthralled. But when she picked up a book belonging to one of the girls and asked the meaning of a printed word, the girls snatched it from her, shouting, "Don't you touch that book with your black hands." Reading was for whites only in Mayesville, as in many other places in the South.

Nevertheless, Mary was determined to learn to read. And in October 1886 with the establishment of the Presbyterian mission school at Mayesville, the opportunity to do so arrived. She made rapid progress, too, under the guidance of Miss Emma Wilson, a young black teacher from the Scotia Seminary at Concord, North Carolina, who was the sole teacher in the little one-room mission school. In fact, despite the shortness of the school year, which lasted only four months, by the end of her third year Mary was helping Miss Wilson teach the newcomers to the school to read.

Indeed, Mary McLeod was so good a scholar that her teacher selected her to attend Scotia on a scholarship provided by Mary Crissman, a Quaker seamstress from Denver, Colorado. When the young student left for the seminary in Concord in the fall of 1889, black people from miles around came to the railroad station in Mayesville to see her off. It was an important event in their lives. For Mary, it was the beginning of a new life.

Concord was an eight-hour train ride from Mayesville in those days, but Scotia Seminary was a whole world away from the cabin in the cotton fields and the one-room schoolhouse Mary McLeod had known. The vastness of the difference was apparent to Mary on the night of her arrival at Scotia, when she sat down to a table set with knives and forks. Turning to

Rebecca Cantcy, one of the teachers who had met her at the station, Mary said, "You'll have to show me, ma'm. Forks are just for white folks in Mayesville."

There were other wonders besides forks and toothbrushes and the curtained bedroom with two beds that she shared with a roommate. There were Latin and Greek and algebra for her to master. There was "moral philosophy," too, as well as music, literature, and penmanship. In addition to the formal curriculum, there were household duties to be performed, part of her education, too. In fact, summing up her experience at Scotia the summer following her first year there, she said: "Education, it's Greek and a toothbrush. Learning for the sake of learning but learning for life's sake, too."

Mary McLeod spent seven years at Scotia. Upon graduating, in 1895, she left for Chicago, where she continued her studies at the Moody Bible Institute. She had been much influenced by the foreign missionaries who had visited Scotia during her years there and dreamed of becoming a missionary herself, hopefully in Africa. But that dream was not to be. After two years at the Moody Institute, Mary returned home. Under pressure from plantation owners, who didn't want sharecroppers' children educated "beyond their station in life," the Mayesville school year had been reduced from four months to two, and Emma Wilson had not yet returned to resume classes. Mary opened the school. And her experience in teaching the twenty or so black children who came from the surrounding farms determined her lifework. She would not be a missionary. She would be a teacher.

When Miss Wilson returned to resume her duties in Mayesville, Mary McLeod sought a regular teaching position for herself. By Christmastime she had a good one, at the Haines Normal and Industrial Institute in Augusta, Georgia, a school that had been founded ten years earlier by Miss Lucy Laney, a former slave. Starting with five students in a rented cottage, Miss Laney had built the school up to a point where, when

Mary McLeod joined the staff, there were more than one hundred students and fifteen teachers. Developed during the period following Reconstruction, when bigoted whites had converted public schools created after the Civil War for the education of all children into "white only" institutions, Haines was thus an island of learning in a sea of enforced ignorance.

Mary's special subject was mathematics, but she loved singing and enjoyed working with the choir, too. That work was important, for the spirituals the choir sang served as a reminder to the youngsters of the significance of their black heritage. Moreover, the concerts given by the choir contributed substantially to the support of the institute, attracting patrons with funds for buildings, scholarships, and books.

After three years at Haines, Mary decided to move on. She had enjoyed working with Lucy Laney and had learned much from her about the development of a successful school. But that was just the point: Haines was a successful school. Throughout the South there were so many places having no schools at all for black people that Mary decided she would use her abilities to start a school of her own. But that was a big step to take. First she would go to Kendall Institute in Sumter, South Carolina, to see what she could do to make a small, backward school flourish.

At Kendall, however, there was a distraction: Alburtus Bethune, a young teacher with a fine tenor voice who sang in the choral society Mary organized in a nearby church. In January 1900 Mary and Alburtus Bethune were married. Shortly thereafter, Alburtus had an offer to teach in a church school in Savannah, Georgia. There was a place on the faculty for Mary, too, so the young couple packed their few books and other belongings and left for Savannah.

After the birth of her son Albert, Mary became restive in Savannah. She loved the ocean and the wide vistas of the country surrounding Savannah, but she was dissatisfied with the school. It had a meager library, taught no science, and largely ignored the plight of the black man, who was confronted by bigotry and oppression in a racist world that ignored his heritage and denied him the opportunity for advancement. The school taught only the academic fundamentals. At Scotia Mary had learned about schools like the Hampton Industrial Institute in Virginia and the newly formed Tuskegee Institute in Alabama, with their emphasis on vocational skills that would prepare the black man to take his place in the world of modern agriculture and industry. However, she did not share the reservations of Booker T. Washington, Tuskegee's guiding spirit, about academic training that went beyond the teaching of specific trade skills. "Vocational training," she wrote later, "includes not only the technique of actual work, but intelligent comprehension of duties as a citizen and the ability to partake of the higher spiritual life of the world."

Mary wanted a school that would prepare black children for a vocation *and* prepare them to become an integral part of their communities. That would be risky, for it would require the black man to speak out and to vote in white-dominated communities determined to prevent such efforts. The school must therefore make the black man aware of the risks by informing him of the way things were in the world. He would have to know about lynchings, race riots, disenfranchisement, and the myriad of repressive measures taken by whites against blacks in America. He would also have to know something about the things he had accomplished, something of his heritage here in America and earlier, in Africa, something of the culture of the people from whom he had sprung. And it was not only the black man who must be so educated. Mary McLeod Bethune was a woman, a married woman with a child. That didn't make her into a mere domestic drudge. She was a teacher, an educated woman who had a place and a voice in the community. Her school would educate women as well as men to take their places in the world.

The school in Savannah was no place for the realization of

her dreams, and when she learned of two openings for teachers in a little mission school in Palatka in Florida, she talked Alburtus into moving. The salaries were similar to those they were getting in Savannah—small. But living in a small town would be less expensive than the city. Perhaps they could save something toward the realization of Mary's dream: the establishment of a school of her own.

But no money was saved in Palatka. Nor, alas, were any dreams realized there. And within a couple of years, Mary was restless again. In fact, at almost thirty, she was more restless than ever, impatient with a dream too long deferred. It was 1904. Throngs of black people were moving south, coming off plantations in Georgia and Alabama to work on the railroad that was being built along the Florida coast. Most of them were heading for Daytona, where the railroad yards were located. There were large encampments of workers and their families, with no provision for the education of their children, who were growing up in ignorance. That would be an ideal place for the realization of Mary's dream.

However, Alburtus was tired of moving. Moreover, he was head of the Palatka school choir, happy with his work. There was good fishing in the Saint Johns River. So Alburtus remained behind. Perhaps he would follow later, perhaps not. In any case, Mary went, taking little Albert with her. She had $1.50 in her pocket when she left. With it she would build her new school.

And she did build it. Starting from small beginnings in a run-down shack on the edge of a dump heap near the ocean, she built a school for the railroad workers' children. The dump heap was a convenience, providing lumber and other cast-off materials with which to refurbish the dilapidated building. For money, she made sweet potato pies and baked yams which she peddled at the railroad yards when the whistle blew for lunch. Rich winter tourists who stayed at the new hotel erected by Mr. Flagler, the railroad magnate, also bought the pies which she and her students hawked outside the landscaped grounds of the hotel.

James N. Gamble, the wealthy soap manufacturer, became one of her regular customers. Listening to Mrs. Bethune's talk about the needs of black people and the high aims of her school, about plans for a new brick hall and a chapel, a science laboratory and a library, about the place of her school in the community and its lovely site on the shore, he agreed to become a trustee of the Daytona Educational and Industrial Training School. Shortly thereafter, he visited Mrs. Bethune in her shack on the dumping grounds by the sea. "Where is the school of which you want me to be trustee?" he inquired. She confessed that her school was "in my mind, my spirit. I'm asking you to be trustee of a . . . dream," she said, "trustee of the hope I have in my heart for my people."

Mr. Gamble accepted trusteeship of the dream and helped to bring it to fulfillment. Moreover, he interested others in helping, particularly Thomas White, the millionaire sewing machine manufacturer, who contributed money for classroom buildings and dormitories. By 1914 Mrs. Bethune had a full high school curriculum in operation at Daytona, one of two such curricula for black people in the whole state of Florida.

Later, with the development of better grade school facilities for black children in Florida, some of the lower grades were abandoned by Mrs. Bethune and two years of college training were added to the program. In an effort to provide manual training workshops and other facilities and staff that would attract more than the half dozen or so young men who attended Daytona, in 1924 Mrs. Bethune consolidated her school with Cookman Institute of Jacksonville, a merger that brought Bethune-Cookman College into being, a comprehensive coeducational school under Mrs. Bethune's direction as president.

But Mrs. Bethune was not concerned with the education of young people alone. She opened the school library to anyone who cared to use it, an important service in the South, where black people were denied access to public libraries. She instituted adult education classes to prepare black people to qualify as voters and urged them to make whatever sacrifices were necessary, such as payment of the burdensome and unfair poll tax. She organized mission schools in the wretched turpentine camps in the piney woods of the state, sending out her student teachers to work in them. Discovering that black people were not accepted in Daytona's all-white hospitals, she established a hospital at the school.

Nor were Mary McLeod Bethune's activities limited to Daytona and its environs. She was a force in marshaling the National Association of Colored Women to fight for the betterment of black people in the South. During the depression, she was called upon by President Roosevelt to serve on the advisory board of the National Youth Administration, developing programs to help young people get on their feet in a period of economic crisis. Later she was made director of minority affairs in that government agency. During World War II, she served as special civilian assistant in the War Department, where she worked toward eliminating Jim Crow in the armed forces. While in Washington, she organized the National Council of Negro Women, raised money for its clubhouse on Vermont Avenue, and helped the organization grow to more than eight hundred thousand members. After the war she helped work for the establishment of the United Nations, participating in the charter conference at San Francisco in April 1945 at the specific request of her friend Mrs. Franklin D. Roosevelt.

In view of the range of her activities and the quality of her service to humanity, it is small wonder that the popular journalist Ida Tarbell named Mary McLeod Bethune in 1932 one of the "fifty greatest women in American history." Other marks of recognition followed, including the Spingarn Medal in 1935; the Francis A. Drexel Award in 1936; the Thomas Jefferson Medal of the Southern Conference for Human

Welfare in 1942. The list of her honorary degrees included those from, among other institutions, Tuskegee, Wilberforce, Xavier, Wiley, Howard, Lincoln, Atlanta, and Rollins. She was particularly proud of the doctor of humanities degree from the latter, not because she was the first black woman so honored by a southern white college but because the degree signified her accomplishment in establishing at Bethune-Cookman the Florida Inter-Collegiate Interracial Conferences for the study of mutual problems among black and white educators.

Perhaps the memento Mrs. Bethune cherished most, however, was the gold-headed cane of Franklin D. Roosevelt that Mrs. Roosevelt gave her after the death of the President, in recognition of her intimacy with and service to him and to the country over the years. After her retirement, at the age of seventy-five, she used the cane regularly as she strode across the Bethune-Cookman campus, where, as president emeritus, she continued to live in a memento-filled cottage until her death at ninety-two on May 18, 1955.

A. PHILIP RANDOLPH

During World War I one of the greatest population shifts in the history of the United States commenced. Eventually, more than a million black people left the ramshackle cabins in which they had lived in the South. There they had been exploited sharecroppers in a backward agricultural economy, an economy that had deteriorated steadily since Civil War times. During the war they flocked northward to the industrial centers, driven by poverty, prejudice, and fear—an average of fifty-six black people were being lynched every year—and lured by extravagant promises of riches, glowing reports of good conditions, and naïve hope in the future. The first great wave of the northward migration occurred between 1916 and 1919, when industry, its labor force depleted by the draft and its production enormously increased, was searching for a plentiful supply of cheap labor to produce war matériel. The second wave—between 1921 and 1923—was the result of stringent immigration laws, which cut off the European labor supply of still-expanding industry.

Some of the expectations of the migrating black people were fulfilled in the North. Enough of their hopes were realized to keep a northward trickle flowing during the thirties, a trickle that would swell again into a steady stream whenever the demand for labor exceeded the supply. The black person did, for example, gain the right to vote when he left the South. His

A. Philip Randolph

children attended school, many for the first time. But he was forced to live in overcrowded, segregated areas. And northern race riots were as productive of anguish as southern lynch mobs. Moreover, unemployment, an ever-present specter to the workingman in our industrial economy, resulted in starvation just as surely as did crop failure.

Of all the evils that the black person faced in the North, the most widespread, and one of the most serious, was unemployment. Hired during an emergency at minimum wages, he was the first person to be dismissed when conditions changed. And although employers used him and cast him aside, organized labor refused to have anything to do with him. The constitutions of at least twenty-two unions (more than half of the American Federation of Labor's affiliates) banned black people. And as the number of black workers in industry rose, many unions became more and more hostile. Some of them insisted upon special anti-black clauses in their contracts with employers. One such contract, negotiated by the Brotherhood of Locomotive Firemen and Engineers, specified that "at least 51 percent of firemen on this line must be white and the road agrees not to employ Negro engineers and in the future all vacancies must be filled by white firemen."

Samuel Gompers, who headed the AFL, suggested that unions should encourage separate local unions and central organizations for blacks—Jim Crowing the black worker. When he was accused of intolerance and discrimination, Gompers bridled and later gave lip service to the cause of black workers. In 1916, 1917, and 1918, he introduced resolutions at the annual AFL conventions calling for the organization of black workers. But he never set up any machinery to implement these resolutions. Only when A. Philip Randolph organized the sleeping car porters in 1925 did the black man begin to have a meaningful role in the labor movement in America. And when Randolph finally forced the AFL executive council to grant his Brotherhood of Sleeping Car Porters an international charter—

the first awarded to an all-black union in the forty-seven-year history of the AFL—he was serving not the porters alone, but all black workingmen.

Asa Philip Randolph, the man who did so much for black American workers, was born at Crescent City, Florida, on April 15, 1889. His father, James William Randolph, was a poor man, a preacher in the African Methodist Church, serving three of the poorest parishes in the state. His salary as a minister was so small that he could not support his wife, Elizabeth (Robinson) Randolph, and their two children upon it. So he opened a small cleaning, dyeing, and tailoring shop to supplement his income. The whole family worked in the shop as occasion demanded, for James was frequently forced to rush out on parish business. And in this fashion they got on.

Even with the help of the shop, however, the Randolphs did not have smooth sailing. As soon as they were able, the children got odd jobs after school, mother taking over the duties of the shop when her preacher husband made sick calls or went out to officiate at a country wedding or a wake. Young Asa's first independent contributions toward the welfare of the family were earned as errand boy and general helper to a white grocer in town. So anxious was he to help out that he didn't even stop at home to eat his dinner after school. He had his mother prepare the food and put it in a bucket, which he snatched up and carried off to his job. Then, when a break in his duties gave him time, he sat down behind the counter and gobbled his meal.

As he grew older, Asa sought better-paying jobs. For a while he worked as a clerk in a grocery store; his experience as errand boy helped him to get the job. Then he took a job one summer as a section hand on the railroad, digging and shoveling dirt, loading flatcars, and laying crossties and rails. When school resumed, he left the railroad to drive a delivery wagon, after class, for a large chemical and drug company. Later, he worked for fertilizer and trucking concerns. And he supplemented his earnings whenever he could by selling newspapers, or helped at odd moments between work and school in the family tailor shop. Nor did he let up on his studies. After grade school, he went on to high school at Cookman Institute in nearby Jacksonville. Then, when he had finished at the institute, he looked around for greater opportunities.

Asa decided that his best chance for success lay in leaving his hometown and trying to continue his education in the North. The opportunity for advanced study was limited in the South, particularly for a black man. And if Asa remained at home he would be a burden to his struggling parents, for books and supplies cost money, and the boy would have to limit his working hours in order to attend college. Perhaps on his own he could live cheaply and eke out the money for the desired education. Anyway, it was worth a try. So the young man set off for New York.

Settling down in Manhattan, Asa found a job and enrolled at the College of the City of New York, taking courses in political science, economics, and philosophy. Soon, however, he discovered that earning a living interfered with his studies. He worked as a porter for the Consolidated Edison Company of New York, and could only snatch at his studies as he rushed from job to school. So he tried other types of work, as an elevator operator, then as a waiter in a railroad restaurant. Indeed, he took any job he could land, for his interest in the condition of the workingman, stimulated by his studies and fostered by his own plight, was getting him into trouble with employers. He already had a reputation as a "troublemaker." For example, while a waiter on a Fall River Lines ship plying between New York and Massachusetts, he organized a protest against conditions in the "Glory Hole," the foul living quarters of the crew. He was dismissed for his efforts, and reports of his activities were circulated from employer to employer. Neither work nor study went smoothly for young Asa.

Despite his difficulties, however, and the increased responsibility he shouldered in 1915, with his marriage to Lucille E. Green, he did not knuckle under to unscrupulous employers. Such employers, fanning the flames of war hysteria for the sake of larger profits, aroused Asa's antagonism. He established contacts with workers in the shipyards of the Virginia Tidewater area during the early years of the war and tried to organize them, hoping to win for them a larger share of the tremendous profits that were being reaped on war contracts. But the shipping interests proved too strong for him. Black workers, particularly, were brutally intimidated by gangs of thugs hired by the employers, and efforts at unionization were viciously crushed.

When America entered the war, Randolph and a friend, Chandler Owen, launched a monthly magazine called *The Messenger*. Its purpose was to arouse the black worker to an awareness of his critically important position in mass-production industries and in the army. Take advantage of this position, the editors argued, to force the government to correct some of the worst abuses from which you suffer, even though this meant relentless criticism of the government for its discriminatory practices in the draft. Asa was arrested and thrown into jail for his stand, but charges could not be made to stick and he was released after a couple of days.

After the war A. Philip Randolph, as he was beginning to be known, participated in a number of organizational campaigns among laundry workers, motion-picture operators, and members of the garment industry. He said, "The Negro should organize himself because with organization he will be better able to break down the barriers and prejudices of white workers against him than he will without. . . ." But until 1925, it was primarily as a writer and lecturer that Asa functioned. At the Rand School of Social Science in New York, where he taught for a while, he lectured to labor, radical, and liberal groups on the evils of intolerance and discrimination. And in *The Messenger* and other periodicals for which he wrote, he demanded unconditional social, political, and economic equality for all men, black and white. Joining the Socialist Party to implement his demands, he was that party's candidate for secretary of state for New York in 1921. And he has since run for other offices on the Socialist ticket.

In August 1925 Randolph joined a small group of men in a Harlem recreation hall to outline a campaign for organizing the sleeping car porters of America. A long history of failure lay behind them. As early as 1915 an attempt had been made to unionize the porters, but the leaders of the effort had all been dismissed by the Pullman Company and the effort came to nought. Most recently, the company, sensing the discontent among its employees, had sponsored an employee representation plan known as the Pullman Porters' Benefit Association. The porters, as Randolph pointed out, "innocently accepted it as a declaration of justice by the Pullman Company . . . , unable to realize that an organization which is handed down by the boss to wage earners is for the benefit of the boss and not the wage earner." Dues collected from the porters—$26 a year from each man—were being used by the company to pay labor spies who rode the trains on the lookout for union "agitators" and "troublemakers."

A. Philip Randolph took on a tremendous job when, at thirty-six, he was elected president of the newly organized Brotherhood of Sleeping Car Porters. Of course, the Pullman Company, a national carrier operating over every railroad in the country, did all it could to stop the new union, distributing anti-labor news free to the porters and firing more than five hundred men for union activities during the first ten years of the Brotherhood's existence. Luckily, President Randolph was not dependent on the Pullman Company for a job. But most of his assistants were. Fortunately, they were men like M. P. Webster, Bennie Smith, C. L. Dellums, Ashley L. Totten, and E. J. Bradley, who, with or without jobs, pushed the fight for unionization, putting up with extreme poverty, many of them, rather than abandon the Brotherhood. The attitude of the majority of porters toward the union was far different, however. "If it succeeds, we are for it," they said. "If it doesn't, we are against it."

Under the leadership of A. Philip Randolph, the Brotherhood did succeed. Pleading his case before the Interstate Commerce Commission, the Federal Mediation Board, and a federal court, Randolph finally won recognition for the Brotherhood, establishing it, in law, as the porters' union. Then, backed by increasing numbers, he pressed for revision of the Railroad Labor Act, insisting that the porters should be included within the scope of that act. Victory came in 1934. By 1937 the Brotherhood was strong enough to strike directly at sources of trouble within the Pullman Company itself, demanding a new contract for the men, with provision for $2 million in long-overdue pay increases. Once again victory went to the union, and skeptics were finally convinced of its importance.

Down through the years, Randolph was elected president of the Brotherhood time after time, until his retirement at the age of seventy-nine in 1968. Building the union from a once-struggling young organization to its peak of power and influence in the forties and fifties, with a membership in the neighborhood of fifteen thousand, Randolph continued to win advances for the porters. Never one of the very large unions, the Brotherhood was, nevertheless, extremely influential, serving as a spearhead of black mass political action in the middle years of the century and propelling its chief into a position of national leadership in the labor and civil rights struggles. Reflecting on the significance of the Brotherhood's role in areas beyond its particular service to the porters, its founder and president noted that it "exerted great moral influence." It was, Randolph saw, a stimulus to black participation in unions everywhere and a powerful force in the fight to end discrimination in the labor movement.

One of the most significant illustrations of the pervasiveness of this moral influence is provided by events growing out of the merger of the AFL and the CIO in 1955. A. Philip Randolph was named a vice-president of the giant new labor organization. Along with Willard S. Townsend, president of the CIO United Transit Service Employees, who also became a vice-president of the newly merged group, he became one of the first black men ever to attain so high a rank in labor circles. Randolph used his position on the executive council of the joint labor organization to demand that immediate action be taken against segregated local unions, against discrimination, and against unions that had many black members but kept blacks out of leadership positions. Despite nondiscrimination pledges contained in the charter of the new labor federation, union members were outraged by his demands.

Therefore, early in 1960, Randolph organized the Negro American Labor Council. Made up of black union members from all over the country to advance the cause of black labor, it was the voice of black people within the AFL-CIO. Through the NALC, Randolph was able to organize black labor caucuses, set up training programs for black youths, and work for the elimination of racial discrimination in a number of unions. Among its other accomplishments, NALC helped to integrate the musicians' union, which had separate black and white locals in many cities, and assisted in the unionization of underpaid hospital workers in New York, pressuring the state legislature to enact a law in 1963 permitting such workers to join unions.

In 1964 Randolph founded the A. Philip Randolph Institute, with Bayard Rustin as executive director, to develop the "Negro-Labor alliance" and to strengthen "the political coalition needed to assure democratic social change." Working closely with COPE (Committee on Political Education), the political arm of the AFL-CIO, the AFL-CIO Civil Rights Department, and the Workers Defense League, the institute organized black trade unionists around the country to conduct voter registration drives, fought discrimination, and sponsored the Joint Apprenticeship Program to recruit, tutor, and place blacks in the predominantly white training programs for building trades apprentices. Since 1965 this latter program alone has brought more than four thousand black and Puerto Rican trainees into the building trades.

Important as his role in Brotherhood and AFL-CIO affairs has been, however, Randolph's influence has not been limited to those roles alone. In the 1930s he served on Mayor La Guardia's Commission on Race in New York. During the forties he threatened to organize fifty thousand black workers and lead them to Washington in protest against the sidetracking of efforts to establish a Fair Employment Practices Committee. His threat brought results, and the committee was promptly instituted. Throughout his career, Randolph has been active in opposing segregation in the armed services, and his continuing protests have had much to do with the lowering of the barriers of race in our military organization. He has served as a representative to the Second World Congress of the International Confederation of Free Trade Unions and presented North American views on the creation of free trade unions in underdeveloped areas. Perhaps the proudest accomplishment of his life was the March on Washington for Jobs and Freedom on August 28, 1963, of which he was director.

To be sure, Randolph's career, particularly in its later phases, has not won praise from all segments of the black community. In fact, militants have dubbed him Tom No. 2, second to Roy Wilkins of the NAACP, for what they take to be too close an embrace of white-dominated organized labor, which has been pitifully slow in opening its ranks to black laborers. Irritation over his attitude grew when, in 1968, the seventy-nine-year-old leader supported the United Federation of Teachers' strike in New York City after thirteen teachers had been summarily dismissed or transferred by Brooklyn's black-controlled Ocean Hill-Brownsville school district. The strike aroused great hostility in New York's black community, where many saw the UFT's action as hostile to their interest—the control of their own neighborhood schools—and an expression of labor union racism.

In fact, Randolph sees the problems that the black man faces as "fundamentally economic problems which are caused by the nature of the system in which we live," a system geared to the expectation of profit rather than to the desire to achieve social justice. His own battle for social justice, to which he has devoted his life, has been fought largely on the economic plane, where progress is inevitably slow. But it is, he believes, the surest ground on which to achieve lasting results for black men and white men alike.

RALPH J. BUNCHE

*All human beings are born free and equal in dignity and rights.
They are endowed with reason and conscience and should act
towards one another in a spirit of brotherhood.*

So reads the first article of the Universal Declaration of Human
Rights adopted and proclaimed by the General Assembly of the
United Nations on December 10, 1948.

*Those of us who believe in the United Nations and who are
closely associated with it know that . . . if the United Nations is to
achieve its fundamental objectives, there must be substantial
improvement in the lot of vast millions of people throughout the
world. We know that international peace cannot be achieved in a
vacuum. Peace must be paced by human progress.*

So spoke Dr. Ralph J. Bunche. As Undersecretary General
in the United Nations Secretariat, the administrative organ of
the United Nations, he was the highest-ranking American in
the U.N. His ideas about the ways in which the fundamental
objectives of the U.N. should be achieved were significant ones.
They were put to work by Dr. Bunche in a variety of situations
after he joined the U.N., on leave from the United States
Department of State, in 1946. As director of the Department of
Trusteeship and Information from Non-Self-Governing Territories, from 1947 to 1954, he was directly concerned in the

Ralph J. Bunche

United Nations' continuing attempt to improve the lot of vast millions of people, the aspiring subject peoples of the world. As acting U.N. mediator in Palestine in 1949, he helped forward the cause of international peace by negotiating an armistice between the warring Arabs and Jews. For this work, which enormously bolstered the prestige of the U.N. and confirmed it as a force in world affairs, Dr. Bunche was awarded the Nobel Peace Prize for 1950. As U.N. Undersecretary for Special Political Affairs, he headed U.N. peace-keeping operations in the Congo, in Kashmir, and again in the Middle East after the Suez crisis of 1956. Having served as number two man at the U.N. under both Dag Hammarskjöld and U Thant, whose most influential adviser he was, Ralph Bunche was described as "the heart, brains, and right arm" of the United Nations.

Even before Dr. Bunche left the State Department he was active in the U.N.'s behalf. Actually, he was active in behalf of the world organization before it became the United Nations. A participant at the Dumbarton Oaks Conference in 1944, he was among those representatives of the four powers who sponsored the proposals out of which grew the U.N. as we know it. Dr. Bunche was also present at the San Francisco Conference on International Organization which drew up the U.N. charter in 1945. As a matter of fact, the sections of the charter dealing with trusteeship are largely his work. He was also present, as an adviser to the U.S. delegation, at the meetings of the Executive and Preparatory Commissions of the U.N. in London in 1945. And when the charter had been approved by a majority of members and the General Assembly held its first meeting, in London in 1946, Ralph Bunche was there, too. His knowledge of world affairs, particularly of colonial affairs, made him a logical choice for inclusion at all of these meetings and made him an extremely effective member of the Secretariat.

What were the origins of this man who rose so high in international affairs and made himself such a force in the U.N.? They were inauspicious enough, to be sure. Ralph Johnson

Bunche was born "very much east of the railroad tracks in . . . Detroit, . . . in and of the working class" on August 7, 1904. His father, Fred Bunche, was a barber from Ohio. "He was a good barber, too," Dr. Bunche asserted, "and he worked in high-class shops in downtown Detroit."

Ralph's mother was the daughter of Thomas Johnson, a teacher who died of malaria in Indian territory, leaving a family of five children to be raised by his widow. This widow, Lucy Johnson, was Ralph's maternal grandmother. She later played an important part in Ralph's life. He has described her as "the strongest woman I ever knew, even though she stood less than five feet high."

After ten years in Detroit, Ralph and his parents moved to Toledo, Ohio, where his sister was born. It was this event, Dr. Bunche declared, that impaired his mother's health. Before his sister's birth, Ralph's mother had been a fine amateur pianist; after that day she rarely had sufficient strength to play for half an hour at a time.

The stay in Toledo was a brief one, and they were soon back in Detroit with the Johnson clan. Shortly after, they moved again. Mrs. Bunche's health continued to be poor and doctors advised her to move to the warm, dry climate of the Southwest. Hence, in 1914, the "advance party," as it was called in the family, moved to Albuquerque, New Mexico. The group consisted of young Ralph, his mother, sister, and Grandma Johnson and Uncle Charlie Johnson. Ralph's father, who could not afford to take a chance on finding employment in the sparsely settled Southwest, stayed behind. Later on he joined them in their comfortable adobe house at 621 North Fifth Street in Albuquerque.

When he was a grown man, Dr. Bunche revisited Albuquerque. He sought out the house he had lived in as a boy. It was still standing, but its adobe walls were now covered with a layer of stucco. The city of Albuquerque itself had changed since young Ralph attended the Fourth Ward School and played with the Mexican and Indian children in the small community. It had grown much larger since the day in 1917 when Ralph and his sister, accompanied by their grandmother, left for Los Angeles. The children's parents had died within three months of one another and lay buried in a small New Mexican cemetery.

In Los Angeles Mrs. Johnson set up a home with her two grandchildren. Later she was joined by other members of her family, Ralph's Aunts Ethel and Nelle and his Uncle Tom. It was a full and happy home. Ralph completed his intermediate school training and entered Jefferson High School in Los Angeles. He was an excellent student and delivered the valedictory address for his class when he was graduated in 1921.

In September 1922 Ralph Bunche enrolled in the freshman class at the University of California at Los Angeles. Within a short time, however, he was forced to drop out because of ill health. After an ear operation he resumed his college career in the fall of 1923. It was an active career, combining scholarship and athletics and supplemented by part-time employment. Dr. Bunche always prized the three miniature gold basketballs he won as star guard on three championship varsity basketball teams at UCLA. Of all his awards, those gold basketballs were the hardest to win, he said, for, though he was a lithe 160 pounds in his college days, he was of medium height.

Ralph played football and baseball as well as basketball at UCLA and his efforts on behalf of the school teams won him a part-time job as janitor in the women's gymnasium. The duties were slight, however. Someone else swept the floors, for Ralph's real work for the school was accomplished on the basketball court.

Nevertheless, he did exercise a broom while at college—and a mop, too. After classes each day, he and a friend piled into a Model T Ford they had bought for $25 and went to work. With their brooms and pails rattling behind them, they drove through

Los Angeles, stopping here and there to give a "fast lick" to the stores and shops of their customers—one more way to earn extra pocket money.

Ralph majored in political science, and served as a student assistant in that department during his last two years at college. He was elected to Phi Beta Kappa. At graduation in 1927 his A.B. was conferred "with highest honors." Furthermore, he was awarded a scholarship for graduate study at Harvard University. In addition, the Iroquois Friday Morning Civic and Social Club, a black women's club of Los Angeles, raised $1,000 and presented it to Ralph to help him pay his living expenses at Harvard.

Later Ralph came by additional help in a curious fashion. The story is an amusing one.

I was friendly with the proprietor of a U.C.L.A. bookstore. And before I left for Harvard I stopped to see him and say good-by. Aware of the fact that books are an expensive item in the scholar's budget, he gave me a letter of introduction to a friend of his who owned a bookstore in Cambridge. The letter requested I be given a discount on the books I would need.

Naturally, when I arrived in Cambridge I looked up the friend and presented my letter. He took it, peered at it from behind thick-lensed glasses and immediately offered . . . to hire me! He thought the letter was one of recommendation for a job. I didn't bother to correct him. I accepted the job.

Ralph took his master's degree in government at Harvard in June 1928. In the fall he was appointed an instructor at Howard University in Washington, D.C. There he set up the Department of Political Science before returning to Harvard, on an Ozias Goodwin Memorial Fellowship, for the year of residence required of doctoral candidates. In June 1930 he married Ruth Ethel Harris, an attractive young schoolteacher from Montgomery, Alabama. She had been one of his students in an evening class at Howard University the year before.

After their wedding trip Mr. and Mrs. Bunche settled in Washington, where Ralph resumed his duties at Howard University. As chairman of the department he had helped to fashion, he rose, successively, from assistant to associate and ultimately, in 1937, to full professor. His teaching career was interrupted and enriched during this time by periodic leaves for travel and research. One trip came with the winning of a Rosenwald Fellowship in 1932. He visited Africa and made a comparative study of rule in a mandated area, French Togoland, and in a colony, Dahomey, in French West Africa. The study was submitted as his doctoral thesis at Harvard in 1934. It was so well written and so scholarly that it won him his Ph.D. and the Toppan Prize as well, as the best essay in social science.

In 1936 Dr. Bunche was given the opportunity for further travel and study. He was awarded a fellowship of the Social Science Research Council, and for two years he traveled around the world, visiting Africa once again, Europe, Hawaii, the Philippines, Indonesia, and Malaya. His firsthand observation of the ways in which man's institutions and customs have developed in various sections of the globe was checked and guided by formal study under distinguished anthropologists at Northwestern University, the London School of Economics, and the University of Cape Town, South Africa.

Dr. Bunche's studies resulted in his publication of the booklet *A World View of Race* in 1936. In this short study he comes to the conclusion that there is no valid reason for assuming men are basically different from one another just because the color of their skin, the texture of their hair, or some other equally superficial physical characteristic differs. Yet elaborate theories of imaginary differences have been developed on such slight grounds. Why? Because such theories serve as an excuse for otherwise unjustifiable exploitation.

So long as . . . society endures an economy which demands and thrives on human exploitation, race will be employed as an

effective device in the promotion of the process of group exploita-
tion. . . . In such a society and under such an economy attempts at
solving the "race problem" will be futile.

As applied to our own society here in America, Dr.
Bunche's conclusions are particularly interesting.

The status of the Negro in present-day America is conditioned
by the historical fact that he was brought to these shores as a slave.
. . . The Negro was enslaved not because of his race but because
there were very definite economic needs which his enslavement
served. The New World demanded his labor power. . . . But his
race was soon used as the basis for rationalizing a justification for
the inhuman institution of slavery.

Continuing his analysis of the relationship between the
institution of slavery and present-day attitudes toward the
black man in America, Dr. Bunche points out the fact that

During years of bondage certain fixed social patterns, stereo-
types and beliefs were crystallized in respect to the relations
between the white and black peoples in the society.

Because of his rich background of knowledge and experience, Dr. Bunche was appointed co-director of the Institute of
Race Relations at Swarthmore College in Pennsylvania in 1936.
He continued as a member of the faculty at Howard University
until 1950. And his teaching was supplemented by further field
research experience. During the period from 1936 to 1938, for
instance, he worked with the Swedish sociologist Gunnar
Myrdal on a survey of the black man in America. This survey,
sponsored by the Carnegie Corporation, resulted in the comprehensive study titled *An American Dilemma* (1944). Dr. Bunche's
contribution to this classic work was a significant one.

During World War II the United States Government called
upon Dr. Bunche for information concerning colonial areas.
His work in the Office of Strategic Services, where he became

chief of the Africa Section in the Research and Analysis
Branch, helped to make the allied invasion of North Africa
successful. Later Dr. Bunche was transferred to the State
Department, becoming area specialist in the Division of
Territorial Studies in July 1944. He was, thus, the first black
man to assume a desk in this important branch of the
government. And he rose to the position of acting chief in the
Division of Dependent Area Affairs in the department. He also
served, by appointment of President Truman, as U.S. Commissioner on the Anglo-American Caribbean Commission from
September 1945 to June 1947.

When Dr. Bunche entered the United Nations "on loan"
from the State Department in May 1946, the New York *Herald
Tribune* commented editorially, "He is as well qualified as is
humanly possible for the post. . . . Americans must regard
[him] with pride and humility."

Dr. Bunche demonstrated, time and time again, the validity
of this judgment. As director of the Division of Trusteeship in
the United Nations, he fulfilled an important function not
only for the two hundred million people who lived in non-self-
governing territories, but for all the world. For, as Dr. Bunche
has asserted, "In the pattern for world peace the well-being and
aspirations of the subject peoples of the world figure promi-
nently."

The role that Dr. Bunche played in helping to secure an
armistice in the Holy Land in 1949 is well known. It was this
achievement as acting U.N. mediator that brought him to wide
public attention. Yet the significance of that achievement is not
so generally recognized. Even though tension has increased in
that section of the world since 1949, the U.N. has generally
been able to keep the situation under some sort of control.
Moreover, the U.N. has been generally regarded as the
appropriate agency to turn to in the event of international
crisis. The success of Dr. Bunche's mission in Palestine had

much to do with establishing this healthy attitude toward the world organization.

In 1950, as a consequence of Bunche's role in the Middle East, President Truman offered him the post of Assistant Secretary of State of the United States. It was a high honor and a fitting post with the opportunity for useful service. However, after careful consideration, Dr. Bunche declined the job. His reason? "Frankly," he said, "there's too much Jim Crow in Washington for me. I wouldn't take my kids back there." His was a sad commentary on the prevalence of bigotry in the very seat of American government, but a true one.

Happily, the American government's loss was the U.N.'s gain—and the world's. For with the renewal of warfare in the Middle East, Dr. Bunche returned to the scene of his former efforts for what he later described as "the single most satisfying work I've ever done." That work was containing violence for eleven years, from 1956 to 1967, in one of the most volatile areas of the world. The satisfaction resulted from helping to organize a six-thousand man peace-keeping force recruited from ten countries and supervising every detail of its activity. "For the first time," as Dr. Bunche said of his work, "we have found a way to use military men for peace instead of war."

Alas, the peace did not endure. But the instrumentality that Bunche had developed was available. And it was used again, successfully, in 1960, in the Congo, when Belgium granted independence to its former colony and pulled out precipitously, inviting anarchy and disaster by leaving no trained personnel behind to run the country. Katanga province attempted to secede. An army of twenty thousand men, without leadership, erupted in undisciplined violence. And Ralph Bunche, dispatched by the U.N. to restore order, worked nineteen hours a day for weeks and months on end at the head of a twenty thousand-man U.N. peace force to bring tranquility to the chaotic country. When peace finally came, Dr. Bunche, breathing a sigh of relief, described what he had accomplished in the Congo as his "most difficult task."

There were to be other difficult tasks and long hours of hard work in the effort to preserve and maintain peace in a world seemingly bent on its own destruction. Hence, in 1962, at the age of fifty-eight, ill and tired from overwork, Dr. Bunche contemplated retirement. But U Thant entreated him to reconsider. President Johnson added his entreaties. And Dr. Bunche stayed on. He stayed, in fact, until two months before his death, at the age of sixty-seven, in 1971, exercising until the end what he wryly described as his biases—

I have a number of very strong biases [he said]. I have a deep-seated bias against racial and religious bigotry. I have a bias against war, a bias for peace. I have a bias which leads me to believe in the essential goodness of my fellow man; which leads me to believe that no problem in human relations is ever insoluble. And I have a strong bias in favor of the United Nations and its ability to maintain a peaceful world.

To name all of the honors that were bestowed upon Dr. Bunche for the important part he played in world affairs would require another chapter, so numerous are they. Here is a list of some of the more significant ones: Fifty-odd American and foreign universities bestowed honorary degrees upon him, among them Lincoln, Fisk, Howard, Atlanta, Columbia, Princeton, Harvard, UCLA, McGill (Canada), and Delhi (India). He was decorated by the republics of Haiti and Cuba, and feted by more than a dozen American cities. Scrolls, plaques, and citations were conferred upon him by civic, labor, youth, religious, black, and international organizations. He was awarded the Spingarn Medal, the Francis Drexel Medal, the Third Order of St. Francis Peace Award, the Theodore Roosevelt Association Medal of Honor, and the Medal of Freedom, America's highest civilian award, bestowed upon him by President Kennedy in 1963.

Most significant of all was the Nobel Peace Prize in 1950, for it honored Dr. Bunche's devotion to the belief that sustained him and the organization for which he worked, the belief that "All human beings . . . should act towards one another in a spirit of brotherhood."

MALCOLM X

Malcolm was our manhood, our living, black manhood! This was his meaning to his people. And, in honoring him, we honor the best in ourselves. . . . he was and is—a Prince—our own black shining Prince!—who didn't hesitate to die, because he loved us so.
—Ossie Davis

He died at the hands of a trio of assassins, who shot him as he started to speak from the stage of the Audubon Ballroom in Harlem on February 21, 1965. He was not quite forty years old, but he had lived so variously and so intensely that he might have lived half a dozen lives in that limited span. In fact, it can be said that he did live six different lives, the differences between one and another denoted by the several names by which he was known.

Born on May 19, 1925, in Omaha, Nebraska, he was christened Malcolm Little. When he grew up he went east—to Boston and New York—where he became a hustler, a drug addict, and a small-time criminal known as Big Red, or Detroit Red. Then the life of crime paid off—in a jail sentence that kept him in prison for seven years. The inmates called him Satan. However, while in jail he learned of Mr. Elijah Muhammad and the Nation of Islam, or the Black Muslims as they are sometimes called, and he was, in a sense, reborn as Malcolm X. After twelve years of devoted service to Mr. Muhammad,

Eve Arnold/Magnum

Malcolm X

Malcolm left the Black Muslims and, following a trip to Mecca, was converted to Islam, the religion of the Moslems, as El-Hajj Malik El-Shabazz. Then, visiting black Africa on a journey that would result in the formation of the Organization of Afro-American Unity, Malcolm was greeted as Alhajj Omowale by the Nigerians, *Omowale* meaning, in Yoruba, "the son who has come home."

To be sure, Malcolm was called other names as well—traitor and hypocrite by the Black Muslims he outgrew, extremist and racist by the white men he frightened, demagogue by newspaper and television reporters who played up the sensational aspects of his work, saint by his devoted followers among the black masses, and prophet by those who saw in his charismatic leadership a new force created in the black world. Perhaps it is the latter name that fits him best; for however particular individuals or groups saw him, he did, by word and example, help to effect a profound change in the psyche of black Americans. Conditioned by generations of oppression to accept themselves as inferior, the black masses developed a new level of consciousness of themselves largely through what Malcolm said and was. "He was," as Ossie Davis said in his eulogy for Malcolm, "our manhood, our living, black manhood! This was his meaning to his people."

Malcolm's father, the Reverend Earl Little, was a very black, six-foot-four giant of a man from Reynolds, Georgia. A Baptist minister, he was also an organizer for Marcus Garvey's Universal Negro Improvement Association. Garvey, with headquarters in Harlem, was an early black separatist with a large following who believed that freedom and self-respect could not be achieved by the black man in America, that his best chance lay in becoming completely independent of the white man, with a view to returning, ultimately, to Africa. Malcolm's father strove for such independence, seeking always a place to live where the family could raise its own food and putting by a little money each week in the hope of one day buying a store and building his own business. He also preached Garvey's "Back to Africa" message in secret meetings of small groups of black people held at night in various locations to avoid detection and harassment by white vigilante organizations like the Ku Klux Klan and the Black Legion.

But word of the Reverend Little's views did get about, and shortly before Malcolm was born the Klan visited the Little home one night when Earl was off preaching, terrifying his pregnant wife with their threats and their weapons and breaking every window in the house before riding off.

Earl Little was not easily frightened, though. The Littles remained in Omaha until after Malcolm was born. Later they moved to Milwaukee, Wisconsin, and, after a brief period there, to Lansing, Michigan, always in pursuit of independence. Again, in Lansing, a white hate group struck. The family—Malcolm's mother clutching a new baby, Yvonne, his father shooting his pistol, the children crying and wailing—managed to escape from their burning house just before it collapsed in a shower of sparks and smoke.

Settled in East Lansing, the Littles were harassed again. Finally, Malcolm's father moved the family two miles out into the country, where he built with his own two hands the sturdy four-room house in which Malcolm and his seven brothers and sisters grew up.

Despite their removal so far from town, the Little family was still threatened from time to time by the Black Legion. Then one night in 1931 the Legion struck—fatally. At any rate, Earl Little's friends and neighbors were convinced that they did. There was no direct evidence. The independent Reverend Little simply went into town and didn't come home one evening. He was found later with one side of his skull crushed by a blow from a heavy instrument and his body cut almost in two by a streetcar that had run over him. One of the insurance companies with which he had a policy claimed it was suicide— and refused to pay any death benefits. Apparently he had bashed in his own skull and then walked over and lay down on the tracks!

So Louise Little and her eight young children were left to make it on their own. Eventually, Mrs. Little suffered a breakdown and was hospitalized. The family was split up, the children, as wards of the state, going to foster homes in and around Lansing.

Malcolm, who was around twelve at the time, was sent to the Gohannas family, where he remained for about a year. Then truancy at school brought him to court, where he was sentenced to reform school. However, at the detention home in Mason, a sort of way station where children await hearings and an assignment to reform school, Malcolm made a good impression on the white couple in charge, Mr. and Mrs. Swerlin. Malcolm describes the Swerlins in his *Autobiography* as "very good people."

They treated him well, providing him with a room of his own, enrolling him in the Mason Junior High School, and helping him to get a job washing dishes in a local restaurant after school But they also discussed him as though he were not there. And they talked about black people and their problems— real and imagined—in his presence as though he were completely insensitive or could have no fellow feeling for the human beings they discussed so condescendingly. Later Malcolm would come to recognize that such treatment, ignoring his humanity, reducing him to the status of a pet canary, was, however well-intentioned, demeaning. He would conclude that even well-meaning white people—a rare enough phenomenon, generally, in a black man's experience—simply did not accept black people as fellow creatures, entitled to the same consideration and respect and having the same dignity as they themselves enjoyed.

Malcolm's treatment in Mason, where there was only one black family, was pretty much the kind of treatment he got from the Swerlins. An oddity, he was viewed with tolerant bemusement. In fact, as an oddity he was much in demand. He was asked to join the school debating society, cheered as "our coon" or "Rastus" on the basketball team, permitted to stand on the sidelines at school dances. He was even elected president of his seventh-grade class. And he accepted—welcomed—such treatment. Then one day Ella, one of three of his father's children by an earlier marriage, came to visit him from Boston, where she lived. Jet black, like Malcolm's father, Ella was "the first really proud black woman" Malcolm had ever seen in his life. Her pride was infectious. Moreover, when he accepted her invitation and visited her the following summer, on vacation, in Roxbury—the Harlem of Boston—he discovered a new sense of identity with the masses of black people there. The visit marked a turning point in his life.

Malcolm returned to Mason vaguely troubled by his peculiar status in the little town. Shortly thereafter an episode occurred that was to clarify his role as Mason's black mascot. Interviewing students on their career prospects, Mr. Ostrowski, Malcolm's kindly English teacher, had urged all of the bright white students to strike out for whatever high goals they conceived for themselves. Then Malcolm's turn came. Malcolm was one of the top three students in the school. He said he wanted to be a lawyer. Mr. Ostrowski was dumbfounded. "A lawyer—that's no realistic goal for a nigger," he said. "You need to think about something you *can* be." And he urged Malcolm to take up—carpentry.

Carpentry represented what patronizing white people thought "fitting" for Malcolm, and he would have none of it. Instead, he went to stay with Ella in Roxbury. She also had ideas about what would be fitting for him: a steady job and rising status among the black élite on Sugar Hill, where wealthy black people made a kind of ghetto aristocracy. But he rejected that role, as too tame and conventional, for the life of poolrooms, bars, and dance halls, gambling, drugs, and petty crime, first in downtown Roxbury and later in Harlem, where he graduated from marijuana to opium and cocaine, began to carry a gun, and quickly moved from petty crime to armed robbery, breaking and entering, and drug peddling. When things got too hot for him in Harlem, Malcolm went back to Roxbury, where he organized a burglary gang that proved his undoing. Picked up by the police in a jewelry store where he had taken a "hot" watch to have it repaired, he was tried on fourteen criminal counts and sentenced to ten years in prison in February 1946. He was not yet twenty-one years old.

Angry, mean, and rebellious, Malcolm earned his prison nickname, "Satan," and long spells of solitary confinement by his behavior. Then, impressed by the intellectual power of a fellow convict in the Charlestown State Prison in Massachusetts, he started taking correspondence courses. Transferred to the Norfolk Prison Colony, a model prison in Norfolk, Massachusetts, he educated himself in the prison's excellent library and by reading in his cell through the night, by the dim light of a bulb in the corridor outside his cell door. "I don't think anybody ever got more out of going to prison than I did," says Malcolm in his *Autobiography*. "In fact," he says, "prison enabled me to study far more intensively than I would have if my life had gone differently and I had attended some college."

The motivation to study came from another source: the Nation of Islam, a black separatist organization based in the Midwest and headed by a man known as Elijah Muhammad, the Messenger of Allah. Claiming to have been inspired by a visit from Mr. Wallace D. Fard, a black man whom he described as "God in person," Elijah Muhammad preached that the white man is the devil. Produced by a mad scientist named "Mr. Yacub," the bleached white race had been exiled by black people to the caves of Europe, where they gradually achieved dominance. But the white devil's domination, lasting six thousand years, had reached its end. Soon, out of the tribe of Shabazz from which all black Americans have descended, an all-knowing black man would come to lead his people.

Mr. Yacub's history is fanciful enough, and, in its black racism, remote from Islam, the Mohammedan religion upon which Elijah Muhammad's Nation of Islam sect is based. However, the concept of an evil race of white devils appealed to oppressed black people, particularly to convicts like Malcolm, who could in fact document the evil of the white man from extensive personal experience. In any case, Mr. Yacub's history gave downtrodden black men a psychological lift, providing, as it did, an alternative to "whitened" history, which ignored the black man, his accomplishments, and his culture almost completely. Moreover, the disciplined morality of Elijah Muhammad's followers, with its emphasis on clean and wholesome living, self-respect, and independence, resulted in happy and productive lives.

Malcolm was introduced to Elijah Muhammad's Nation of Islam by his brothers and sisters, three of whom were members of the sect's Detroit Temple Number One. Soon he became a devoted disciple, writing daily letters to Elijah Muhammad, whose headquarters were in Chicago, receiving instruction from him and teaching his fellow convicts the tenets of the faith. When he got out of prison, on parole, in August 1952, Malcolm went to Detroit, where he lived with his brother Wilfred and joined the temple to which his brother's family belonged. It was at this time that he took the name of Malcolm X, the "X" replacing the name which "some blue-eyed devil named Little had imposed upon" his forebears and symbolizing "the true African family name that he never could know."

Malcolm rose rapidly in the Nation of Islam to be a minister and an organizer of new temples, or mosques as they came to be called. Soon one of Elijah Muhammad's most trusted lieutenants, he was sent east to organize mosques in Boston and Philadelphia. Appointed minister of key Temple Seven, in New York, Malcolm went "fishing," as he describes it, for converts in Harlem. Highly successful, he was able to spur the growth of the Nation of Islam in New York and to organize or enlarge other temples in Springfield, Massachusetts; Hartford, Connecticut; Atlanta, Georgia; and other cities as far west as Los Angeles. In fact, Malcolm either directly established or helped to establish most of the one hundred or more mosques in the fifty states. He started a newspaper called *Muhammad Speaks,* putting it together at first almost single-handedly in the basement of his Temple Seven. He traveled to Africa as Mr. Muhammad's spokesman, visiting Egypt, Arabia, the Sudan, Nigeria, and Ghana on a three-week trip. Back home, he traveled widely in the car provided him by the Nation, or by jet plane, crisscrossing the country in his visits to black communities where Elijah Muhammad's teaching might be spread.

In 1956 Malcolm met an intelligent young woman named Sister Betty X, who gave instruction in health care to the sisters at Temple Seven. A native of Detroit originally, Sister Betty had been educated at Tuskegee Institute in Alabama and was a nursing student at a big New York hospital. More and more drawn to Sister Betty, Malcolm observed in her what he thought were qualities that would make a good Muslim wife, and on January 14, 1958, they were married. As their family grew—there were ultimately to be four girls: Attilah, Qubilah, Ilyash, and Amilah—the Nation of Islam provided them with a seven-room house in East Elmhurst, Long Island.

But all was not well between Malcolm and the Nation of Islam. For one thing, Malcolm's popularity with the black masses aroused jealousy among Elijah Muhammad's inner circle. Malcolm was later to learn that Mr. Muhammad himself, while continuing to praise Malcolm to his face, criticized him privately, characterizing him as "dangerous." Ever more widely covered in the national media for his harsh criticism of the white establishment and what he described as "integration-mad Negroes," Malcolm began to be ignored in *Muhammad Speaks,* his own paper, now published in Chicago by Muhammad's son Herbert. Moreover, Malcolm discovered other evidence of Mr. Muhammad's hypocrisy.

Finally, an open break came. Following the assassination of President Kennedy on November 22, 1963, Malcolm gave a speech at the Manhattan Center in New York. The title of the speech, which had been prepared a week before the assassination, was "God's Judgment of White America." Its theme, a common one for Malcolm, was "as you sow so shall you reap," a commentary on white violence and hypocrisy. In the question and answer period following the speech, reporters asked Malcolm what he thought about President Kennedy's assassination. His response was that it was a case of "the chickens coming home to roost," meaning that America's climate of hate had been responsible for the President's death. Widely reported and misinterpreted—people said he had condoned the assassination—the remark brought severe criticism to Malcolm. And Mr. Muhammad seized upon the opportunity to silence him. He was forbidden to speak for ninety days. Malcolm heard rumors that the Nation of Islam would permanently silence him. In fact, in the concluding pages of his *Autobiography* he says, ". . . I do not expect to live long enough to read this book in its finished form."

He did not, but he did live long enough to do several things. Doubtless the most important of these was his completion of the *hajj,* the pilgrimage to Mecca that every orthodox Muslim strives to make at least once during his lifetime. It was another major turning point in his life. On the pilgrimage he encountered hundreds of thousands of pilgrims of every color—black, white, brown, and yellow. He observed that all behaved as brothers, for all are brothers in Islam, a faith that knows no color discrimination. All are one before Allah. This ran counter to what Mr. Muhammad had taught and Malcolm, in the Nation of Islam, had believed. Now a true Muslim, Malcolm came to see that it is not in our color that we are devils or angels, good men or villains, but in our actions that we are one or the other. To be sure, the majority of white Americans, obsessed with the mistaken notion of their superiority, behaved villainously toward black Americans. And Malcolm saw no reason to change his tactics in his continuing attack on that villainy. Nor did he believe in token integration. The brotherhood of all men was possible. Allah so taught. But it could only be based on the brotherly feeling and behavior Malcolm had observed on the pilgrimage, not on slogans, promises, or even laws that were recorded in books but not observed by actual men and women.

Malcolm had experienced a spiritual rebirth in the Holy Land. And on the way back to America, traveling through Ghana and Nigeria, he experienced another kind of renewal, a discovery of his cultural roots.

The following year he returned to Africa to take part in the Second Organization of African Unity Conference, where he was regarded as a head of state speaking for twenty-two million black Americans. On his next trip he visited fourteen nations and had extended audiences with seven heads of state, including Jomo Kenyatta of Kenya, Milton Obote of Uganda, Sekou Touré of Guinea, and Kwame Nkruma of Ghana. Naturally, Malcolm drew a political lesson from his experience in Africa. The lesson was that the black problem in America could be internationalized. In the face of oppression, support for the black minority in America could be found among the newly independent states of Africa. Indeed, with African backing, a case could be made in the United Nations indicting the United States for its suppression of the human rights of American blacks.

Such was Malcolm's hope. And some preliminary steps were taken in pursuit of that hope. For example, the Organization of Afro-American Unity was founded by Malcolm in America between his African journeys. Chapters of the new organization were established in various African countries on his next trip with a view to cementing ties between American black people and their African counterparts. The groundwork was laid for a large-scale cooperative effort. But international cooperation takes time, and Malcolm didn't have much time left. On the afternoon of February 21, 1965, time ran out in a hail of bullets and a trail of blood on the Audubon Ballroom stage.

MARTIN LUTHER KING, JR.

Doctor of philosophy, minister, head of the Southern Christian Leadership Conference, orator, scholar, teacher, author, disciple of Mohandas K. Gandhi, champion of civil rights, Nobel Peace laureate—all of these men were killed by an assassin's bullet on Thursday, April 4, 1968. All of these men were Martin Luther King, Jr., a sort of modern Moses who saw the Promised Land for his people but, like his great predecessor, never got there himself.

We have got difficult days ahead. But it doesn't matter to me because I have been to the mountain top. . . . I just want to do God's will, and He has allowed me to go up the mountain. I see the Promised Land. I may not get there with you, but I want you to know tonight that we, as a people, will get to the Promised Land. I am happy tonight that I am not worried about anything. I'm not fearing any man. Mine eyes have seen the glory. . . .

These were his last public words, uttered less than twenty-four hours before the bullet cracked from the assassin's rifle and killed King as he stood on the porch of a motel in Memphis, Tennessee. A massive civil rights demonstration had been planned for the following Monday in downtown Memphis. Up the road ahead lay a gigantic march of the poor on Washington, D.C., an activity meant to focus attention on the economic plight of the nation's underprivileged. Recently, Dr. King had

Martin Luther King, Jr.

begun to take part in protests against the war in Vietnam, and more peace drives were planned. Yet to be resolved was the question of Dr. King's role in relation to the growing militancy of the civil rights movement.

King had been the unquestioned leader of the first phase of the struggle, which had begun in the mid-fifties. During that phase blacks had sought redress for grievances under law, using peaceful methods patterned on those of Mohandas Gandhi, the Indian apostle of nonviolence. They sought the cooperation of enlightened white people. Their goal had been complete integration of black and white citizens with freedom and equality for all, in accordance with the ideals of the United States Constitution, ideals far from realized for the black portion of our population.

Under the Reverend King's leadership, hundreds of thousands of black people stood up to proclaim publicly their discontent with their lot. Demonstrating peacefully, they were beaten and jailed, cursed, reviled, and spat upon. Their houses and places of worship were bombed and burned. Their leaders were threatened and killed. There was, unfortunately, nothing especially new about all this. It had happened before. The difference was that now it was happening in full view of television cameras and members of the international press. All America—indeed, the entire world—saw the shocking brutality.

"We must learn to meet hate with love," said King. It was difficult to sing hymns in response to chants of hate, though, to pray for the men who beat you with clubs or threw sticks of dynamite into your bedroom windows, to go to jail for rights already guaranteed by the Constitution. Discipline was required to demand service firmly but courteously in segregated restaurants when the demands were met with contempt. Discipline was required to return again and again to voter registration lines in the face of denial, equivocation, and delay. But the discipline helped to forge a spirit and a determination among black people best summed up in a line from a song that became the unofficial anthem of the movement—"We shall overcome."

Characterizing later the temper of the spirit he had been instrumental in mobilizing, Martin Luther King said: "Three simple words can describe the nature of the social revolution that is taking place and what Negroes really want. The words are 'all,' 'now,' and 'here.' " The question was whether or not the techniques that he had used in forging that spirit—techniques of Christian nonviolence—would bring about the necessary changes.

Many black leaders said that they would not. They were tired of gradualism and disappointed with the small gains blacks had made. They questioned the need for a people who had suffered so long to suffer even more. They questioned the wisdom of assuming the white man's burden of guilt. After all, he had inflicted the suffering, they said; let him take care of his own guilt. They challenged Dr. King's concern about matters like the war in Vietnam. That was Whitey's war, not theirs. Nevertheless, everyone—or almost everyone—recognized the crucial significance of Martin Luther King's work in the first phase of the civil rights struggle.

Martin Luther King was born in Atlanta, Georgia, on January 15, 1929, to the Reverend Martin Luther King, Sr., and Alberta Christine (Williams) King. The Kings had two other children, Christine, who was a year older than Martin, and A. D. (Alfred Daniel), who was a year younger. They lived in an ample two-story frame house on the residential end of Auburn Street, a street that became a few blocks farther west one of the principal black business streets in America. The house had been the residence of the Reverend Adam Daniel Williams and his wife Jennie when King married their daughter and the young couple moved in with the Williamses. King became his father-in-law's assistant at the Ebenezer Baptist Church, also on Auburn Street, where the older man had been pastor for more than thirty years. When Adam Williams died, in 1931, Martin's father took over the leadership of the solid brick church with its prosperous flock. Mrs. Williams continued to live with the family, becoming by virtue of her softhearted tenderness, a second "Mama" to her grandchildren. Such was Martin's devotion to her that on two occasions—once when she had an accident that knocked her unconscious and again at her death in 1941—he attempted suicide by jumping from his second-story bedroom window.

Martin's mother came from an affluent and influential segment of the black urban South. She had attended Spelman College, even then one of the finest black women's colleges in the country, and Hampton Institute and was teaching school in Atlanta when she met Martin's father. His background was very different indeed from hers. The second of ten children of a poor sharecropper, he had hoed cotton and curried mules on the plantation his father "cropped" near the small town of Stockbridge. At sixteen, when he left home and started walking to Atlanta with his shoes strung around his neck to save them from the road, he had but a sixth-grade education. But he had great determination. Working during the day at whatever jobs he could get—carrying freight in the railroad yards, serving as a mechanic's helper, doing duty as a fireman—he continued school at night, graduating from high school and eventually taking his degree from Morehouse College when he was already married and had started to raise a family.

Two stories that Martin Luther King used to tell reflect his father's strong character and his attitude toward white racism. On one occasion, Martin and his father went into a white-owned shoe store to buy a pair of shoes. Father and son sat down in the front of the store. A clerk asked them to move to the rear if they wanted to be waited on. Reflecting that the benches in back were no more comfortable than those they were sitting in and that the shoes would be the same no matter where they tried them on, "Daddy" said they'd remain where they were or get the shoes elsewhere.

On another occasion Martin was riding with his father in the family car when the elder King inadvertently passed a stop sign without halting. A policeman pulled up to the car and said:

"All right, boy, pull over and let me see your license."

With icy dignity the Reverend King turned in his seat and pointed to young Martin. "That is a boy," he said. "I am a man."

The ticket was written in stony silence and the vehicle moved on.

At home Martin was taught by his mother and soon discovered a love of books, of which there were many in his father's library. He also liked to listen to visiting preachers and was particularly fond of "big words," a childish enthusiasm he never outgrew. He was, in fact, a precocious young boy, and when he was eleven he was transferred from the regular elementary school to an Atlanta University-sponsored school for especially bright students. By the time he was fifteen he had been accepted as a freshman at Morehouse College.

At Morehouse Martin read avidly, particularly in American and black history. He also played basketball and football, driving himself to become quarterback of the football team despite his small stature and light weight. While still at college, King was ordained a Baptist minister, and after he received his degree from Morehouse, he continued his religious studies, on a scholarship, at Crozer Theological Seminary, in Chester, Pennsylvania. It was at Crozer that Martin first became aware of Mahatma Gandhi's teachings, teachings that were to have a profound influence upon his own career.

In 1951 Martin was awarded his degree. Besides being class valedictorian and the president of his senior class, he won two awards, one in the amount of $1,250 for two years of study at the graduate school of his choice. That choice was Boston University, where he enrolled as a candidate for the Ph.D. in the fall of 1951.

While at Boston, King met Coretta Scott, a poised and

pretty music student at the New England Conservatory. Coretta was from the small rural town of Marion, Alabama, but she had graduated from Antioch College and, at twenty-five, was studying voice, intent on a career on the concert stage. Her plans were changed, however, by her meeting with Martin. After a whirlwind courtship, he married her on June 18, 1953. A year later, in September 1954, he took up full-time duty as pastor of the Dexter Avenue Baptist Church in Montgomery, Alabama, and he and Coretta moved into the newly redecorated parsonage at 309 South Jackson Street.

Martin's first ministry was a happy one. He soon got to know his parishioners and developed a routine for dealing with church business—counseling, marriages, funerals, visiting the sick, attending meetings of the various church committees. But above all, Martin was a preacher. He spent as much as fifteen hours preparing each of his Sunday sermons, some of which were later collected in a book, published in 1963, called *Strength to Love.* A moving orator, he won the hearts of his congregation with his sermons. And his warm and lively personality won him the friendship of a neighboring minister, the chunky, good-humored pastor of the First Baptist Church, Ralph David Abernathy. Of course, later Abernathy would become King's right hand in the civil rights movement and, at the leader's death, by King's expressed wish, his successor as head of the Southern Christian Leadership Conference.

Other matters occupied the new pastor of the Dexter Avenue Church as well. For one thing there was his doctoral thesis. That was completed and his Ph.D. was awarded in the spring of 1955. Meanwhile, Coretta had given birth, on November 17, 1954, to the Kings' first child, Yolande Denise. A chubby, lovable baby, she was called "Yoki" in the family, a family that was to grow over the years ahead with the coming of two brothers and a sister—Martin Luther King, III, Dexter, and Bernice Albertine.

However, it was neither family nor study nor regular church

duty that occupied most of Martin Luther King's time now. Rather, he was occupied with events growing out of an episode that took place early on the evening of December 1, 1955. What happened was that Mrs. Rosa Parks, a forty-two-year-old black seamstress, refused to get up out of her seat on a Montgomery bus, as she was summarily ordered to do by the bus driver, and turn the seat over to a white rider who had just boarded the bus. Mrs. Parks had not planned her action as a protest against segregated facilities. After a long day of work and shopping, she had boarded the bus to go home. When she was commanded to get up, she explained later, "I was just plain tired and my feet hurt." She refused to budge. The bus driver summoned a policeman. Mrs. Parks was arrested and escorted to jail.

For years black people in the South had been required to ride in the rear of buses. Mrs. Parks's refusal to comply with that requirement represented a turning point in history and had symbolic value in organizing public opinion far beyond its importance as an isolated event. Hence, when Mrs. Parks was arrested, there was a spontaneous outburst of indignation among the black people of Montgomery. A meeting was called and a one-day boycott against the bus company was agreed to. Black people, who comprised 70 percent of the bus company's passengers, simply did not ride the buses the following Monday, December 5, the day of Mrs. Parks's trial. And when Mrs. Parks was convicted, there was a general agreement that the boycott would continue. And so it did, until December 21, 1956, the day following the receipt in Montgomery of a U.S. Supreme Court order declaring Alabama's state and local laws requiring segregation on buses unconstitutional.

Montgomery was the beginning of the modern civil rights movement. From there the movement spread, spearheaded by the Southern Christian Leadership Conference, formed in 1957 with Dr. King as its head. Operating out of Atlanta, to which city King returned in 1960, the SCLC organized voter registration drives, freedom marches, and selective buying campaigns against stores practicing discrimination throughout the South. There were major confrontations with segregationists in, among other cities, Raleigh, North Carolina; Albany and Atlanta, Georgia; Selma, Birmingham, and, once again, Montgomery, Alabama; and St. Augustine, Florida. Perhaps the most dramatic confrontation occurred in Birmingham, Alabama, in April and May 1963, where Commissioner "Bull" Connor mobilized police forces as for a city under siege to combat peaceful civil rights demonstrators; employing high pressure water hoses and police dogs against marching schoolchildren, Connor personified the brutality of racism in the South. Ultimately, the SCLC organized demonstrations in northern cities with large black ghettos, in Detroit and Chicago, where segregation exists in fact if not in law. These activities, widely covered by the news media, stung the conscience of America and the world. They also gave black people a new sense of unity and strength. And they made Martin Luther King, Jr., world famous.

The fruits of that fame were both bitter and sweet. They were sweet in that they brought prestige and power to King, who traveled across America and around the world—in 1957 he helped Ghana celebrate its independence; in 1959 he made a pilgrimage to Gandhi's homeland; in 1964 he had a private audience with Pope Paul VI in the Vatican. His "I have a dream . . ." oration, the culmination of the March on Washington on August 28, 1963, reduced 250,000 people to awed silence and was followed by thunderous applause. Then on December 10, 1964, he was awarded the Nobel Peace Prize.

But there were bitter fruits on the tree of fame, too. An event that was an omen of just how bitter they were took place on September 19, 1958, while Dr. King was autographing copies of his book *Stride Toward Freedom* in a Harlem department store. A demented black woman emerged from the crowd surrounding Dr. King, pulled a long, razor-sharp letter-opener from her dress, and plunged it into King's chest. A team of three doctors operated on King, whose calmness through the ordeal insured his survival.

Indeed, the attack on Dr. King was but the prelude to a storm, a wave of violence that was to shake America to its very foundations in the years to come, with the murder of President John F. Kennedy, his brother Robert, Medgar Evers, Malcolm X, and ultimately King himself; with the burning of Watts; and, in the long hot summers of the mid-sixties, bloody rioting in the ghettos of many of the major cities in the country. In his last book, *Where Do We Go from Here: Chaos or Community?* published the year before he died, King reflects on that violence. "These," he asserts, "are the deepest causes for contemporary abrasions between the races":

Every civil rights law is still substantially more dishonored than honored. School desegregation is still 90 percent unimplemented across the land; the free exercise of the franchise is the exception rather than the rule in the South; open-occupancy laws theoretically apply to population centers embracing tens of millions, but grim ghettos contradict the fine language of the legislation. Despite the mandates of law, equal employment still remains a distant dream.

Commenting, toward the end of his twelve-year crusade for civil rights, on continued white indifference or hostility to the condition of black people in America, King said: "Cries of Black Power and riots are not the causes of white resistance, they are the consequences of it."

King knew whereof he spoke. He had relied on nonviolent confrontation, but within his own movement those who believed in the use of force and violence had come into power. Their voices had been listened to because the very hopes that King had done so much to raise had been frustrated again and again by white people who were either indifferent to those hopes or actively against their fulfillment.

Many people call Martin Luther King, Jr., a dreamer. They

see irony in the concluding words of his famous speech, the words that are carved on his tombstone:

> *Free At Last, Free At Last*
> *Thank God Almighty*
> *I'm Free At Last*

But in a moving tribute to King, two of his devoted followers express the feelings of millions of people around the world:[1]

In a nation tenaciously racist, a black man sensitized its somnolent conscience; in a nation sick with violence, a black man preached love; in a world embroiled in three wars in twenty years, a black man preached peace.

And they conclude:

He was incontestably one of history's preeminent black leaders. Yet he was, as well, a leader to millions of white people who learned from him that in degrading black men, they diminished themselves, that in supporting black liberation they enriched themselves.

[1] Quoted in Coretta Scott King's *My Life with Martin Luther King, Jr.*

Science

In the early days of our country science was not the important discipline it has since become. As a matter of fact, it was looked upon with scorn by most cultivated people. Experiments were considered "messy." Scientific apparatus was thought to be mere "gadgetry." Scientists were called "charlatans."

It is not surprising, therefore, that the black man, though he was a slave and denied access to many pursuits, was permitted to investigate the phenomena of nature. Living close to the soil, he learned to compound medicines from roots and herbs and to treat the sick with these remedies. Frequently, he was called upon to treat his white masters when they became ill. And gradually his skill won for him a new dignity.

Medicine was, thus, one of the first branches of science to attract the black man. James Desham, a slave born in New Orleans in 1762, became America's first black doctor. From that time to this, black Americans have been among our country's finest physicians.

Daniel Hale Williams (1856–1931) was the first surgeon to operate successfully on the human heart. He was also instrumental in establishing the first training school for black nurses at Chicago's Provident Hospital.

William A. Hinton (1883–1959) developed a test for the presence of syphilis in the human body which is one of the most reliable known to science. He was head of the Wasserman

Laboratory of the Massachusetts Department of Public Health from its establishment in 1915 until his retirement in 1953 at the age of seventy.

Louis T. Wright, who died in 1952, was the first black police surgeon appointed in New York City and the first black doctor to join the staff of a city hospital there. A specialist in the treatment of head injuries, he was recognized as one of the outstanding physicians in the United States. In 1969 the Louis T. Wright Surgical Building of Harlem Hospital in New York City was named for him.

One of Dr. Wright's two doctor-daughters, Dr. Jane Wright Jones, is a cancer researcher and chemotherapist. The first black woman to be named dean of a medical school (New York Medical College), she has also served as director of Harlem Hospital and was appointed in 1964 to the President's Commission on Heart Disease, Cancer, and Stroke.

Dr. Hildrus Poindexter, born in 1901, has been for many years a leader in the study of tropical medicine.

One of the leading skin specialists in the country is the Chicago dermatologist Theodore K. Lawless. In fact, Dr. Lawless, born in 1892, has an international reputation. The dermatology clinic at the Beilinson Hospital Center in Israel was erected largely through his efforts and bears his name.

Of course, the black man's contributions to science have not been limited to medicine. He has turned to all branches of science. Ernest E. Just (1883–1941) made his reputation as a zoologist, specializing in marine biology. James C. Evans, the inventor of a device that prevents ice from forming on aircraft in flight, has been honored for his work in electronics. W. Montague Cobb, a distinguished anthropologist, helped, through his research, to overthrow some fantastic myths about race. A pioneer in food chemistry, Dr. Lloyd A. Hall has devised new ways of curing and preserving foods and methods for preventing fats and oils from becoming rancid. Dr. Percy L. Julian has synthesized drugs used in the treatment of glaucoma and arthritis, as well as hormones that protect expectant mothers from miscarriages and help sustain the virility of aging men. Known as the "soybean chemist" for his important work in deriving useful products from the soybean plant, he has created paper coatings, textile sizings, cold water paints, and a substance known as Aero-Foam, which is used to put out oil and gasoline fires by forming a "blanket" over the fire, thus cutting off oxygen.

The black man has kept pace with the rapid development of science in America and has contributed greatly to that development. Let us examine some of his contributions as we look at the lives of three of the greatest of black scientists.

DANIEL HALE WILLIAMS

Today heart surgery has become commonplace, a matter of daily occurrence. The heart is opened so that defects within may be repaired. And, of course, badly defective hearts are sometimes replaced by healthy ones in transplant operations. But it was not always so. In fact, up until the end of the nineteenth century a serious heart defect or a wound in that vital organ meant certain death, for no doctor would dare to perform so delicate and critical an operation as one upon the human heart. The necessary techniques had not been developed. No doctor felt that he had sufficient skill. Moreover, the heart was considered the very organ of life, and there was a good deal of superstition about tampering with so fundamental a life process as that controlled by the heart.

Then, on July 9, 1893, a skillful black surgeon named Daniel Hale Williams made a six-inch incision in the chest of a wounded patient at the Provident Hospital in Chicago. Detaching the fifth rib from the patient's breastbone and working through a 1½-by-2-inch opening into the chest cavity, he repaired a torn artery and stitched up the pericardium, or membranous sac enclosing the heart, which had been punctured by a knife wound. The patient survived the delicate operation and regained full health. Dr. Williams had achieved a landmark in the history of surgery and opened the door to a new epoch in medicine.

Daniel Hale Williams

The man who accomplished that surgical feat—"Dr. Dan" as he came to be called—was born on January 18, 1856, in Hollidaysburg, Pennsylvania, a flourishing town of three thousand inhabitants at the head of the heavily traveled Pennsylvania Canal. His father, Daniel Williams, Jr., was a light-skinned man of mixed black, Indian, and white ancestry dating back to pre-Revolutionary days. He had settled as a barber in the town after marrying Sarah Ann Price, the daughter of a well-to-do Annapolis, Maryland, family of similar ancestry to his own. Dan's father's shop prospered, and, in addition to other property, he bought a house at 315 Blair Street, near the Town Hall. There Dan was born, the fifth of seven children who survived to maturity in a family of nine.

A trustee of the African Wesleyan Church in Hollidaysburg, Dan's father was also active in the abolitionist cause, fighting slavery and working for the advancement of black people everywhere through the Equal Rights League, an organization of black people devoted to winning civil rights and better education for all blacks. A vigorous man until he was forty-seven, Mr. Williams was stricken with tuberculosis at that age and died in Annapolis, where he had taken his family to visit his wife's relatives, on May 5, 1876.

Dan was eleven when his father died. His brother, already twenty and a man, was teaching school and studying law in the North. Soon the family was split further when his mother left for Rockford, Illinois, where some Williams cousins had a wig-making business. She left her youngest daughter in Annapolis with her widowed mother, placed two of the girls in St. Frances's Academy, a Baltimore convent school, and apprenticed young Dan to C. M. C. Mason, a Baltimore shoemaker.

Dan's skill with a needle, acquired in Mason's cobbler's shop, would serve him well later as a surgeon. But he didn't remain a shoemaker's apprentice long. Lonely separated from his family, within a year he fled to Rockford, using a railroad pass borrowed from one of his father's friends.

Surprised at his arrival, his mother took the twelve-year-old's journey as a sign of the fact that he could take care of himself. Therefore, when she decided to return east again, as she soon did, she left Dan and his sister Sally behind to fend for themselves.

Dan worked as a barber, as a roustabout on the docks of several Great Lakes ports, and as a deckhand on the lake boats, where he learned to sing sailor's chanteys and play the guitar. By the time he was seventeen, he was running his own small barber shop in the village of Edgerton, Wisconsin. However, when his sister Sally got work in Janesville, a town of 10,000 people a few miles away, he joined her there, rooming with Harry Anderson and working in his Tonsorial Parlor and Bathing Rooms. The barbershop, a fancy six-chair establishment, also provided facilities for hot baths, since even the wealthiest homes lacked plumbing in those days. With a good school in town, and mindful of the importance his father had placed on education for the black man, Dan enrolled at Jefferson High School.

Soon, however, Sally got married and left Janesville for Portage, in the north, with her husband. Lonely and neglected, Dan came down with a series of heavy chest colds. He had to drop out of school. Things looked pretty glum. But Harry Anderson, who was to help Dan over many rough spots and who, in fact, became a sort of second father to him, encouraged him to forget his troubles. He urged Dan to join his string band, which played at musical events all over Wisconsin. Dan went to rehearsals, learned to play the bass, and was soon a regular member of the band.

Dan also returned to school, attending Dr. Haire's Classical Academy. Upon graduating, he followed briefly in his older brother's footsteps, reading law while serving in a Janesville lawyer's office. But he found the law dull. Within a year he had quit the law office and apprenticed himself to Dr. Henry Palmer, a fine physician with a large practice and a busy office on the corner of Main and East Milwaukee Streets in down-town Janesville.

In 1878, when young Dan Williams entered Dr. Palmer's office, the way to a career in medicine was through an apprenticeship with a practicing doctor, followed by from one to three years at a medical college. Dan read medicine—Gray's *Anatomy* and *The National Dispensatory*—in the doctor's office under his tutelage and observed and assisted him in his daily practice, helping to set broken bones, deliver babies, make up prescriptions. By the fall of 1880, Dr. Palmer felt that Dan was ready for medical school.

So were two other apprentices of the doctor, Frank Pember and James S. Mills, with whom Dan had become fast friends. Pember and Mills had decided to go to the Chicago Medical College, one of the best medical schools in the country at that time, to complete their training, and Dan was determined to accompany them. The question was, How? He had saved a little money barbering on weekends for Harry Anderson, and during his final year as an apprentice he had made some extra money stringing wires for the new telephone exchange and the electric street lights that were being installed in Janesville. But he needed about a hundred dollars for fees and books, and he didn't have enough. Harry Anderson, however, agreed to back him on a bank loan for the money required. Moreover, when Dan's mother wrote to inform him that she could not help him with his living expenses in Chicago, as he had hoped she would, Anderson also assisted him with those expenses.

So Daniel Hale Williams went to Chicago to continue his studies. He arrived in the fall of 1880, when American medicine was undergoing revolutionary change, particularly in the area that was to be Dan's special interest, surgery. Heretofore surgery had been resorted to with great apprehension, generally as a last desperate remedy, for the vast majority of patients operated upon—without antiseptic safeguards of any sort—suc-cumbed to infection and died. Surgical instruments were not sterilized, for example, and doctors generally washed up in those early days after an operation, not before. Hence students who received their degrees in the year Dan entered Chicago Medical had observed but six abdominal operations in the course of their three-year training period, and every one of the patients operated upon had died.

While Dan was at medical school, however, the theories of Joseph Lister, the great English founder of antiseptic surgery, were introduced at Chicago and put into practice there, with a dramatic reduction in the incidence of postoperative infection. Moreover, with infection controlled, surgery became feasible early in the history of an illness, when the probability of success is greatest. And, of course, a vastly greater number of conditions than were formerly thought operable were treated successfully by surgery.

Hence when Daniel Hale Williams got his doctor of medicine degree, in March 1883, and set up his own office in Chicago, at 3034 Michigan Avenue, he had already acquired considerable experience in the operating room. He was thoroughly familiar with the techniques of antisepsis, and was prepared to use surgery not as a last resort but as a regular and dependable method of countering illness and saving lives. He soon had many opportunities to demonstrate the adequacy of his training and the usefulness of modern antiseptic surgery. In addition to his regular office practice he was appointed as attending physician at the Protestant Orphan Asylum; he joined the surgical staff of the South Side Dispensary; and he was hired as surgeon to the City Railway Company. He also became an instructor in clinical medicine and demonstrator in anatomy at Chicago Medical College, his alma mater, where he helped to train Charles H. Mayo—one of the founders of the famous Mayo Clinic—Coleman Buford, Andrew Hall, and other outstanding surgeons.

In 1889 Dr. Williams was appointed to the Illinois State Board of Health, where he helped to draw up public health measures for the control of epidemics like typhoid, diphtheria, and scarlet fever, which swept the state, and the nation, in those days with terrible frequency and much loss of life. He was also instrumental in drawing up a set of standards of medical practice for the profession and in controlling unscrupulous "quacks" and fast-talking "medicine men" who preyed upon gullible patients, selling them worthless concoctions as cure-alls.

There was ready patronage for such unscrupulous practitioners in Chicago, particularly among the black population, for there were few enough doctors who would attend black people and the limited hospital facilities available were generally denied to them. When blacks were admitted to hospitals, they were generally put in the charity wards, regardless of their ability to pay, and there they were often ill treated or subjected to unauthorized and sometimes dangerous experiments by white doctors who had little regard for them as people. The few black doctors in the city found it almost impossible to get regular staff appointments in the hospitals.

Dr. Williams was, of course, aware of these problems. The first operation he performed in Chicago, a hemorrhoid excision, had been done on his patient's dining-room table. He had long thought about establishing a hospital where black people could get adequate medical attention, where young black interns could get professional experience and serve as staff physicians when their training was completed. Moreover, there was a dire need for trained nurses familiar with the new techniques of modern antiseptic surgery. A hospital could provide such training, and it would be a marvelous opportunity for young black women to find a profession, earn a living, establish independence, and make a contribution toward raising the health standards of their people.

The final impetus toward the establishment of such a hospital was provided one snowy December day in 1890 when the Reverend Louis H. Reynolds, pastor of St. Stephen's

African Methodist Church, asked Dr. Dan to try to get his sister Emma placed in a nurses' training program. A bright young woman, she had come to Chicago from Kansas City for that purpose, and everywhere she applied she had been rejected, simply because she was black.

Dr. Dan's answer to the Reverend Mr. Reynolds was no. He would not beg a place for a qualified black woman in an institution where she had been unfairly rejected. He would establish a hospital with a nurses' training school where she would not be rejected on racial grounds. And within little more than a year, having mobilized the whole black community in support of the effort, he had, in fact, established such an institution, the Provident Hospital and Training School Association. When its articles of incorporation were drawn up on January 23, 1891, it was the first interracial hospital to be established in America.

Located at Twenty-ninth Street and Dearborn, the Provident opened its doors for service to all the suffering, irrespective of color, on May 4, 1891. It was only a twelve-bed hospital. But it was owned, staffed, and managed by blacks. It was a beginning. And it would provide a pattern for others to follow. Moreover, it had an excellent nurses' training division for black women, beginning that first year with seven trainees, Emma Reynolds among them.

Thereafter, Dr. Williams operated regularly at the Provident. It was there, in fact, that James Cornish, a young black expressman, who had been stabbed in a knife fight, was rushed on July 9, 1893. He had a one-inch gash in his chest, near the heart, and had collapsed from loss of blood and shock. It was evident that he was on the point of death.

For a doctor to enter the chest cavity in those days was still a daring and dangerous procedure. He had no X-ray pictures to show him the area beneath the wound. He could give no blood transfusions, for they were unknown. He had no antibiotics to administer to fight infection. Major abdominal surgery was dangerous enough; operating upon the heart itself was unthinkable. Yet that is precisely what Dr. Williams discovered he had to do to save Cornish.

Surrounded by six doctors anxious to witness the daring operation, Dr. Williams quickly went to work. He saved Cornish's life. Fifty-one days after he entered the hospital, a dying man, Cornish left, fully recovered. Twenty years later he was still alive and well. Nor was Cornish's case merely a happy accident. Dr. Williams later performed other operations on the heart. One of his patients, George Albert Cotten, lived for fifty years after the operation.

Soon after the epic feat of surgery on Cornish, Dr. Williams was appointed to the position of chief surgeon at the Freedmen's Hospital, a 200-bed institution on the grounds of Howard University, in Washington, D.C. This job called upon another aspect of Dr. Williams' talent—his administrative ability. Established at the end of the Civil War by the Freedmen's Bureau to give medical assistance to emancipated slaves, the hospital suffered from indifference and neglect in the post-Reconstruction period and was in sad condition when Dr. Williams assumed control in February 1894. It had no trained nurses, an inadequate staff, outmoded methods of care, and a mortality rate in exess of 10 percent.

Dr. Williams completely reorganized the hospital, introducing high medical standards, enlarging the staff, and developing a nurses' training program. He even established an ambulance service. Demonstrating and lecturing in surgery himself, Dr. Williams attracted doctors and medical students from Johns Hopkins and the University of Pennsylvania, who came to watch him operate. During his tenure the number of surgical cases increased almost 200 percent while the mortality rate dropped to less than 3 percent. In four short years, Freedmen's was reborn, under Dr. Williams' direction, as a major modern surgical hospital for black people.

Missing the free interchange of professional information

and experience that he had enjoyed in Chicago in the more restrictive, racist environment of Washington, where such interchange was not forthcoming, Dr. Williams was instrumental in forming the interracial Medico-Chirurgical Society of the District of Columbia in 1895. Later that same year he helped to establish the National Medical Association, for many years in most parts of the country the only medical association open to black physicians. Declining the presidency of the organization because of the pressure of his own work, Dr. Williams was elected vice-president of the association.

Not all of the good doctor's time in Washington was spent in surgery or related professional duties, however. He had the opportunity for a bit of courting, too. And in February 1898, he married Alice Johnson, the beautiful daughter of an ex-slave and the English sculptor Moses Jacob Ezekiel. Black poet Paul Laurence Dunbar celebrated the marriage in verse. After the wedding, Dr. Williams, who had resigned his job at Freedmen's, returned with his wife to Chicago, where he resumed his place as chief surgeon at Provident Hospital, now enlarged to sixty-five beds.

In Chicago patients flocked to Dr. Dan. In addition to his work at Provident, he served at Mercy Hospital and was attending surgeon at Cook County Hospital. He operated on a wide variety of cases, removing fibroid tumors, delivering babies by Cesarean section, saving torn and mangled limbs from amputation after accidents through corrective surgery. Some of his operations were highly unusual for the time; such as, for example, his repair of a hernia of the bladder through the groin, his removal of a damaged kidney, or his successful suturing of a ruptured spleen, the latter operation being one of the first ever performed on that soft, pulpy network of vascular tissue.

As his practice grew and his fame spread, he was called upon to travel widely to lecture and demonstrate his skill, particularly among black doctors and medical students with little opportunity to observe highly sophisticated medical procedures. One such call took him to Meharry Medical College in Nashville, Tennessee, where he encouraged the faculty to establish an interracial hospital and training school for nurses patterned on his own Provident in Chicago. Thereafter he returned annually for many years to give the Williams Clinics week-long surgical demonstrations that were the high point of the school's calendar and a source of inspiration to many young black doctors.

Long acquainted with Booker T. Washington, the founder and president of famous Tuskegee Institute, Daniel Hale Williams tried to pursuade the black leader to build a medical and surgical center at Tuskegee that would serve the black people of the South, where such care was sorely needed. In this effort he failed, however. Washington was not interested. Nor was he interested in another project proposed by Williams, the reorganization and expansion of Freedmen's Hospital, which since Williams' departure had again fallen into its old slipshod ways. Booker T. Washington had the political power to make Freedmen's into a demonstration center of black medical expertise, but such a plan seemed to Washington too closely allied to the tactics of Williams' friend W. E. B. Du Bois. Washington did not wish to assert black power by too great a display of accomplishment in medicine or any other field. He feared such demonstrations would frighten off the white man upon whom he depended for much of his support. So Dr. Williams' proposal was ignored and Freedmen's was neglected.

In 1912 Dr. Williams' outstanding accomplishments won him appointment as associate attending surgeon at St. Luke's Hospital, the largest and wealthiest hospital in Chicago and one second to none in the country in quality. Old enemies, headed by Dr. George Hall, whom Williams had once refused to put on the Provident staff as unqualified, seized the opportunity to make life difficult for him, ultimately forcing him to resign from the staff of Provident, the hospital that he had done so much to create. That was a grievous blow to Dr. Dan. There was, however, compensation for that deprivation in the signal honor accorded Williams in 1913. In that year, upon its foundation, the American College of Surgeons made Daniel Hale Williams a charter member. He was the only black man to be selected.

Daniel Hale Williams spent the rest of his surgical career at St. Luke's Hospital, where he served for fourteen years, performing a wide variety of difficult operations. At the same time, he also ran the largest gynecological service in Chicago. And he continued to be an active contributor to scientific societies like the distinguished Chicago Surgical Society, of which he was a member.

In 1920, Williams, who loved to hunt and fish, built a summer home at Idlewild, in the north Michigan woods. There he spent long vacations with groups of friends who enjoyed outdoor sports, doing the things that, next to surgery, he loved best. It was to Idlewild that he retired in 1926, following a stroke that partially paralyzed him, effectively ending his surgical career. His wife had died of Parkinson's disease five years earlier. So he was lonely. Diabetes added to the burden of his last years. Other strokes followed. Then on August 4, 1931, at the age of seventy-five, Daniel Hale Williams died.

He will always be remembered as a pioneer of medicine who was the first man to sew up a human heart. But he was more than that. A distinguished surgeon, he spent his life in service to mankind, using his skill to reduce suffering and prolong life. Devoted to his race, he sought and found ways to foster the aspirations of black men and women of science by establishing facilities where black doctors and nurses could study and work. A skillful teacher, he shared his great gift with others so that they, too, might acquire something of his skill and make contributions to humanity that would outlast one man's brief days.

GEORGE WASHINGTON CARVER

Toward the end of the Civil War in Diamond Grove, Missouri, news spreads in the village that night riders—slave thieves who strike by night—are in the vicinity. Then, toward midnight, Moses Carver hears the sounds of galloping hooves and screams, shots, and curses. Grabbing his rifle, he rushes into the darkness, half-dressed. A little black girl lies in the yard, bleeding from a head wound, her brother Jim bent over her, trying to stop the flow of blood. Before Moses Carver can get his horse from the barn to ride to the village, the little black girl is dead. Her mother and infant brother have been carried off by the night riders, who will head for Arkansas or Texas, where slaves still bring high prices.

Mrs. Carver sits up through the stormy night, waiting for her husband. Toward morning the weather clears, and her husband returns, drenched and carrying a soggy bundle. Mary, the slave woman whom her husband had bought for $700, is lost. This is her baby, rain-soaked, clammy, almost dead.

Nursed through the next several days by Mrs. Carver, the baby survived, but it developed a racking cough. The cough hung on for months, then disappeared. But the baby was spent. Still it grew—not much, but little by little. It was a boy, thin, puny, spindly—and mute. His father, now dead, a slave from a neighboring plantation, had been called "Big George." The Carvers named the frail, mute child George—George Washing-

George Washington Carver

ton, in fact. He would grow up to be Dr. George Washington Carver, honored by his race, his country, and all the world for his knowledge of the natural world and his contributions to humanity.

With the end of the war and the abolition of slavery, George's brother, Jim, left the Carver farm to find work on his own, but George was too small and frail for that. He stayed on with the Carvers, helping with the household chores. Quick-witted, he picked up skills rapidly, and before he was ten years old he could sew, knit, make candles and soap, prepare spices for seasoning and medicines, cook with great success, and make designs for hooked rugs, patchwork quilts, linens, and lace. He could darn and mend faultlessly; his stitching was so deft that Mrs. Carver couldn't distinguish it from her own. But little George's greatest skill was with plants. He could make anything grow. Mrs. Carver's garden was the envy of her neighbors for miles around, with a rich profusion of blooms on a great variety of plants, many of them transplanted from the woods and fields and domesticated in the garden by George, under whose loving care they throve and multiplied.

Mrs. Mueller, a friend of the Carvers in whose garden he sometimes worked, gave George an old spelling book, and he taught himself to read and write a bit. Gradually, too, his voice developed and he was able to speak, at first in treble squeaks and halting phrases, later in normal sentences, although his voice would always be high-pitched and he would stammer when excited or in strange company. As a matter of fact, he was generally shy of people and preferred solitude. For him, however, the woods and fields were a peopled solitude, for he talked and sang to the small animals and birds and even to the plants and flowers that he loved to be among. There was, in fact, only one stranger to whom little George responded enthusiastically at first meeting. That was Hermann Jaegar, a Swiss farmer who lived in neighboring Newton County, where he had great success in cultivating grapes, developing new disease-resistant strains in his extensive vineyards.

Moses Carver had been given some cuttings from Hermann Jaegar's vines, which he cultivated. Or rather, George did so, training the vines himself with remarkable results. So when Moses went to visit the man who had given him the cuttings, he took George along. George was mightily impressed by the sight of Hermann Jaegar's vineyards, stretching row after row along the hillsides, and awed at the glass house with green plants in it, the first greenhouse he had ever seen. He was intimately touched by the man, who shared his reverence for growing things and who recognized immediately an affinity with the little boy. Taking George's small hand in his own, Hermann Jaegar said: "The hand of a gardener—his touch brings life." Before his visitors left, he gave the boy a book on plants and told him about a school for black children in nearby Neosho, which he urged George to attend.

George needed no urging. Within a week, he had left the Carver farm, with the blessing of Moses and his wife. Mrs. Carver gave him a pair of almost-new shoes and a warm old shawl, in which he carried his spelling book, a small knife that he used in cutting and trimming plants, a lunch with two apples, and the plant book given him by Mr. Jaegar. In the pocket of his made-over pants he had a dollar in change. When he reached Neosho, Mrs. Carver advised him, "Go to some big house and tell them you can tend fires, cook and wash. Help is hard to get and they will take you in." Thus equipped with supplies, money, and advice, he set out for Neosho and school. He was perhaps a little over ten years old.

No one took him in at Neosho, at least not for a while. But he did go to school. After school he worked at a variety of jobs around town, earning enough money to buy food. At night he slept in a barn, rising early enough in the morning to leave before the farmer caught him there. Thus he spent the winter, half-starved and almost frozen, in pursuit of learning.

In the spring he was caught by a farmer, John Martin. But John and his wife, Lucy, were good people who took him in and fed him. He stayed with the Martins for two years, until John Martin lost his job at the flour mill when it shut down and he and his wife left their farm for California.

"Aunt Mariah" Watkins, a black woman whom George had met at the church on the edge of town, took him in next. She and her husband Andy shared their one-room cabin with the boy. In return for food and lodging, George helped with the laundry Aunt Mariah took in and read to her from the Bible in the evening.

Within a year, however, George had left Neosho for Fort Scott, Kansas, where there was a better school. There he progressed rapidly, earning his living by washing linen for hotel guests at the Wilder House and reading everything he could get his hands on. He particularly impressed Miss Long, the drawing teacher at the Fort Scott school, who rewarded his skill with a box of water colors, thereby initiating a lifetime of drawing, painting, and sketching from nature.

When George was about sixteen he took a summer job as cook's helper, working west with a railroad construction crew. When the job ended, he traveled farther west, down into New Mexico. Back in Olanthe, Kansas, he worked weekends for "Big Nat," a giant barber with a fund of tall tales, and lived with "Aunt Lucy" Seymour, an aristocratic black lady from Virginia, and her stern Presbyterian husband. Aunt Lucy did fine laundry and pressing. When she and her husband moved to Minneapolis, Kansas, George went with them, helping Aunt Lucy with her work and finishing high school in that city.

Having decided to continue his education, George Washington Carver applied to Highland College in northeastern Kansas. On the basis of his excellent high school record, he was accepted as a scholarship student and instructed to report for classes on September 15, 1886—only to find that, as a black man, he was inadmissible. Bitterly disappointed and penniless, he took up "homesteading" for a while in western Kansas, where he shot up to six feet working his claim of 160 acres but almost perished in a fierce prairie blizzard his first winter there.

Still seeking higher education, Carver drifted to Winterset, Iowa, where he met the Millholland family. Mrs. Millholland particularly was a cultivated and sensitive woman. A gifted musician, trained in Europe for the concert stage, she taught George to play the piano, an accomplishment that he mastered quickly and one that became a lifelong source of joy to him. Moreover, Mrs. Millholland introduced George to her nephew Dan Brown, a student at Simpson College in nearby Indianola. The boys became friends, and soon George joined his new buddy at Simpson as a fellow student.

Supporting himself by establishing a laundry business in an old abandoned woodshed, George Carver developed as a painter at Simpson under the guidance of Miss Etta Budd, director of the School of Art. Four of the paintings he did there were later selected to hang in the art exhibit at the World's Columbian Exposition in 1893. However, Carver was increasingly attracted to science, and he soon discovered that laboratory facilities at Simpson were inadequate for his needs. So he transferred to Iowa State College at Ames, where he majored in botany and agricultural chemistry.

In 1894 George Washington Carver received his bachelor's degree in science from Iowa State. Having trained as a cadet in the Officers Reserve, he was commissioned captain in the National Guard at commencement, one of the first black men to hold this commission in the United States Officers Reserve. And in recognition of his scholarship, he was immediately appointed to the faculty of the college, where he taught agriculture and bacterial botany while working for his master's degree.

Carver was happy teaching at Iowa State. But he was needed elsewhere more urgently. Fifteen years earlier Booker T. Washington had gone to Tuskegee, Alabama, to take over as head of the new Normal and Industrial Institute for Negroes. He had success in winning support for the new school. Buildings were erected. Students came for instruction. Washington taught them to read, to write, to make shoes and bricks. He taught the elements of mechanics and engineering, but up to now the school had offered no courses in farming. Agricultural methods in rural Alabama were primitive. There was a need for the courses, but Washington had no skill in these matters. Then, learning of Carver's work at Iowa State and of his ability to "raise corn on a wooden floor," he wrote the agricultural scientist, asking him to come to Tuskegee. "I cannot offer you money, position, or fame," he said in his letter. "The first two you have. The last, from the place you now occupy, you will no doubt achieve. These things I now ask you to give up! I offer you in their place work—hard, hard work—the task of bringing a people from degradation, poverty and waste to full *manhood*."

When Carver received the letter, he read it over twice. Pulling out a small notebook from his pocket, he tore a sheet from it on which he scribbled three words and a signature. He placed the note in an envelope and addressed it to Dr. Booker T. Washington, Tuskegee Institute, Alabama. Then he went back to his laboratory to work.

Four days later the envelope arrived on Dr. Washington's desk. Opening it, he read: "I will come." It was signed G. W. Carver. A compact had been made that would change the history of the South.

When Carver came to Tuskegee in the fall of 1896 he was bewildered and appalled. The campus itself was harsh and ugly, traversed by "erosion gullies in which," as Carver put it, "an ox could get lost." But in wayside fields there were more wild flowers than he had ever seen, and the state of Alabama had more varieties of trees than could be found in all of Europe. Asked to come to Tuskegee to teach agriculture, Carver found upon arrival no laboratory, no greenhouses, and no gardens.

Moreover, there were hardly any agriculture students, for the rural blacks who came to Tuskegee came to learn a trade or skill that would get them off the farms. Anybody could farm! And most did—poorly. When Carver asked for a two-horse plow to clear the twenty-acre patch of rubbish-littered "no good" ground assigned to him, he discovered that no one at Tuskegee had ever seen such an implement. Then, when the plow was procured, and Carver hitched it up to turn the soil, they laughed at the idea of a professor plowing.

The laughter turned to dismay when Carver gathered muck from the swamps and manure from the stables to add to the soil. Dismay gave way to indignation when, after all this work, he sowed not cotton but cowpeas. Rotating crops, he planted sweet potatoes the next year, and the students' indignation increased, mollified only slightly when his harvest yielded an incredible eighty bushels an acre. Finally, after the land was refreshed and enriched, Carver did plant cotton. The plants were perfect, the bolls large, and from one acre he harvested a five-hundred-pound bale of cotton—an unheard of yield in that area. Indignation was replaced by respect. Agriculture students multiplied. A lesson had been taught in the use of fertilizer, in crop rotation, and in multi-crop farming.

But the lesson needed to be more widely learned, particularly in the back country where isolated families farmed with primitive methods and lived wretchedly. The lesson had to be brought to them. Carver had an idea, but neither money nor facilities with which to carry it out. Then, as he played the piano one day in a dormitory lounge, students gathered to listen. He had another idea. Why not give a concert—even a series of concerts—to raise money for his project? When school closed, he set out on a concert tour of the South, returning in August with enough money to buy farm implements for a demonstration wagon. If the farmer couldn't come to Tuskegee, he would take Tuskegee to the farmer. That is just what he did, bringing modern equipment and techniques to help improve the lot of the impoverished, pellagra-ridden, ignorant farmers throughout the state.

Still cotton was king in the South. Carver said: "Plant other crops that will enrich the soil instead of depleting it. Plant sweet potatoes. Plant peanuts, highly nutritive legumes that are easy to raise and have a wide variety of uses." Some followed his advice and prospered. Then the boll weevil struck, destroying the cotton crop. More and more farmers turned to peanuts for economic salvation. The market was glutted. Prices fell. Catastrophe threatened.

Carver went to his laboratory, the laboratory that he had put together himself out of castoffs and make-dos. There he took the peanut apart chemically, separating out water, fat, oils, gums, resins, sugars, starches, amino acids—all the various components. Then he began recombining them under varying conditions of pressure and temperature, synthesizing new substances out of what he had decomposed. Within a week he had created two dozen substances. Before he was through he had synthesized more than three hundred different products, including wood dyes, linoleum, soap, flour, oils of several kinds, paint, ink, butter, coffee—all from the lowly "goober," as the peanut was called in Alabama, where all it had been thought fit for was food for hogs. And what had come close to being an agricultural disaster turned into a bonanza, putting $45 million annually into the peanut farmers' pockets and $200 million a year into the peanut business.

The sweet potato proved almost as fruitful when Carver got to work on it. From it he derived milk, glue, ink, paint, flour, a kind of rubber—125 different products in all. Thus from this tiny makeshift laboratory in the Deep South, Carver effected an agricultural and economic revolution, creating in the process a whole new industry of synthetics—the reconstruction of decomposed substances. Characteristically, he took no credit himself. "The great Creator gave us three kingdoms," he said, "the animal, the vegetable, and the mineral. Now he has added a fourth, the synthetic kingdom."

News of Carver's work quickly spread across the country and around the world. He was invited to speak at colleges and universities. Congress called upon him to testify before the Ways and Means Committee concerning pending legislation. Membership in the distinguished Royal Society for the Encouragement of Arts, Manufactures and Commerce of Great Britain was conferred upon him in 1916. In 1923 he was awarded the Spingarn Medal for service to his race. Simpson College and the University of Rochester granted him honorary doctor of science degrees. Famous people sought him out at Tuskegee, including the Crown Prince of Sweden, Henry Ford, and the Prince of Wales. Thomas A. Edison invited him to join the staff of his well-equipped laboratories at Orange Grove, New Jersey, reportedly at a salary in excess of $100,000 a year. But Dr. Carver turned the offer down, preferring to remain at Tuskegee. "They need me here," he said simply.

Dr. Carver was not tempted by offers of money, to which he paid little heed. In fact, his modest salary checks were left in an office safe at Tuskegee, often for years. He had few expenses, except for books, which lined the walls of his rooms in Dorothy Hall. His clothing was nondescript. Indeed, rumor had it that after more than forty years at Tuskegee, he wore the same old, threadbare, greenish-black jacket and baggy pants that he had arrived in. The only variation in his costume was the daily fresh flower in his lapel, often a wild one picked on his regular before-breakfast walk in the woods and fields.

Those walks were walks of discovery from which Dr. Carver brought back, in the tubular tin can divided into sections that he carried with him, thousands of specimens of plant life for study and analysis. He was, as plant pathologist L. T. Pammeau observed, a "systematic botanist of rare ability," and there wasn't a flower, plant, tree, vine, weed, bit of moss, lichen, seed, or fruit in the state of Alabama, or indeed throughout the whole

South, that he didn't know. But his daily walks were more than walks of scientific discovery. They were opportunities for communication with the world of nature, occasions of reverence for a man who loved every living thing.

For more than forty-five years, until his death on January 5, 1943, George Washington Carver worked at Tuskegee, sharing his learning and wisdom with students; bringing efficient, economically useful agricultural practices to the poor farmers; enlarging human opportunity with information on everything from the maintenance of fertility in soils, the cultivation of the peanut, and the profitable raising of livestock, to methods for drying fruit and vegetables and recipes for dishes made from peanuts and healthful salads made from common weeds. As a synthetic chemist his contribution to mankind was incalculable, with thousands of useful products developed from peanuts, wild plums, sweet potatoes, cotton, cowpeas, from other indigenous plants, from the clays of Alabama, and even from waste materials.

It was for the creation of these new things that Dr. Carver was honored by the world, his birthplace at Diamond Grove made into a national monument, his laboratory at Tuskegee converted to a memorial museum. But as Carver himself observed, reflecting on a new product he had created through synthetic chemistry, "It is perhaps less a new thing than a new way of looking at old things." George Washington Carver was a great looker-at-things, a careful observer. If we could learn that ability from him, perhaps that would be the greatest gift of all the gifts he gave us.

CHARLES DREW

For a while he wanted to be a jockey. Later he thought he would be a professional athlete. He did some teaching. And for a couple of years he was a collegiate athletic coach. But his real profession was medicine, where he made his mark in laboratory and clinical research, surgery, and high-level medical administration before he was killed, in the prime of life, in an automobile accident on April 1, 1950. How high a mark he had made before his untimely death may be indicated in several ways. His study on "Banked Blood," completed in 1940, was described by Dr. John Scudder, a blood-studies expert, as "a monumental work and a guide to the founding of blood banks." In 1944 he was made an examiner by the American Board of Surgery, a position given to few of the outstanding surgeons in American medicine and one never before held by a black man. Most significant of all, it was Dr. Drew's pioneer work in organizing the collection, processing, and transport of huge quantities of blood in the Blood for Britain project early in World War II that made that project a success, thereby saving the lives of countless soldiers and civilians during the Battle of Britain and preparing the way for other massive blood-transfer efforts wherever disaster struck.

Charles Richard Drew was born on June 3, 1904, in Washington, D.C., the eldest of five children of Richard Thomas Drew and Nora (Burrell) Drew. His father, a carpet

Charles Drew

layer by trade, was an independent man, firm in his convictions. "Do what you believe in," he urged his children. "Take a stand and don't get licked." His mother, a graduate of the Miner Normal School, was a teacher whose respect for learning was to be an important ingredient in her son's rise to success.

The District of Columbia that Charlie grew up in was not the District that most tourists see, a city of majestic marble buildings set on broad avenues and spacious malls, planned by Washington and Jefferson and executed by the great French engineer Major Pierre L'Enfant. He lived instead, with thousands of other blacks, in a district of ramshackle old wooden buildings and unpaved streets known as Foggy Bottom. However, in those early days of the century when Charlie was young, conditions in Foggy Bottom were not so bad as they were later to become. There were still open spaces between the small houses and shops. The country was not far off, where a boy could ramble. The Potomac River was unpolluted, and Charlie often sat on its banks with his pole and line, waiting for catfish to bite. There were farms off nearby country lanes where horses were trained for racing. In fact, Charlie was friendly with one of the trainers, who let him water and exercise the horses. At ten years of age, Charlie hoped against hope that he might stay small so that he could be a jockey and ride in flaming silks before thousands of people on a great track instead of around the meadow in his old clothes before a cluster of indifferent, ruminative cows.

But Charlie grew and the dream passed. In any case, responsibility pressed. Carpet installers did not make much money, even when they were expert, as Charlie's father was. With five children to feed, every penny counted. So, at twelve, Charlie helped out by taking a newspaper delivery route. Soon he had charge of several routes, with six boys working for him.

Sports always interested Charlie, and he was good at most of them. When he was only eight years old, he won a swimming tournament at a local pool in the annual Fourth of July competitions. After school at Stevens Elementary, from which he was graduated in 1918, he played football and baseball with the neighborhood kids before starting on his paper route. And at Dunbar High School, a segregated school, as all schools in our nation's capital then were, he was a four-letter man, starring in football, baseball, basketball, and track. During his last two years at Dunbar High, he was awarded the James E. Walker Memorial Medal as outstanding all-round athlete.

Despite work and sports, Charlie's grades were excellent, and he was graduated from Dunbar High with honors in 1922, winning admission to Amherst College. Amherst was beginning a great era in its athletic history the year that Charlie Drew entered; he contributed to its success from the start, playing on the freshman football team and becoming the only member of the freshman class to win a major letter in track. As a sophomore, he surpassed himself, starring at halfback on the varsity football team. He was, in fact, named all-American halfback in 1924. As a junior he was awarded the Thomas W. Ashley Memorial Trophy as the football team's most valuable player. Reflecting on Drew's years at Amherst in an article in *The Saturday Evening Post*, D. O. "Tuss" McLaughry, his football coach during those years, called him "the best player I ever coached." He was, said McLaughry:

. . . lightning fast on the getaway and dynamite on inside plays, plowing on with a "second effort" that brought him yardage long after he should have been stopped. He threw the old pumpkin-shaped football farther and with more accuracy than anyone else I ever saw, and was also an excellent receiver. He was equally effective on defense, a true tackler and pass stopper.

The six-foot-one, 195-pound all-American halfback also won the junior national AAU hurdles championship while at Amherst, where he was elected captain of the track team in his senior year. An all-round athlete, Charlie won the Cobb Pentathlon Award for his triumphs in five different sports each year at college. When he was graduated, in 1926, he was presented the Howard Hill Mossman Trophy as the man who contributed most to Amherst in athletics during his four years as an undergraduate.

Along with the awards and triumphs, the cheers and congratulations, Charlie Drew took some bitter memories with him when he left Amherst. One in particular rankled in his heart. The episode took place when the track team went to Brown University for a meet. After the meet, the team set off for the Narragansett Hotel for dinner, only to learn that the hotel would not serve Charlie and three other black members of the team. Angry and humiliated at the rejection, Charlie asked, "Well, where *is* the team going to eat?" He was advised that he and the other "boys" could go back to the University Commons for dinner. The rest of the team went to the hotel. That was an example of team spirit Charlie never forgot.

Charlie was good enough at sports to be a professional athlete, and some opportunities—though not many—did exist for the black athlete, particularly in football. For a while, Charlie toyed with the idea of becoming a professional football player, but such careers are generally short, limited to a man's prime physical years. Charlie wanted something more enduring on which to ground his life. In any case, he was interested in science. Before he left Amherst, he had decided to become a doctor. He had saved some money from his summer job as a lifeguard, but not enough to see him through medical school. Therefore, when he received his degree from Amherst, he accepted a position at Morgan State College, a black school in Baltimore, as director of athletics and teacher of biology. He stayed there for two years (1926–28), raising Morgan's mediocre football and basketball teams to college championship class.

It looked as though, willy-nilly, Charlie was bound for a career in sports, particularly so when, applying to the Howard University School of Medicine in 1928, he was denied admission because of a minor insufficiency in undergraduate English credits. Howard offered him instead the post of assistant football coach. But Charlie was determined to be a doctor now. So he turned down the offer and applied for admission to McGill University Medical School in Montreal, Canada, where he was accepted.

At McGill, Charlie made friends with a young British doctor, John Beattie, his instructor in anatomy, who was interested in the problems of blood transfusion. Some of those problems had been solved by Karl Landsteiner, who in 1930 received the Nobel Prize for his work in blood grouping. Landsteiner had demonstrated that all persons have one of four different blood types: A, B, AB, or O. Transfusions can be given between persons of the same blood type, providing that their blood is compatible, a fact determined by a simple "cross matching" test in which two drops of blood are mixed on a glass slide and observed for coagulation, or "clumping," an indication of incompatibility. However, despite the advances made possible by Landsteiner's discoveries, many people still died through blood loss in accidents before the appropriate typing and matching could be effected. Beattie was trying to find an alternative method of providing blood for instant use in such emergencies, and he interested Drew in his work.

The year 1931 almost brought an end to the association of these two young men and to Charles Drew's medical career. He ran out of money, and because it was a depression year, money was scarce and jobs were hard to find. Charlie was resigned to dropping out of McGill. Then he received a fellowship from the Julius Rosenwald Foundation, which enabled him to continue at school. He finished second in a class of 137 students. He also won the annual prize in neuroanatomy and the Williams Prize, a senior year award granted on the basis of competitive examination among the five highest ranking students in the class. And he was elected to Alpha Omega Alpha, the honorary medical fraternity.

Upon receiving his degree, Dr. Drew interned for a year at

the Royal Victoria and Montreal General hospitals. Then he served for a year as resident in medicine at Montreal General. Dr. Beattie worked there, too, continuing his research on blood transfusion. Thus the association between the two young doctors continued, with Drew's interest in the problems of blood storage and transfusion developing, until 1935, when Beattie returned to England and Drew left for Howard University Medical School as an instructor in pathology.

At Freedmen's Hospital in Washington, the teaching hospital of Howard University, Dr. Drew was quickly promoted, first to assistant in surgery, later to assistant surgeon. Then, in 1938, he was awarded a Rockefeller fellowship by the General Education Board. Seizing the opportunity to continue his research on blood, Drew left for New York, to enroll for graduate study at Columbia University, where, in 1940, he became the first black man to be awarded a doctor of science. (Sc.D.) in medicine.

Through his research, Dr. Drew discovered that plasma, the liquid portion of blood, without the cells, could be stored for considerable periods of time without spoiling. Moreover, plasma could be administered at once to people suffering massive blood loss, without the necessity for blood typing or cross matching, as with whole blood. His discoveries led him to further experiments with all aspects of blood collection and preservation and to the establishment, in August 1939, of a blood bank, funded by a grant from the Blood Transfusion Association, at Presbyterian Hospital in New York, where Drew served as resident in surgery and conducted much of his research while studying for his degree.

Dr. Drew's thesis on "Banked Blood" established him as an authority on the subject. Even before it was published, however, his work at Columbia was widely known and recognized. In April 1939 he was called upon to present a report on blood transfusions at the annual meeting of the John T. Andrews Memorial Clinic at Tuskegee Institute in Alabama. The invitation had unexpected personal consequences for Dr. Drew. On his way to the conference, he stopped overnight in Atlanta, Georgia, where he met Lenore Robbins, a pretty young home economics teacher at Spelman College. On his way back from Tuskegee, four days later, he stopped in Atlanta again and proposed marriage. The wedding took place on September 23, 1939.

With the outbreak of World War II, blood plasma became crucially important in saving the lives of the wounded. Soon it was in short supply in England. In desperation, Dr. John Beattie, now director of research laboratories of the Royal College of Surgeons, where he was in charge of shock treatment and transfusions for the Royal Air Force, cabled Drew:

Could you secure 5,000 ampules dried plasma for transfusion work immediately and follow this by an equal quantity in three to four weeks Stop Contents each ampule should represent about one pint whole plasma

It was a big job to be accomplished in a short time, but Dr. Drew did it. Shortly thereafter, he was named Medical Supervisor of Blood for Britain, a blood supply project sponsored by the Blood Transfusion Association in New York with the cooperation of major American hospitals. Dr. Drew came to New York and plunged into the mass production of plasma, standardizing procedures for the collection and processing of blood to avoid contamination, organizing the handling of volunteer donors, centralizing collection in one depot, and dealing with the thousand and one details of a pioneer cooperative medical effort on a huge scale between two countries.

The project was a great success and saved many lives. In 1941, when the American Red Cross assumed control of the blood bank program, Dr. Drew was made director of the blood bank in New York and assistant director of blood procurement for the National Research Council. In this capacity he was in charge of the collection of blood for use by the United States Army and Navy, a tremendous wartime responsibility.

Ironically, racists succeeded at this time in forcing medical authorities in charge of blood collection to adopt a policy of blood segregation. Scientists have determined that there is no significant difference between the blood of people from various races. But while America was engaged in a life-and-death struggle with Nazi proponents of racism, some Americans insisted that blood taken from black persons and blood taken from whites be collected, stored, and administered separately— with great additional expenditure of time, money, and effort. The only reason for such a dangerously wasteful procedure was ignorance and prejudice. Yet Charles Drew, the black doctor who had been responsible for the success of the blood plasma program, was asked to Jim-Crow blood! Refusing to accept this policy of segregating blood, he resigned as director of the program.

In May 1941 Dr. Drew returned to Howard University. In July of that year he was elevated to a full professorship and made head of the department of surgery in the medical school. He was also made chief of staff at Freedmen's, where he continued his work, begun earlier, to build up an outstanding program of surgical resident training.

In April 1942 the American Board of Surgery made Dr. Drew an examiner, a great distinction. In the same year he was given the E. S. Jones Award for Research in Medical Science. He was awarded the Spingarn Medal in 1944. In 1946, he was elected Fellow of the International College of Surgeons. The United States Government appointed him surgical consultant for the Army's European Theater of Operations in 1949, a job that involved touring occupied Europe as part of a four-man medical team with responsibility for improving medical conditions in hospital installations there.

Returning to America upon the completion of his work for the army, Dr. Drew resumed his responsibilities as one of the outstanding surgeons in America. His work often involved traveling great distances from his home in Washington, D.C., where he lived with his wife and four young children, to attend scientific conferences and meetings at which his knowledge was always in demand. Driving to one such medical meeting at Tuskegee Institute in Alabama, Dr. Drew, tired after a speaking engagement that delayed his departure until two o'clock in the morning, dozed at the wheel of his automobile. The car ran into the shoulder of the road near Burlington, North Carolina, and overturned. Three doctors who accompanied the pioneer in blood plasma work escaped with minor injuries. Dr. Drew was killed. The day was April 1, 1950, a sad day for science.

Sports

On October 23, 1945, Branch Rickey, president of the Brooklyn Dodgers, broke baseball's "unwritten law" and signed a young black athlete to a playing contract. The player was Jackie Robinson, who went on to become an all-time major league great. Rickey's action was deemed "the most significant development in fifty years of sport," for it brought the black man into our national game. Of course, there had been outstanding black baseball players before 1945. Satchel Paige is one of the most famous, a legend in black baseball. But no black athlete, no matter how good a ballplayer he was, had been permitted to play in the major leagues.

Since that historic day in 1945, many great black players have starred on major league teams, among them Hank Aaron, who in 1974 broke Babe Ruth's all-time record of 714 home runs; Lou Brock, who in the same year broke the major league record for stolen bases; Roy Campanella, the Brooklyn Dodger's great catcher; Willie Mays, who made baseball history for the New York Giants with his outstanding fielding; Bob Gibson, the strike-out king of the St. Louis Cardinals; and Monte Irvin, Elston Howard, Willie Stargell, Willie McCovey, Reggie Jackson, Cleon Jones, Vida Blue, Joe Morgan, Frank Robinson, and a host of others. At the end of the 1974 baseball season, Frank Robinson was named manager of the Cleveland

Indians, the first black man to become manager of a major league team.

In football, the early years of the century saw Fritz Pollard and Joe Lillard star. Later Marion Motley made his reputation on the gridiron. In 1957 Jimmy Brown, who had been an All-American at Syracuse University, joined the Cleveland Browns, where he was described as "the greatest offensive back in the history of football." Today there are more black men playing football than any other sport in America. Among the outstanding players of recent years are Emerson Boozer, Ron Johnson, Paul Warfield, O. J. Simpson, Gale Sayers, Leroy Kelly, and Joe Gilliam, to name but a few.

Black players abound in professional basketball, too. Bill Russell, the champion rebounder of the Boston Celtics, after helping his team to a record number of National Basketball Association championships was named coach of the team, the first black man in professional basketball to achieve such a position. Other superstars of the court include Wilt "The Stilt" Chamberlain, Willis Reed, Walt "Clyde" Frazier, Kareem Abdul Jabbar, Julius "Dr. J" Ervine, and Earl Monroe, among many.

Since 1936, when Jesse Owens returned from the Olympic Games in Berlin, Germany, with four gold medals, there have been many black stars of track and field, including hurdlers Harrison Dillard and Rod Milburn; Reggie McAfee, the first black American to crack the four-minute mile; Bob Beamon, who set a broad jump record of 29 feet 2½ inches; and sprinters John and Tommie Smith, John Carlos, and Dr. Del Meriwether.

Milt Campbell was the first black man to win the Olympic decathlon, a test of all-around athletic ability in ten field events, a feat repeated by Rafer Johnson, who compiled an 8,392-point Olympic record in 1960 and earned the title of "the greatest all-round athlete in the world."

Black women, too, have been among the world's great

athletes. Among the finest have been Mildred McDaniel, former women's high jump champion; Wilma Rudolph, one of the world's outstanding women runners; and Willye White, five times Olympic broad jump champion.

It was Althea Gibson who broke down the barriers of race in tennis and went on to win both the United States Women's Singles Championship and the Women's Singles Championship at Wimbledon, England, the top prize in world tennis, in two successive years.

Boxing fans can look back to the days of George Godfrey, Peter Jackson, Joe Gans, and Jack Johnson, the first black heavyweight champion. And John Henry Lewis, "Sugar Ray" Robinson, Joe Frazier, and George Foreman continue the championship tradition down to present times. But it is to Joe Louis, the "Brown Bomber," and Muhammad Ali that all thoughts turn as the most powerful and the most colorful of champions. Joe Louis will always be remembered for his mighty punch and great boxing skill. And Ali, who boasted and then made his boasts come true, will go down in prizefight history as the master of the "psych-out," enraging his opponents, dancing around their rage on flying feet, and then, when they had tired themselves out, picking them off with well-placed blows.

JESSE OWENS

It was August 1936. The Olympic Games were being held in Berlin, Germany. Adolf Hitler, the Nazi dictator, was in the stands. Lutz Long, one of Germany's best athletes, had just broken the Olympic record for the broad jump in one of his trial jumps to qualify for the event. Now it was Jesse Owens' turn to take his qualifying jumps.

The Nazis believed in the racial superiority of the white peoples of Northern Europe, and as Jesse got ready to run, Hitler left the stands, a gesture of contempt for the black athlete. Seething with anger, Jesse raced for the takeoff board and threw himself into a soaring leap. Before he hit the ground, he heard the referee shout, "Foul!" His run had taken him six inches past the takeoff board before he leaped.

He had two more chances to qualify for the event. Returning to the starting point, he controlled his anger. Knowing that he had plenty of power for a jump long enough to qualify, he was determined to be very careful this time. He would not try for great distance but would concentrate on not fouling. He would play it safe. He did play it safe, too safe. He fell short of the qualifying mark. His second jump was no good.

He had one jump left. If he failed to make it, he would not even be able to compete in the event. He was nervous, shaky, close to panic. As the other finalists made their jumps, Jesse walked round and round in a tight circle, trying to keep his legs

Jesse Owens

from trembling. Then the athlete whose turn preceded his own was jumping. He was next, and he wasn't ready. He would fail in his third attempt to qualify. He would be laughed at, humiliated.

Suddenly, a hand was laid on his arm. Someone was speaking to him in broken English.

"Hello, Jesse Owens," he said, "I am Lutz Long."

They talked briefly, waiting for Jesse's name to be called for his last jump. In fact, Lutz did most of the talking. He told Jesse that he knew he was capable of a better jump. He said Jesse should not fear fouling again. He should put everything he had into his jump. But the words were not important. It was the spirit that counted, the spirit of good sportsmanship. The human spirit, even there in Nazi Germany, could not be altogether stilled.

Jesse did qualify on his third jump. And he went on to win a gold medal for the event, beating Lutz Long and breaking Long's Olympic record by establishing one of his own. He won three other gold medals, too, demonstrating thereby the emptiness of the Nazi myth of racial superiority. But he also learned something, something about the vitality of the human spirit and its surprising way of appearing even in the most unfavorable of circumstances.

Circumstances had generally been far from favorable to the development of the human spirit in Jesse Owens, or James Cleveland Owens, as he was named at birth. (His parents called him "J. C.," which was mistaken for "Jesse" when the family later moved north to Ohio.) He was born on September 12, 1913, on a tenant farm in Oakville, a tiny hamlet in Morgan County, Alabama. Oakville consisted of little more than the general store owned by John Clannon, the white man who also owned the two hundred and fifty acres of cotton cropped on shares by eight black families. The families had to trade at the store. It was the only one nearby. Moreover, they didn't have to pay cash for the few tools or the weekly supplies of potatoes, beans, and cornmeal (meat was bought only twice a year, at the holidays). The supplies were entered in the store's books as debts against whatever share they made on their cotton. And though the work of the eight families enabled Clannon to send more than six thousand pounds of cotton north each year, none of the families ever earned enough to pay off the debts they incurred at the owner's store during the year.

Henry Owens, Jesse's father, was luckier than most. Of his seven children, four were boys. Jesse was sickly, but his three brothers were strong enough to help their father in the fields. So they farmed the largest plot on the plantation—fifty acres. Moreover, Mr. Owens owned five mules that he had scrimped and saved for over the years. And Emma, his wife, kept a small vegetable garden behind their house. Occasionally, too, Jesse's father and his older brother Prentis got up before their usual 4 A.M. rising time and hunted rabbits for their supper. Nonetheless, each year they went a little deeper into debt at Clannon's store.

Jesse was frail and skinny, and each winter when the winds whistled through the Owens' thin-walled house, he would come down with pneumonia. His mother had always been able to nurse him through his illnesses with home remedies. But during one bout, he had spit blood each time he coughed and was unconscious for a week. Although his mother pulled him through again, she knew it would be the last time she could do so. His lungs were too weak. He needed more and better food, warm clothes, medicines, a doctor's care. Frantic, Emma urged her husband to pull up stakes and go someplace where these things could be had.

But where would they go? In Oakville, at least, they had a roof over their heads. They had their garden patch and their mules. As a matter of fact, this year—it was 1921—they had made enough on their cotton to wipe out their debt. Things were looking up. Or so it seemed, until John Clannon's agent called Henry Owens in. Mr. Clannon was no longer satisfied with half the profits on the crop Henry farmed. He would take 60 percent. The Owens would receive 40.

So Henry sold his mules and took his family north to Cleveland, Ohio. There things were not much better. Henry Owens was over forty years old and untrained for any job but cotton farming. He couldn't read or write. He could get no regular employment. To be sure, he worked whenever he could. Emma hired out as a domestic servant. The boys, Prentis, Quincy, and Sylvester, all got jobs. Even skinny little Jesse had a job. In fact, he had two jobs. After school he delivered groceries and on weekends he worked in a greenhouse. So the family ate—beans, onions, potatoes, and bread. There was even an occasional piece of meat, the lion's share of which generally went to Jesse, to help build him up.

But the big change in Jesse's life was school. There he met coach Charles Riley, who thought him the skinniest boy he had ever seen. When he learned that Jesse had had pneumonia four times in the past three years, he urged him to run—for survival. Running would develop his lungs and enable him to withstand the Cleveland winters. He asked Jesse to come out for track, but Jesse couldn't. He had to work after school. So Riley had him come out in the morning, an hour before school started. He brought the boy a substantial breakfast, too, urging him to eat and "put some meat on your bones."

Jesse ate. And he ran for three-quarters of an hour each morning on the sidewalks around the school. His lungs strengthened. In fact, his whole body did. He survived the Cleveland winters. And he got faster and faster, becoming Coach Riley's "sidewalk champion."

At East Technical High School, where Charles Riley continued to coach him, Jesse broke the world's record in the 100-yard dash in 1936, running it in 9.4 seconds, a record that endured for twelve years. Thereafter, he was besieged with offers of scholarships and other inducements to enroll from colleges and universities all over the country. Many of the offers were very attractive, but Jesse turned them all down. His father had been laid off a job that required him to load hundred-pound crates at $12 for a sixty-hour week. Jesse, as he told Coach Riley, couldn't accept the idea of living in comparative luxury while his family went hungry.

However, Riley was eager to have Jesse go to college. As a matter of fact, he wanted him to attend a particular school, Ohio State University, where he knew Larry Snyder, perhaps the best track coach in the country. So one spring weekend in 1930 Riley drove over to see his friend Snyder. Naturally, Snyder wanted Jesse for his team, but he could offer no scholarship. He could, however, arrange for Jesse's father to get a permanent job with the state of Ohio.

When Jesse heard the news about his father's job, he threw his arms around Riley and kissed him. Then he enrolled at Ohio State. Instead of a scholarship, he paid his way by working at the school. In fact, since he had married his grammar school sweetheart, Ruth Solomon, at sixteen, while they were both in high school, he needed three jobs to support himself and Ruth. So in addition to studying, training, and running for the track team, he waited on tables in the college dining hall, worked in the library, and ran an elevator from five to midnight six days a week.

In his book *I Have Changed*, published in 1972, Jesse Owens names his "greatest day in sports": May 25, 1935. That was the day of the Big Ten track meet at Ann Arbor, Michigan, when he tied the world record for the 100-yard dash and broke three world records—for 220 yards, for the low hurdles, and for the broad jump. The new record of almost 27 feet that he established for the broad jump that day lasted for twenty-four years.

Not all the days were good days, however, even for a world champion track star. There was, for example, the terrible day in February 1936 that Jesse speaks of in *Blackthink* (1970). A cavalcade of cars containing the Ohio State track team was headed for a track meet in Indianapolis. At nine o'clock in the morning, they stopped for breakfast. Everyone went into the restaurant except the occupants of the last car in the cavalcade, Mel Walker, Dave Albritton, Ralph Metcalfe, and Jesse Owens, the black members of the team. They would not be served, so a couple of teammates brought out food for them. This was humiliating enough, but a few minutes later, the owner of the restaurant reached into the car and yanked their plates away, spilling eggs all over the boys and the car, shouting that the waitress had made a mistake and bellowing, "I don't want money to feed no *niggers*."

In 1936 Jesse went to the Olympics in Berlin as a member of the United States track team. He came back with four gold medals, and there was a ticker-tape parade for him in New York. He was named Athlete of the Year by the Associated Press, the second black man ever to win that award. But in Cleveland there were responsibilities. His wife was expecting the second of their three daughters. With a family of four to feed, Jesse could not return to finish his last year of college. He quit and sought a job. Despite the gold medals and the ticker tape, the best offer he had was a $30-a-week job as a Cleveland playground instructor. He and his family could live on what he earned, but he certainly couldn't save anything against his return to school.

Then a couple of white promoters of black baseball offered him a deal. They wanted the fastest man in the world to race against a thoroughbred racehorse to increase attendance at the baseball games they had scheduled. It would be no contest, they assured Jesse, since the starter's gun would be held close to the horse's ear, frightening him and allowing Jesse to get off to a healthy start. Before the horse could cut his lead, Jesse's speed would enable him to finish in front at 100 yards.

Jesse was repelled at the idea of competing with a horse. It was degrading, beneath human dignity. Worse, it was, to all intents and purposes, a rigged race, dishonest. In fact, it was no race at all, simply a spectacle. But the promoters offered Jesse five cents on every dollar paid for attendance. The amount would enable him to return to college in the fall to get his degree. So he did it, hating himself for being exploited.

Back in college, Jesse was approached by another group of men who wanted to exploit his name and reputation. This time it was for a chain of cleaning stores. Jesse was made a partner in the chain in exchange for the use of his name, and Jesse Owens Cleaning Stores sprang up all over Cleveland. For a while he made a good deal of money, enough to buy a fifteen-room house for his parents. Then one day in the fall of 1939 Jesse's partners disappeared. The cleaning chain was bankrupt, and Jesse found himself responsible for its debts—in the amount of $55,000.

It took Jesse five years to pay off the debts. But he did pay them off. In order to do so, he moved to Detroit, where he was in charge of recruiting black help for the Ford Motor Company. Traveling widely, Jesse recruited almost fifty thousand black workers for Ford during the years of World War II.

In 1949 Jesse, his wife, and their three daughters moved to Chicago. For more than twenty years Chicago was to be home base for Jesse as he traveled hundreds of thousands of miles back and forth across the country and around the world, speaking to young people about sports, his role in the Olympics, civil rights, and brotherhood. In 1955 President Eisenhower named Jesse Ambassador of Sports, and he made a world tour under the auspices of the State Department. Back in Chicago, he started a radio program featuring jazz music. He developed a profitable public relations agency. And he continued to travel and lecture to young people. Perhaps his most satisfying work during this period was the six years he spent as Sports Specialist for the Illinois Youth Commission, between 1955 and 1961, helping to combat juvenile delinquency by showing young people in trouble how to find satisfaction and a sense of accomplishment through sports.

Traveling widely on the lecture circuit and working hard at a variety of other jobs, including executive responsibilities for the American League and the Harlem Globetrotters, among other athletic organizations, Jesse Owens made as much as $100,000 a year during his more successful years in Chicago. He had a ten-room apartment in a high-rise building on the city's South Side and a summer home in Michigan. But as he approached sixty years, his heavy schedule and the cold Chicago winters began to tell on him. As in his early youth, he had several bouts with pneumonia. After the most serious of these, in 1971, his doctor urged him to take the entire month of September off to recuperate or he wouldn't be here in October.

Jesse complied with the doctor's orders. And he got well. It had been the first time in more than fifty years that he had spent more than a day or two idle, unemployed. He was anxious to return to work. But Ruth was frightened. She urged him to abandon his rigorous schedule and move to a less severe climate, one that would be easier on his lungs. Ruth had asked for very little over the years. Now, however, she insisted. So they moved to Phoenix, Arizona, where the winters are mild and golf can be played year round. Jesse still travels a good bit to talk to young people about sports and sportsmanship. He has never forgotten the lesson he learned from Lutz Long in the Olympic Stadium in Berlin in 1936. But he spends more time on the golf course these days. And more time with Ruth, his grammar school sweetheart whom, after more than forty-three years of marriage, Jesse still describes as "the most worthwhile human being I've ever known."

JOE LOUIS

Braddock, Schmeling, Sharkey, Baer, Carnera, Levinsky, Conn, Farr, Uzcudun, Lewis, Galento, Pastor, Walcott—all fell to the Brown Bomber, Joe Louis. His sledgehammer jab and explosive left hook, delivered in combinations befuddling to his opponents, made him, at the age of twenty-three, heavyweight boxing champion of the world. On June 24, 1948, eleven years and twenty-five victorious fights later, he knocked out "Jersey Joe" Walcott with a smashing right to the jaw in the eleventh round at Yankee Stadium in New York and retired shortly thereafter, at thirty-four, undefeated champion.

Born on May 13, 1914, in a sagging, unpainted sharecropper's shack in Chambers County, Alabama, to Monroe and Lillie (Reese) Barrow, Joseph Louis Barrow was the second youngest of eight children. His father, a big man, six feet three inches tall and weighing more than 200 pounds, he hardly remembers. When Joe was only two years old his father was taken to the Searcy State Hospital for the Insane at Mt. Vernon, where he was to spend the remainder of his fifty-nine years sunk in profound, immobilizing melancholy.

Before Joe was six, his mother remarried. Pat Brooks, her new husband, a widower with five children of his own, moved the large family to Mt. Sinai, a hamlet deep in Alabama's Buckalew Mountains, where they became tenants on the Walton plantation, farming cotton on shares. The tenant's

Joe Louis

"share" of the crop he worked to produce was small indeed under conditions laid down by the landowner. Although the whole family worked in the fields, they made hardly enough to live on. And conditions in the rough plank house they lived in were very crowded with the children sleeping three to a bed.

In 1926 Pat Brooks went north to Detroit, seeking work in the automobile industry. Soon after he was settled with relatives on the East Side, the family joined him. Barney Nagler, in *Brown Bomber* (1972), quotes Joe's recollection of the move. "We went up after him," Joe recalled. "The place we lived in on Macomb Street was crowded, but it had something we didn't have in Alabama, an inside toilet. And there were electric lights. It was nice."

When his stepfather got a job at a Ford Motor Company plant, the family moved to larger quarters in a frame tenement house on Catherine Street. Joe was enrolled at the nearby Duffield School, but he soon transferred to the Bronson Trade School. However, most of his time he spent in the street, running with a gang from Catherine Street and getting into fights. In an effort to get him off the streets, his mother started him on violin lessons with a teacher on Woodward Avenue. Joe lasted for five or six lessons. Then, having discovered at school that he could box, he used the money for the lessons to join the Brewster Recreation Center, where he could work out, use the boxing ring, and get some instruction. Unbeknown to his mother, he had traded a violin teacher for a boxing coach. "Fellow's name was Alter Ellis," says Louis. "He was the first man showed me how to hold my hands up. He taught me a lot about boxing."

When Joe's mother discovered the use to which he had put her money, she wasn't angry. "Joe, if you want to keep on boxing, you keep on with it," she said. "I'll work for you to get it." But Joe didn't want to spend his mother's money. Instead, he quit school and got a job for $25 a week at the Briggs auto-body plant. "I pushed truck bodies to the sprayer on the assembly line," he recalled later. "The tape would come off the body covers and land on the floor sticky side up. The tape would gum onto the dolly wheels, and you'd get a real workout pushing those truck bodies. . . . Working that hard kind of made me forget about boxing."

But the lapse was only temporary. Late in 1932 Joe was matched against Johnny Miler in a bout at the Edison Athletic Club. It was his first big amateur bout, and it was a disaster. Miler, an experienced amateur fighter who had participated in the 1932 Olympics, knocked Joe down seven times in the two rounds Joe was able to last against him.

Humiliated and sore from the beating he had taken, Joe hung up his gloves again, determined to fight no more. He got himself a new job at Ford's River Rouge plant, and he stayed away from Brewster's—for a while. But the lure of the ring was too great. Joe heard that Holman Williams, a professional middleweight boxer, was working out at Brewster's. Joe returned there to work out, impressing Williams, who took him in charge and taught him how to move in the ring. The results were impressive. In Joe's second amateur bout, two blows were struck, both by Joe Louis, who won by a knockout. As a matter of fact, in his two-year career as an amateur light heavyweight, Joe won fifty of his fifty-four fights, forty-three by knockouts.

Early in 1934 Joe met John Roxborough, an enterprising black man who was to have a profound effect on his career. Roxborough took Joe under his wing, determined to make a professional heavyweight out of him. Realizing that that would take some doing and would involve considerable expense, Roxborough introduced Joe to Julian Black, a friend who knew the professional fight game. The result of the meeting was an agreement. Joe would turn professional under the management of Roxborough and Black. They would guide his career, arranging matches with successively more and more highly rated boxers, until he could challenge the heavyweight champion. They would also provide for publicity, see to Joe's training, hire a staff, and handle all business arrangements for half the proceeds from each fight, after expenses had been deducted. Normally prizefight managers got one-third of a purse, but Black and Roxborough were shrewd. They were gambling on Joe's becoming heavyweight champion. However, no black man had done that since Jack Johnson had been defeated by Jess Willard nineteen years before. Prejudice against the black man in sports was so profound that it would be eleven years more before Jackie Robinson would break the color line in baseball. And Joe Louis was still untried as a professional boxer. The managers' gamble was a real one, against considerable odds. In any case, Joe's acquaintance with money was slight, his knowledge of financial arrangements sketchy. He was glad to take what Black and Roxborough offered.

In Chicago Joe lived in a rented room on Forty-sixth Street, near South Parkway, in the apartment of Bill Bottoms, a chef who cooked for Joe and later became his regular training camp cook. However, most of Joe's day, after three miles of roadwork in Washington Park at 6 A.M., was spent at George Trafton's gymnasium under the beady eyes of Jack Blackburn, who was hired as his trainer.

Blackburn, whom Joe called "Chappie," had been a professional lightweight himself before becoming a trainer. And he had trained two champions—Bud Taylor, a bantamweight, and Sammy Mandell, a lightweight—before taking on Joe. "Chappie" found Joe clumsy-footed in the ring. Moreover, he saw that Joe couldn't follow a left hook with a right without picking up one foot, a dangerous practice. Blackburn pointed out that a fighter had to keep both feet planted firmly on the canvas in order to get power in a punch or to take a blow without being knocked down. He also taught Joe not to rely on single, isolated punches but to put his hits together in a series, for their cumulative effect on opponents and to hamper counterpunches. "Whatever he told me to do in the ring, I did," Joe said. "He was the best teacher anybody ever had."

Joe learned fast. Within six months he had won a dozen fights in and around Chicago and Detroit, ten of them by knockouts. As his reputation grew, he traveled farther afield— to Los Angeles, where he knocked out Lee Ramage in two rounds for a purse of $3,000—and San Francisco. His impassive face began to appear in victory photos on the sports pages of newspapers from coast to coast. And money began to flow into his hands—and out—in larger and larger amounts. He bought and furnished a home for his mother on McDougal Avenue in Detroit. He made substantial down payments on two other homes, one for his sisters Susie and Emmarell, and another, in Wayne, Michigan, for his stepbrother and close childhood companion Pat Brooks, Jr. He had a car, and he began to dress like a dude, in striped suits with wide lapels and broad-brimmed, high-crowned, light-colored hats. Soon he had an extensive wardrobe, with more than one hundred high-priced suits.

But he was in the big time now. He was to fight in New York at Yankee Stadium on the night of June 25, 1935. His opponent: the six-foot-six, 250-pound Italian giant Primo Carnera, who had been heavyweight champion before his defeat by Max Baer on June 14, 1934. Louis trained for the fight at Pompton Lakes, New Jersey, working out against huge sparring partners. "You're fighting a big man in that Carnera fellow," Blackburn told Joe. "You got to hit a big man in training to get the feel of it."

The night of the fight Blackburn instructed Joe: "Go out and hit him in the belly. His hands gonna come down. Then you go for his head." Joe followed the fight plan, concentrating his attack on Carnera's midsection. Carnera went into a clinch, attempting to bull Louis into a corner by lifting him bodily. Joe responded by lifting the giant Carnera and swinging him away from him. Carnera gaped in awe at Louis's strength, dropping his guard, and Louis hit him in the jaw with a smashing left. Carnera's eyes went glassy. Joe knew he had him. In the sixth round he battered the buckling giant's head with lightning combinations. Primo went down for a count of nine. When he got up, Joe was on him again, hitting his head with rights and lefts in a tattoo-like rhythm. The huge hulk crumpled to the canvas, and referee Arthur Donovan stopped the fight. Louis was the victor. His take was $60,000. Even more astonishing, he had been a professional boxer for only ten months.

Joe Louis's next fight was with King Levinsky at Comisky Park in Chicago. It lasted two minutes and twenty-one seconds. That was all the time Joe needed to deliver two straight rights and a left hook that sent Levinsky crashing to the canvas. He was paid $53,000.

Meanwhile Max Baer had lost the heavyweight championship to James Braddock in a humiliating fifteen-round decision that saw him, sadly out of condition, completely outboxed by Braddock. Joe had watched the fight and had commented at ringside, "Ain't nobody gonna tell me these are the two best fighters in the world." When a bout was arranged between Baer and Louis, Baer, smarting from his unexpected defeat and stung by Louis's comment, determined to put aside his clownish playboy ways and train seriously for the fight. He did so. Confident, he boasted of his impending triumph. It would be his first step on the comeback trail to the championship, he asserted. Interest in the fight was high. When the gate receipts were counted at Yankee Stadium the night of the fight, they totaled $1,000,832. There had been a long publicity buildup for the fight. But the fight itself was brief. Baer fell under a two-handed fusillade of blows in the fourth round. Shaking his head from side to side as though in disbelief, he took the full count. And Joe walked off with $240,000 as his portion of the unusual million-dollar gate.

Just two hours before the Baer fight, Joe had presented

Marva Trotter with a four-carat diamond ring and had been married to her in a ceremony presided over by her brother, who was a minister. After the fight the newlyweds left for Chicago, where they had a six-room apartment on South Michigan Avenue. But within a few weeks Joe was back at Pompton Lakes, training for his next fight, with Paolino Uzcudun.

Uzcudun had an unorthodox style. He fought from a crouch, with his gloves up in front of his face, ducking under punches. Joe was perplexed at first. But in the fourth round he found his target. He connected with a right that drove two of Uzcudun's teeth through his lip and caused the referee to stop the fight in a welter of blood. "I never threw a better punch," Louis said after the fight. "Or a harder one," added Blackburn.

But a dark-haired boxer with a broken nose and a thick German accent who had watched the fight intently from ringside was neither bedazzled by the punch nor awed by the flow of blood. Commenting on the fight afterward, he said to reporters, "I seez somezing."

The man was Max Schmeling. The something he saw, he didn't reveal, at least not immediately. But when he fought Louis at Yankee Stadium later in 1936 he capitalized on what he had seen. He saw it again, in the fourth round: a gap in Louis's defense as he shifted position to throw a left. Like lightning, Schmeling shot his own right through the gap to catch Joe on the jaw and send him sprawling. Louis was up at the count of three, but Schmeling caught him again early in the fifth. Then he knocked Joe down at the end of the fifth with an unfortunate blow after the bell.

Afterward Louis said, "People put it out that I hated Schmeling for hitting me after the bell. I never hated him. We became friends. After the fight, he sent me one of those German cuckoo clocks. Ain't no reason to hate a man just because he beats you in a fight."

Louis was beaten in the twelfth round, his first defeat in twenty-eight professional bouts. He didn't hate Schmeling for the defeat. He did work with Blackburn to correct the flaw in his defense, preparing for the day when he could redeem himself.

That day didn't come until after Joe had won the world heavyweight championship, knocking out Jim Braddock in the eighth round before forty-five thousand fight fans at Comisky Park in June 1937. Three title defenses followed Joe's victory over Braddock. But with the memory of his defeat by Schmeling rankling him, Joe didn't feel like the world champion. Finally, on June 22, 1938, Joe had the opportunity to even the score. When he met Schmeling in the ring at Yankee Stadium before seventy thousand people, there were no flaws in his defense. At any rate, if there were, Schmeling didn't see them. He was dispatched too quickly—by a knockout in two minutes and four seconds of round one.

During World War II, Joe Louis served for almost four years in the U.S. Army. Touring army camps, he gave exhibition bouts, helping to keep up morale among the troops. For this service Joe won a Legion of Merit medal. But exhibition bouts were not the real thing. "When I came out of the army I wasn't the fighter I was before I went in," Joe observed. It was true. At thirty-one, after four years' absence from the professional ring, his reflexes were off and his punches had less power than they once had. He still had some good fights—with Billy Conn, for example, and, after a near loss, the second fight with Joe Walcott in June 1948. But he was no longer the invincible boxer, the Brown Bomber he once had been. And on March 1, 1949, Joe Louis retired as world heavyweight champion.

There had been other losses besides his boxing skill during the war years. "Chappie" Blackburn, his beloved trainer, had died. Marva had divorced Joe. And though they tried to patch up their differences and remarried in 1946, they were divorced again in 1949, Marva winning custody of the children, Jacqueline and Joe, Jr., and a large alimony settlement. Joe had huge debts, so on September 27, 1950, he came out of retirement to face Ezzard Charles, who beat him badly in a fifteen-round decision. Joe won all six of a series of fights following the Charles bout, but on October 26, 1951, Rocky Marciano hit him through the ropes in the eighth round with a right to the jaw that ended Louis's career as a boxer. He had fought in seventy-one professional bouts, winning sixty-eight of them. Now, at thirty-seven, his boxing days were done.

But his debts persisted. In fact, they increased. There were bad investments. There were taxes owed to the government. Joe was generous with friends. And he continued to spend money lavishly, as in the days when he was making sizable amounts in the ring. Another marriage, to Rose Morgan, in 1955 ended in divorce two years later, with consequent alimony payments. So, in 1956, Joe went back into the ring—the wrestling ring. A friend, recognizing that professional wrestling is a more clownish show than sport, asked Joe, "Ain't you a little ashamed of being a wrestler?" Joe responded, "Beats stealing, don't it?" But his career as a wrestler was to be short-lived. Rocky Lee, a 320-pound opponent jumped on Joe one night in the ring in Columbus, Ohio, crushing several ribs and causing a cardiac contusion. At forty-two, Joe's wrestling days were over.

There was still golf, however, which Joe played avidly, mostly in and around Los Angeles and Denver, in both of which cities he and his third wife, Martha Jefferson Malone, a successful trial lawyer, have homes. Martha helped Joe resolve some of his tax problems with the government, too. But she was unable to help him remove the dark cloud that descended upon him in retirement. For that he required prolonged hospitalization in 1970, first in the Colorado Psychiatric Hospital and later in the Veterans Administration Hospital in Denver.

His mental health improved and Joe was released from the hospital, resuming his normal life, including a certain number of public appearances at sporting events and benefits of various sports, for which he is always in demand. On such occasions, bathed in the spotlight of public acclaim, Joe recalls his years as the Brown Bomber, the invincible king of the heavyweight boxing ring. And the public, recalling those years with him, cheers one of the great prizefighting champions of all time.

ALTHEA GIBSON

"She was always the outdoor type. That's why she can beat that tennis ball like nobody's business." So said Daniel Gibson, Althea Gibson's father, in an interview after one of her big tournaments. He was right, of course. She certainly could beat that tennis ball, with a serve like greased lightning and an overhand smash at the net that turned her opponents to jelly. Speed and accuracy she had, too, enabling her to cover the court in a flash and drop a lob on a pinpoint. But it was her enormous power that made her game, as she charged the net and rifled the ball into the clay, devastating the opposition. On the center court at Wimbledon, England, in 1957 that power won her the tournament that tennis players consider the world's championship. It also brought her the Women's National Singles Championship at Forest Hills, New York, the same year, making her the top international amateur tennis player, since she had already won the French, Italian, and Asian titles.

Althea was thirty years old when she won the world's tennis crown at Wimbledon, having been born to Daniel and Annie Gibson in Silver, South Carolina, on August 25, 1927. It had been a long road to the championship. And a strange one for the daughter of a poor sharecropper, who lived on a five-acre cotton farm in what her father described as a three-store town, none of which stocked so much as a tennis ball. Speed, accuracy, and power alone could not have taken Althea up that

Althea Gibson

road from Silver to Wimbledon. It required something else: determination. That was a quality she had from the beginning, as the title of her autobiography, published in 1958, indicates. The book is called *I Always Wanted to Be Somebody.*

Somebody. But who? Perhaps a female boxer. "She always was a spunky kid and a good scrapper," Daniel Gibson recalled in an interview in the *Amsterdam News* following her victory at Wimbledon. "When she was about thirteen," he said, "I taught her how to box. There were a lot of women boxers then and I thought it might be a good career for her."

Althea didn't become a professional boxer, but she did get into some pretty fierce scraps. Her sister later recalled how "she beat the tar out of me once" in an argument over a scrub bucket. Most of her battles, however, were not domestic but public, street fights that were a part of the struggle for survival in the tough Harlem neighborhood the family moved to when Althea was three years old.

Once when visiting her Aunt Sally, she found her Uncle Junie being mugged in his hallway on 144th Street by the leader of the Sabres, a tough street gang with which she sometimes hung out. She rescued her uncle from the gang leader, who gave her a gash in the hand with a sharpened screwdriver. (She bears the scar still.) Then, after taking her uncle to his apartment, dripping with blood, she went out after the boy who had attacked her. "We had a fight they still talk about on 144th Street," she says in her autobiography. She didn't quite win that fight—which ended in a draw when some adults intervened— but she didn't lose it either. As she says, none of the Sabres "ever tried to use me for a dart board again."

Street-wise, tough, and strong, Althea found school a bore. She played hooky constantly, spending her time shooting baskets in the playground, making fires in the lots with her friends and roasting potatoes snitched from the Bronx Terminal Market, or going to the movies at the Apollo Theatre on 125th Street, where they had a big stage show.

When her father learned of her truancy, he would punish her, but the hooky playing continued. In fact, after she graduated from junior high school in 1941 and started going to the Yorkville Trade School, her truancy increased. Eventually, she dropped out of school, but without a high school diploma, Althea could find few jobs. Those she got were monotonous, and she quickly became bored with them. Within a few years she worked at a dozen or more different ones. She cleaned chickens in a butcher shop. She ran an elevator in the Dixie Hotel in downtown New York. She was a countergirl in a restaurant. She worked in a department store, a dress factory, a button factory. The job that she liked best was as a mail clerk at the New York School of Social Work, where she had a small office of her own and a sense of importance, being in charge of all incoming and outgoing mail for the school. But when she had been there for six months she took a day off to go to the Paramount Theater in Times Square, where Sarah Vaughan was singing. And she got fired.

Meanwhile, Althea had discovered tennis—or tennis Althea. Actually, it started with paddle tennis, a game played with wooden bats, or paddles, and a sponge ball on a court much like a tennis court but about half the size. Paddle tennis was one of the games played on the block where Althea lived, 143rd Street, which was a Police Athletic League play street. It was closed to traffic during the daytime for use as a playground. Naturally, Althea played. And she was good at the game. So good, in fact, that she attracted the attention of Buddy Walker, a musician who eked out his income by working for the city during the summer months as a playground leader. Recognizing her potential, Buddy talked Althea into trying her hand at tennis, starting her off hitting balls against a wall in Morris Park with a secondhand tennis racket he bought her.

Having taught her the rudiments of the game, Buddy took Althea to the Harlem River Tennis Courts at 150th Street and Seventh Avenue to play with some of his friends. Althea ran their legs off. Players on other courts stopped their games to watch this young girl play. She was a phenomenon. One of the spectators, Juan Serrell, a young schoolteacher who was a member of the Cosmopolitan Tennis Club, saw that Althea was tournament material. He urged that she be taken to the Cosmopolitan, where she could get expert instruction from Fred Johnson, the club's one-armed professional.

Now in those days the Cosmopolitan Tennis Club was, in Althea's words, "*the* ritzy tennis club in Harlem. All the Sugar Hill society people belonged to it." And Althea's family was definitely not Sugar Hill. Her father worked in a garage, where he earned just about enough to support his wife and Althea, her brother and three sisters. In any case, Althea wasn't exactly the sort of girl one found on the Cosmopolitan courts. A tough street kid, she would probably have been more at home, she reflected later, training in Stillman's Gym than playing tennis amidst Harlem's élite on the carefully kept courts of the Cosmopolitan Club. But she could hit the ball. Oh, how she could hit it! So the members of the club, hoping they were nourishing a future champion, chipped in to buy Althea a junior membership and provide her with lessons from Mr. Johnson. One of the members, Mrs. Rhoda Smith, even bought Althea a tennis costume, the first one she ever owned. In fact, Mrs. Smith, who had lost her own daughter some years before, treated Althea like a daughter, guiding and encouraging her, helping to polish off some of the rough spots of the girl's personality, often to Althea's irritation.

Within a year, Althea progressed far enough under Johnson's guidance to enter the girls' singles in the New York State Open Championship of the American Tennis Association, a largely black tennis group. It was her first tournament, and she won it. That was in 1942. Later in the year, the club sent Althea to the ATA National Girls' Championship at Lincoln University in Pennsylvania. It was her first national tournament, and she made it to the finals, where she lost to Nana Davis. The following year wartime travel restrictions eliminated the national tournament. But Althea won the girls' singles in both 1944 and 1945. Then, at eighteen, she was out of the girls' class. And the ATA sponsored her to Wilberforce University in Ohio for the National Women's Singles Championship. Again she made it to the finals, where she was "psyched-out" by Roumania Peters, an experienced player whose pretended exhaustion in the third set of their match made Althea overconfident and lost her the match. But she had played well enough to attract the attention of a couple of black doctors, tennis-playing cronies on the lookout for a young black player with the potential to challenge the championship players in the major—and still, in 1946, all white—tournaments. These men, Dr. Hubert A. Eaton of Wilmington, North Carolina, and Dr. Robert W. Johnson of Lynchburg, Virginia, were to have an enormous influence upon Althea Gibson. In fact, they were to change the course of her life, consciously directing it, by way of a detour through the South, on the road to Forest Hills and Wimbledon.

At first the two doctors thought of trying to get a college athletic scholarship for Althea. However, when they learned of her disastrous high school experience, they changed their plans. Dr. Eaton, who had a private court in his backyard in Wilmington, offered to take Althea into his home as part of his family. She could practice on his court all fall and winter and attend high school in town. After she had acquired her high school diploma, they would see about college. Meanwhile, during the summer she would join Dr. Johnson in Lynchburg and tour the ATA tournament circuit with him.

The plan worked well. Given a goal that she wanted to reach, Althea buckled down to schoolwork and finished the Williston Industrial High School course in three years, graduating tenth in her class. She also played saxophone in the school band and with a small jazz combo that played dates around town for pocket money. She was the star player and captain of the girls' basketball team, and she used up the energy left over from her daily tennis practice by working out with the boys' varsity basketball and baseball teams.

During the summers Althea packed into Dr. Johnson's big Buick with five or six other young tennis players to make the rounds of the tournaments, playing in Washington, D.C., Pennsylvania, New York, New Jersey, Missouri, Kentucky, wherever the big matches were held. The first summer out—1947—Althea played in nine tournaments and won the singles championship in every one, the top win being the ATA National Women's Singles. She was to win that title for ten straight years.

Meanwhile, however, after three years with the doctors, Althea was off on her own—to Tallahassee, Florida, where she had won an athletic scholarship to Florida A and M. While she was a college student, Althea made some significant strides in her tennis career. She broke the United States Lawn Tennis Association color barrier, playing at Forest Hills in 1950 where she lost in the second round of the National Women's Singles.

The next spring Althea also played at Wimbledon. But all she got there in 1951 was "more experience." In fact, 1951, 1952, and 1953 were "mostly disappointing" years for Althea insofar as tennis was concerned. *Jet* magazine ran an article calling her "The Biggest Disappointment in Tennis." And in 1954 she dropped in national ranking from number seven to number thirteen. By that time she had graduated from Florida A and M and had a job teaching in the physical education department of Lincoln University at Jefferson City, Missouri. The pay was low, Jefferson City was racist to the core, and Althea had a disappointing romance with an older man, an army captain who almost succeeded in talking her into joining the Women's Army Corps. Even after she dropped the captain, left her job at Lincoln, and returned east in 1955, she still thought of joining the army and seeing the world, abandoning tennis, for she felt she had come to a dead end. The reason

she didn't was Sydney Llewellyn, a Harlem tennis teacher-
cabdriver who had recently taken her under his guidance,
changing her grip and her game. Syd had faith in her, feeling
that she could go right to the top. Althea hated to let him down.

As it happened, she didn't have to, and she got to see the
world—or a large part of it—without joining the army. Invited
by the State Department to be part of a four-member U.S.
tennis team touring Southeast Asia as ambassadors of goodwill,
Althea played tennis halfway round the world, from Burma to
India, Pakistan, and Ceylon. And she played well. Her confidence returned. She enjoyed herself. When the tour ended in
January 1956, she went on to Sweden, Germany, France, and
Egypt, and continued to play well. In fact, she won sixteen of
eighteen tournaments from Rangoon to Stockholm. But victory
at Wimbledon, and at Forest Hills, continued to elude her when
she tried again in 1956.

At twenty-nine, Althea Gibson had been playing tennis for
fifteen years. She had won scores of tournaments and had more
victory trophies than she could keep count of. Still, the
top-ranking titles remained beyond her grasp. It was very
frustrating. But frustrated or not, Althea would not give in. She
had had her moment of doubt the year before when she had
been ready to turn in her tennis shorts for a WAC uniform.
That moment had passed, and she was determined now to
make it to the top. In 1957 she did, beating Darlene Hard in the
finals on the center court at Wimbledon in straight sets. A
furiously competitive woman, Althea kept muttering as she
stepped up the pace of the game in the final set, noting Miss
Hard's errors mounting, "At last! At last!"

At last she had won at Wimbledon. Queen Elizabeth
presented Althea with the gold salver of victory, engraved with
the names of all the previous champions. At the Wimbledon
Ball she danced with the Duke of Devonshire. There was a
telegram of congratulations from President Eisenhower. And
she returned to New York to a ticker-tape parade of victory up

Broadway. She had won at Wimbledon. But there was still Forest Hills.

When the time came for the U.S. National Women's Singles Championship at Forest Hills, Althea was there. She took each of the first five rounds of competition in straight sets. Then, in the final round, she was to meet her onetime nemesis, Louise Brough, who had beaten her at Forest Hills seven years earlier. Louise was the former U.S. champion and three-time winner in the finals at Wimbledon, a formidable opponent. But Althea took her, too, in straight sets.

Althea had always wanted to be somebody, to have an identity. Now, at last, she had one that she could proclaim: "I'm Althea Gibson, the tennis champion," was what she said. And she added, "I hope it makes me happy."

In 1958 Althea duplicated her feat, winning both the U.S. and the Wimbledon Women's Championship in tennis. Then, at the age of thirty-two, with no place higher to go in the world of tennis, she moved from the tennis court to the golf links. Four years later she turned professional, cracking the color line in women's professional golf as she had done in amateur tennis.

Althea, who was married in 1965 to William A. Darben, is a member of the Ladies Professional Golf Association. A strong golfer who generally drives 230–260 yards off the tee, Mrs. Darben has participated in as many as twenty-five tournaments during a single year. However, in recent years she has limited her participation to about six tourneys a season, so that she can devote her time to work as recreation supervisor with the Essex County Parks Commission in New Jersey, a job from which she takes considerable satisfaction.

WILLIE MAYS

In 1954 the New York Giants beat the Cleveland Indians in the World Series in four straight games to win the world championship. But they almost lost the first game. In the eighth inning of that game, with a record Polo Ground crowd of 52,751 people watching and the score tied at 2–2, two Cleveland men got on base. The next man up was Vic Wertz, who had tripled in the first and singled in the fourth and sixth innings. A hit would have meant a run and, probably, the game.

Wertz stepped to the plate. The ball came sizzling in. Wertz swung and connected—hard! The ball soared up . . . up . . . up . . . and out into deep center field. The Giant center fielder had been playing in short. As the ball left the bat he whirled and started to run back toward the bleachers. Running full-speed straight at the center-field wall, he reached up over his head and made the catch with his back to the plate—460 feet away! More amazing still, he got the ball back to the infield so fast that the man on second base only reached third, instead of home plate as might have been expected. The man on first could not advance at all. Commenting on the play after the series ended, Al Lopez, the Indians' manager, said that this catch, followed by a great throw, "broke our backs." Joe DiMaggio, a pretty good center fielder himself, called the catch one of the greatest he had ever seen. The man who made this

Darryl Norenberg/Camera 5

Willie Mays

spectacular catch was, of course, Willie Mays, one of the greatest young ballplayers the sport has ever known.

Willie Mays' skill was not limited to defensive play. In 1954, his first full season in the major leagues, Willie hit forty-one home runs and had a batting average of .345, thereby winning the National League batting championship for the year. This record is particularly impressive when compared with the first-year records of other great players. Babe Ruth and Joe DiMaggio, for instance, each hit twenty-nine home runs and had averages of, respectively, .322 and .323 in their first years. In 1939, his first full season with the Red Sox, Ted Williams got ten fewer hits and ten fewer homers than Willie did in his first full season with the Giants.

But neither hitting nor fielding nor both combined tells the whole story of Willie's greatness as an athlete. Loving the sport, he played it with his whole heart. And because he was more interested in the game than in starring or setting records, he was a great team player. Full of pep and fun, his very presence on the field seemed to inspire his teammates. And even off the field, his infectious good humor kept team spirit high. Charley Grimm, one of the National League coaches for the 1954 All-Star Game, traveled to Cleveland with Mays for that game. After the trip Grimm declared, "Mays is the only ballplayer I ever saw who could help a club just by riding on the bus with it."

Willie Mays was born in Westfield, a steel-mill town about thirteen miles from Birmingham, Alabama, on May 6, 1931. His father, William Howard Mays, Sr., worked as a toolroom attendant in one of the local mills. But it was as outfielder for the mill team that he was known widely; he was called "Kitty Cat" for his lithe grace. Baseball ran in the Mays family, and Willie is probably correct in saying that he was "born to play ball." His grandfather, Walter Mays, had been a fine player too, pitching for amateur teams around Tuscaloosa, Alabama, at the turn of the century. And though Willie's mother, Ann, did not play ball, she was an athlete and had starred at track in her school days. As a matter of fact, she continued to participate in local meets even after her first child was born.

Willie's mother and father did not remain together long. A couple of years after he was born they were divorced. Willie's mother remarried, and Willie went to live with his Aunt Sarah, the wife of his father's brother. His father, who remained single, used to take his meals at Aunt Sarah's, too. There, after supper, he talked baseball to Willie. As his son grew older, he took him along to the ball field where the boy watched him play with the company team. Soon Willie was playing sandlot ball himself. And at the age of ten he was introduced to the pepper game, an exercise he continued even after he entered the major leagues, considering it one of the most valuable aspects of his training. Standing about fifteen feet from his bat-wielding father, Willie would pitch a ball to him, then jump, duck, stretch, run, pounce, or lunge to recover it as it was hit sharply back in his direction. If the game is played at top speed for some time, pepper demands great agility and skill in fielding all kinds of hits.

Judging from the evidence, it would seem that as a youth Willie, or "Buckduck" as he was also called in those days, was more fond of football than of baseball. At any rate, when he was thirteen years old he climbed a tree to watch a football game between Fairfield Industrial High and West View High. He became so interested that he forgot where he was, fell out of the tree, and broke his arm.

Later, as a student at Fairfield Industrial, he played football and became a fine passer. He also played basketball and was county high scorer in his sixteenth year. His high school had no baseball team, but he did play during the summer with local community teams. Willie still remembers one game that he played when he was fourteen, pitching nine innings under a hot Alabama sun and hitting a home run to end the game. As he rounded third for the plate his head began to swim, and by the time he came in to score he was almost swooning. His father, who had witnessed the game, helped him off the field and, warning him against overtaxing himself, advised him to abandon the pitcher's mound for the field. Willie took his advice.

Willie's father, who was still playing ball himself, had some friends in the Negro National League. Before Willie was out of high school, his father arranged a meeting for him with Piper Davis, manager of the Birmingham Barons, one of the best teams in the league. Piper agreed to try Willie out, taking him on as a utility man for the summer. When the center fielder was injured, Willie took over and did so well that he was made permanent center fielder. As soon as Willie won his professional spikes, his father hung his up. "I didn't see any use of playing any longer after the boy went with the Barons," he said. "That was when I knew for sure Willie was going to be a great player."

The big leagues first became aware of Willie's potential greatness in 1950, when a couple of Giant scouts, Bill Harris and Ed Montague, went to Birmingham to size up Alonza Perry, the Barons' first baseman. They soon lost interest in Perry when they saw Willie in action, and on their recommendation Willie's contract was bought from the Barons for $10,000. He was sent to the Giants' Trenton, New Jersey, farm team in the Interstate League, where he ended the 1950 season with a .353 batting average. His smashing drives, miracle throws, and circus catches made him the talk of the circuit.

In the spring of 1951 Willie was promoted to the American Association and joined the Minneapolis Millers. In thirty-five games he hit eight home runs and loosened the boarding on the right-center-field fence of the park with his extra base hits. His batting average ran up to .477. Leo Durocher, manager of the Giants, had seen and liked Willie at spring training in Florida. Having lost eleven games in a row in the first six weeks of the 1951 season, he decided to call Willie up to the Giants for "some sorely needed punch at the plate." Durocher put a telephone call through to Minneapolis, but Willie couldn't be found. (He was at the movies, his favorite form of post-game relaxation.) When he was located, Willie resisted the idea. He felt he was not yet ready for the majors. However, a phone call to "Lippy" Durocher—whose nickname was not bestowed gratuitously—convinced him that he and the Giants would be good for one another. And Willie reported to the Giants for his major league debut at Shibe Park, Philadelphia, on May 25, 1951.

Willie's first two weeks with the Giants were inauspicious enough. In twenty-six times at bat, he got only one hit—a home run. New to the team, he felt like an outsider. As a matter of fact, he didn't even know most of the players' names, and whenever he wanted information he would prefix his question with, "Say, hey . . ." The expression became so familiar that he was nicknamed the "Say, hey kid." And soon his easy laugh and quiet good nature made him a club favorite. The other players began to kid him, a sure sign of his acceptance. They ribbed him because he always lost his hat when he ran. And they joked about his playing stickball with the neighborhood kids on Amsterdam Avenue in Harlem, where he had taken an apartment.

One story about his early days with the club involves a race he had with Earl Rapp, one of his new teammates. It seems that Earl challenged Willie on the way to the clubhouse after the game. "Race you the rest of the way for five bucks," he said. Willie agreed, dug in his cleats and beat Rapp by ten or fifteen feet. As Rapp came up to the clubhouse steps, he held out his hand and said, "Pay me."

"For what?" said Willie. "I beat you."

"Wasn't anything in the bet about anybody *beating* anybody," replied Rapp. "I just said I'd *race* you."

Soon Willie began to hit. And the Giants, who had been in fifth place when he joined them, began to win games and climb toward first place. At one point in the season the team won sixteen games in a row, the longest National League winning streak in sixteen years. The story of how the Giants caught the league-leading Dodgers and won the pennant from them in a series of three play-off games is now history. And Willie's contribution to that history is well known, for he was honored as Rookie of the Year for 1951 in recognition of his efforts. His batting average for the season, which included twenty home runs, was .274.

But it was in the field that he really shone. One play that he made in a crucial game against Brooklyn that season will never be forgotten by anyone who witnessed it. It took place in the top of the eighth inning, with one out, the score tied at 1–1, Carl Furillo at bat, and Billy Cox, a fast man, on third base. Furillo blasted the ball into deep right-center field, well to Willie's left. Willie, running at top speed, caught it, but as a right-hander he was traveling in the wrong direction for a throw to the plate. Pivoting on his left foot, he executed a complete spin-about and rifled the ball to catcher Wes Westrum in time to catch the fleet-footed Cox coming in from third base. Jackie Robinson, though he was on the Dodgers' side, called the throw the greatest he had ever seen.

Willie played in only thirty-four games of the 1952 season before Uncle Sam tagged him for the draft. He spent twenty-one months in the army, most of the time at Camp Eustis, Virginia, in the physical training department. Playing ball with an army team, Willie developed the famous "basket" catch for which he has since become well known. Throwing with more of a side-arm motion than most fielders, Willie felt that he could save a valuable fraction of a second by catching the ball low and having it in position for the throw. So instead of holding his hands up in front of his face, thumbs in, as most fielders do, he held them at midriff height, thumbs out. The catch has since become a Mays trademark.

The Giants had been in first place in their league when Willie left for the army. But, as one team official commented,

"He hadn't been gone ten days and we were in second place, and that's where we finished the season." In 1953 the club dropped even farther, ending the season in fifth place. Hence when Willie, discharged from the army, showed up at the Giants' spring training camp at Phoenix, Arizona, on April 5, 1954, the same official happily announced, "There's the pennant." His prediction was to be more than fulfilled, for the Giants won the World Series as well. Willie contributed more than a little to the result, driving in 110 runs, a record-setting 81 of his hits going for extra bases, and 41 of those for home runs. With the highest batting average in either league, he was named Most Valuable Player in the National League and Major League Player of the Year. And in a year that, among other athletic events, saw man finally run the four-minute mile, Willie Mays was named by an Associated Press poll as "male athlete of the year."

It is silly, however, as well as unfair, to attribute to one man the victories achieved by a whole team. The 1955 season proved that Willie Mays was not the Giant baseball team. For there was no diminution of Mays' effort that year. As a matter of fact, he hit fifty-one home runs during the season, becoming the seventh man in major league history to hit fifty and tying a National League record set by Johnny Mize in 1947. Yet in 1955 the Giants finished the season in third place.

Generous to a fault, Mays contributed a good percentage of his income to the education of his many half brothers and sisters. His one extravagance was automobiles, and he sometimes owned several at once. Popular with girls, he was as much in demand on the dance floor as in the baseball park. Or at least he was until Valentine's Day 1956, when he was married to Margheurite Wendelle, a New York girl. In 1958 the Giants moved to San Francisco, and Willie received the wildest cheers in a ticker-tape reception for the city's new team. When he returned from California to join the New York Mets in 1971, it was New York's turn for wild jubilation, which it indulged in full measure.

Baseball is a team game, and no one recognized this better than Willie. He regretted the legends that grew up about him, attributing them, in his autobiography, *Born to Play Ball*, to "the other Willie Mays," the one who "sleeps with a box of baseballs for a pillow and picks his teeth with a bat." This Mays, of course, existed solely in the minds of the fans. But the fact that he existed at all indicates something about Willie, for legends do not grow up about second-raters. They develop when a man plays, as *Time* magazine described Willie, "with a boy's glee, a pro's sureness and a champion's flare." Once, when the real Willie made a circus catch of an almost certain home run up against the center-field fence and whirled to double a runner off first, a spectator who had missed the play asked who had hit the ball. The answer: ". . . Willie himself. He's so fast he can go get 'em after he hits 'em."

At the end of the 1973 baseball season, Willie Mays finally hung up his spikes after twenty-two years in major league baseball. In a moving "Farewell to Willie" in his sports column in *The New York Times* Arthur Daley called him "one of the most extraordinarily gifted ballplayers ever to step on a diamond." That was high praise from an old pro who had been observing the game, and reporting on it, for many more years than twenty-two. And Willie surely deserved it.

BILL RUSSELL

Bill Russell Breaks National Basketball Association
Rebound Record
Russell Named Player of the Year
Russell Stars in Sixth Straight All-Star Game;
Holds Chamberlain to 17 Points
Bill Russell of Celtics in Fifth Straight
NBA Championship

Over the years in sports headlines from coast to coast the record-breaking performances of Bill Russell have been a regular feature of the basketball season. But neither the headlines nor the impressive playing statistics Bill has compiled tells the whole story of this basketball superstar—far from it. That the Boston Celtics acquired eleven National Basketball Association titles in thirteen years in the course of his career with them suggests another aspect of his ability, particularly in view of the fact that the Celtics had never won top place before he joined them. So does the record of the college team he played for, the previously undistinguished Dons of the University of San Francisco. During his years with them, they won two successive National Collegiate Athletic Association basketball titles—a feat duplicated by only two other teams in the history of the NCAA. And during Russell's last two seasons of

Bill Russell

collegiate play, the Dons won a string of fifty-five straight victories. Bill Russell was a tremendous team player, more concerned with his team's victory than his own status or statistics.

Moreover, Bill Russell was not a great player in the usual sense. Basketball is, of course, a scoring game. Points are won by scoring baskets. And the recognition usually goes to the outstanding shooters—men with a dead eye on the foul line; men who can hit from outside, with soaring shots that arc high to plunk through without even rippling the cords; men who can hook from the corner and zonk the ball in when no one can get near the basket. Bill Russell was not an outstanding shooter, though. To be sure, he was no slouch. And being a thorough professional, he worked on his shooting and improved over the years. But he was not a sharpshooter like "Clyde" Frazier or Wilt Chamberlain, who seemed to be able to hit any time from any place on the court. Bill's game was defense. He was basketball's great rebound man, grabbing the ball off the backboard when an opponent shot and feeding it to a teammate who would race down the court for a score. And he was so good that he revolutionized the game, forcing coaches to pay more attention to defense than they had ever done before and making interesting an aspect of the game that had once been tame or routine.

At six feet ten inches, with enormously long arms and big hands that could grasp a basketball like a baseball, Russell naturally played center, where he controlled the opening tap-off more often than not, giving his team the advantage of first possession of the ball. Husky, at 220 pounds, he was also incredibly fast for a big man, so that he could get down court in a flash and drive in through the tightest defense for a lay-up shot. Most impressive of all were his steel-spring legs, which shot him into the air to stuff the net, capture the rebound, or tap a teammate's wayward shot into the basket. Thus on play after play, Russell was the key man, robbing opponents of scoring opportunities by recapturing the ball, scoring himself, or providing the extra little tip that made a teammate's effort count for a score.

Yet for all his outstanding ability, superstar status, and marvelous team spirit, Bill had a weakness—his stomach. Before most games he would have twinges of nausea, rumblings of gas, and various internal quakes and tremors. Before big games he often got violently ill, breaking into a cold sweat and vomiting profusely. Time after time during an important series, he would get so sick in the locker room that he'd ask Coach "Red" Auerbach of the Celtics to take him out of the upcoming game. Auerbach was alarmed the first couple of times Bill got sick. But he soon learned that no matter how sick Russell might be, when the team left the locker room for the playing floor, Bill got up on his rubbery legs and joined them. And once out on the floor, all signs of illness disappeared.

A nervous stomach is a great equalizer, bringing even the mightiest low. Perhaps it is this that has given Bill Russell his humility—or perhaps it came naturally or from early training. In any case, he has it. Unlike most star athletes, for example, Bill doesn't generally sign autographs, believing the practice to be silly. Nor does he hold press conferences. "I don't have anything to say," he explains simply. And when beaming fathers approach him with their offspring, announcing proudly, "I want my boy to be like you," Bill, feeling that a boy's closest and best model should be his father, usually says, "What's wrong with you?"

Bill's own father, Charlie Russell, was very close to him and to his older brother, Chuck, especially after the death of the boys' mother, Kate, when Bill was eleven. That was in Oakland, California, where the family had settled two years earlier, having come from Monroe, Louisiana, by way of Detroit. After the warm South, Detroit had been too cold and blustery, so the Russells had moved on to California, where Charlie got a job in a foundry and located a pleasant five-room apartment in sunny

Oakland. Kate was delighted. She had hated Monroe, where she had grown up. She hated the segregation, the poverty, the lack of opportunity—everything about it. When her sons were born there—Chuck in 1932 and Bill on Lincoln's Birthday 1934—she feared that they would be as trapped as she had been in the little backwater town. Uneducated herself, she had great faith in education. In fact, she was determined to send her boys to college and named her younger son William Felton Russell in honor of the president of Southeastern Louisiana College in nearby Hammond.

At first, Charlie resisted leaving Monroe, not actively, but passively, for he was a genial, easygoing, quiet man. Monroe wasn't much of a town, to be sure, but at least it was home. Family and friends were nearby. The boys were growing well. Chuck especially was developing into an athlete, and this pleased Charlie, who had played semipro ball around Monroe for several years. Even young Bill, who was awkward and clumsy, was learning to play baseball.

Actually, Bill preferred watching the trains go by on the Southern Railway nearby to playing baseball. In fact, he preferred trains to anything else and longed for a miniature railroad. But when he picked out a set in a store before Christmas, the price was $35, far beyond what the Russells could afford.

Eventually, Kate convinced Charlie to move north. With World War II in progress, there were jobs available in Detroit, where the automobile plants were turning out war matériel, and in the shipyards of the San Francisco Bay area. Hence the Russells' route. Then, when they were settled, happily far from Monroe, Kate suddenly died.

Overwhelmed with grief at the loss of wife and mother, Charlie and the boys carried on. Young Chuck was already a star athlete at Hoover Junior High. In fact, when he set a 100-yard-dash record for the school, he became so high and mighty that his father had to take him down a peg or two. He did so by setting off a course in the park and running away from the new record holder in his heavy work shoes. The lesson deflated young Chuck's ego. It also stuck in his brother's mind.

Not that Bill needed such a lesson at that point in his life. Tall, skinny, and awkward, he was put completely in the shade by his brother's accomplishments. In fact, rather than attend Oakland Tech, where his brother made all-star high school teams in basketball, football, and track in his junior year, Bill decided to go to McClymonds High School. There he would not be compared with his brother, whom he idolized but could not emulate.

The decision was a happy one, for at McClymonds Bill came under the influence of basketball coach George Powles. Stressing mental attitude as well as physical superiority, Powles taught Bill the importance of determination. Moreover, he saw something in the six-foot-two, 128-pound scarecrow and added him to the junior varsity roster as a sixteenth, or extra, man. And he put him into play now and then. These were agonizing experiences for Bill, for the spectators hooted and jeered at him. His very appearance on the court, a beanpole in shorts and sneakers, brought forth mocking applause mixed with catcalls and laughter. He wanted to get off the court and hide, to quit the team, but Powles wouldn't let him. So he persisted, his embarrassment turning to anger, his anger to determination. And gradually he improved, especially under the basket, where Powles taught him to make good use of his height. He also went out for track, where he beat everyone at the high jump and the hurdles. And at Powles's suggestion, he played table tennis regularly, sharpening his eye and perfecting his timing. By his senior year, he was star center at McClymonds, leading the basketball team to victory over Oakland High and the Bay Area high school championship.

He won an athletic scholarship to the University of San Francisco, where he starred on the freshman team. As a sophomore, Bill joined the varsity as center in 1953, leading

USF to a surprising victory in its first game over the University of California, one of the best college teams on the Pacific Coast. He held the Golden Bears' All-Coast center Bob McKeen to 14 points, while scoring 23 points himself and blocking 13 sure baskets. After that opening game, the Dons, beset by injuries, had a rough season, carried almost entirely by Bill Russell, who acquired an enthusiastic following and had the best press of any athlete on the West Coast.

The lesson in humility Bill's father had taught his brother was now forgotten, as Bill, his name in every paper, became the big man on campus. He developed a swagger, clipped his press notices, and even took to quoting them, unsolicited. Charlie Russell worried, for Chuck had never been this bad, but Bill was soon to get his comeuppance. It was provided by a girl he met at a college dance, Rose Swisher. Introducing himself to her, Bill expected Rose to swoon with recognition. Instead, he was met with a blank stare.

"I'm Bill Russell," he repeated. "Did you get my name?"

"You said Bill Russell, didn't you?" Rose responded matter-of-factly, deflating his ego on the spot—and winning his heart. Three years later, having led the University of San Francisco basketball team from obscurity to a remarkable two consecutive years as NCAA champions, Bill Russell, more famous but less conceited, asked Rose another question: "Will you marry me?" This time he got the answer he expected: "Yes."

Before the wedding, Bill traveled to Melbourne, Australia, site of the 1956 Olympics. Russell had been selected for the basketball team representing the United States in the games. As a matter of fact, Bill, who had continued his track work while at college and was a top-notch jumper, had qualified for the second spot on the high jump team as well. He pulled out of the latter event at the last minute, though, so that two of his friendly track rivals, Phil Reavis and Val Wilson, could make the three-man jump team. "It was the most sporting gesture of the year," wrote a reporter. "Russell is not only the best all-round athlete on the Olympic team, but he's the nicest guy."

Bill returned from Australia with a gold medal, having led the U.S. basketball team to victory in the Olympic Games. In mid-December 1956 he married Rose Swisher in Oakland. He would be well able to support a wife, for the night before the wedding he signed a professional basketball contract with Walter Brown, owner of the Boston Celtics. The contract was for $24,000, at the time the top salary ever paid to an NBA rookie. Then, on December 22, Bill played his first professional basketball game, with the Celtics, against the St. Louis Hawks at the Boston Garden. It was a tight game. Before going into the Garden, Bill, feeling confident that pro ball was no tougher than college ball, had said to Rose, "I did all right at USF. I'll do all right up here." Afterward, he was not so sure. Bob Pettit, the Hawks's big center, had run rings around him. He had been roughed up, confused by the Hawks' speed and power and humiliated by his own weakness in shooting. But he had grabbed 16 rebounds in one 21-minute stretch, helping the Celtics to a narrow margin of victory.

Soon rival players were asking, "How do you stop Russell?" And record crowds were flocking to the games to watch the big new Celtic rookie transform basketball. In a league noted for its high-scoring totals, Russell was stopping offensive stars cold. About midway through the season two coaches from opposing NBA teams adopted tactics designed to stop Russell's aggressive defense game. They pulled their centers out from under the basket and had them shoot from outside. Russell pulled out to stay with them, thereby losing his effectiveness as a rebounder. When Auerbach saw what was happening, he told Russell, "Give 'em the outside. . . . From now on, you're not covering these guys—you're going to make them cover you. No matter where they go, you come in close. . . . They'll come in to cover you, and you'll murder them."

And so he did.

As a matter of fact, he "murdered" them for thirteen years, spurring the Celtics to eleven NBA titles in that time span, serving as player-coach the last three seasons, replacing Auerbach himself. In the process he piled up rebound records, Most Valuable Player awards, All-American championships, and accolades from the press, and he won the respect and affection of sports fans and players alike.

At home in Reading, Massachusetts, where he bought a house during his first season with the Celtics, Bill installed an elaborate miniature railroad system in the basement, making up to himself for the $35 train set he had failed to get as a child. There he often entertained himself and later his children, William, Jr., or Buddha as he came to be called, Kenyatta, and Jacob. But he had more serious interests, too, including music, with a collection in excess of four thousand records, and reading, particularly in black history and culture, civil rights, and politics generally. And following his retirement from active play in 1969 he lectured frequently at colleges across the country, for a while speaking an average of three times a week, lashing out at racism, condemning indifference in the struggle for civil liberties, fighting intolerance and oppression.

Ultimately, basketball called Bill back. Covering ABC's "Game of the Week," he was described during his second season at the job as "the wisest, wittiest, and most forthright basketball analyst in broadcasting." And in 1973 he resumed a more active role in basketball, moving to Seattle to take control of the Supersonics as coach and general manager. His job: to build a fourth-place team into champions. Probability of success? Given Russell's ability and determination, excellent.

MUHAMMAD ALI

You're the chump and I'm the champ. It is prophesied for me to win! I cannot be beaten! . . . I am a baaaad nigger. . . . You are too ugly. You are a bear. I'm going to whup you so baaad. You're a chump, a chump, a chump. . . . And I am the Prettiest. The Wittiest. The Greatest. . . . I'm gonna take you in eight to prove that I'm great. . . . I'll float like a butterfly, sting like a bee. . . . I am the onliest. . . .[1]

As he shouts, his eyes bug out, his hands thrash, he jumps up and down and lunges forward, having to be restrained as he tries to get at the other athlete on the platform. Miami Boxing Commissioner Morris Klein fines him $2,500 on the spot for his behavior at the weigh-in. When his pulse is checked, as part of the weigh-in procedure, it registers 120 beats a minute, 66 beats above his normal rate. Jesse Abramson, sportswriter for the New York *Herald Tribune*, comments to friends, "I think they should call it off. He's in no condition to fight tonight." He is described as "scared" by afternoon papers in Miami and New York, where the headlines read: "Hysterical Outburst at Weigh-in."

But he is not scared. And the "hysteria," if that is what it is, is controlled, having been generated to "psyche-out" his opponent. He does fight that night, putting so much leather in

[1] Quoted in Budd Schulberg's *Loser and Still Champion: Muhammad Ali.*

Muhammad Ali

the "invincible" Sonny Liston's face that Sonny can't get off his stool when the bell rings for round seven to begin. There is a new World's Heavyweight Boxing Champion. It is February 25, 1964. Tomorrow he will announce that he has joined the Nation of Islam and will take an Islamic name: Muhammad Ali. Tonight he is still known by his "slave name," Cassius Marcellus Clay, Jr. He has fulfilled the goal he set for himself when he began boxing in Joe Martin's gym in Louisville, Kentucky, at the incredibly early age of twelve. He is, at twenty-two, heavyweight champion of the world.

Born on January 17, 1942, in Louisville, young Cassius was named after his father, a prosperous sign painter who owned his own house and used to boast that he was never out of work one day in his life. "And I never worked for nobody but me," he would add.

Odessa Lee Grady Clay, the fighter's mother, whose maiden name and light skin color indicates mixed Irish and African ancestry, was a quiet rather pious homebody. Describing her, Ali says: "My mother is just another sweet, fat homey mother. She loves to stay home and cook and she goes to Baptist church every Sunday. And she doesn't meddle, don't bother nobody. She's quiet."

Ali confesses that he was "not that bright and quick in school." And this fact is borne out by his marks at the Virginia Avenue Grade School and later at Central High, where, he says, he was "the badest cat" in the school. He was generally too busy showing off to be studious. He liked to run alongside the school bus instead of riding in it, enjoying the attention he got from the kids waving and hollering inside. At recess, he would start fights to draw a crowd. "I always liked to draw crowds," he says. Even in Joe Martin's gym, where his marks were high—generally on the noses and mouths of his young opponents—and won him a place on Martin's weekly televised boxing show, he made a nuisance of himself. "He was always bragging that he was the best fighter in the gym and that someday he was going to be champion," says Martin. Indeed Martin once had to throw young Cassius out, warning him not to come back until he had learned to "toe the line."

Martin matched him carefully against other fighters, leading him along step by step through 180 amateur bouts. He won six state Golden Gloves tournaments in Kentucky, progressing through the various classifications from light to welter to middleweight to light heavy and heavyweight. At seventeen, as a light heavyweight, he won the 1959 National Golden Gloves and the National Amateur Athletic Union titles. Anxious to use his skill to earn money, Cassius considered becoming a professional. But, he says, "Martin advised me against turning pro and trying to fight my way up in clubs and against preliminaries, which could take years and maybe get me all beat up. He said I ought to try the Olympics and if I won, that would give me automatically a number-ten pro rating. And that's just what I did."

Remaining an amateur, Cassius repeated his National AAU and Golden Gloves victories in 1960, boxing as a heavyweight in the NAAU tournament to permit his brother Rudolf, also a boxer, to compete in the light heavyweight class. Cassius' victory in the NAAU tournament gained him the right to participate in the Olympic trials, for which he returned to his normal weight classification—at the time, 175 pounds—winning the light heavyweight spot on the U.S. Olympic Boxing Team that would take him to Rome for the 1960 Olympic Games.

Toeing the line had paid off. Actually, it had been a pretty flexible line. So long as he didn't back-talk Martin or put down his gym, Martin didn't mind Cassius' boasting. As a matter of fact, he recognized the usefulness of Clay's behavior. As the fighter himself put it, "Almost from my first fights, I'd mouth off to anybody who would listen about what I was going to do to whoever I was going to fight. People would go out of their way to come and see, hoping I would get beat. When I was no more than a kid fighter, they would put me in bills because I was a drawing card, because I run my mouth so much."

After he won the gold medal at the Olympic Games, he turned pro, and his mouthing off and other gimmicks, like his rhymed predictions—"This guy must be done/I'll stop him in one"—helped to attract large income-producing gates. His evident boxing skill won him the attention of professional prizefight managers, who approached him with offers to take him under their tutelage and make him into a boxing champion.

The championship was, of course, Cassius' goal, which he had had in view from the age of twelve. But he had his own ideas about how to get to that goal and about the manager who could help him to it. As early as two years prior to his Olympic victory, Clay had gone to see Angelo Dundee, who managed such champions as Willie Pastrano and Luis Rodriguez. Dundee was in Louisville with Pastrano for a boxing match, and young Cassius had barged into their hotel room with his brother.

"He stood there and talked to us for three and one-half hours," said Dundee. "He told me about all the fighters I had. . . . Then he asked me, 'How many miles do your fighters run?' 'Why do they run?' 'What do they eat?' 'Do they eat once a day, twice a day, three times a day?' 'What do they do prior to a fight?' . . . He wanted to know every facet of boxing. See, he's a student of boxing. . . . He studied boxing. . . . He and I got to be very friendly."

But when Clay turned pro, though he was besieged with attractive offers from good professional managers, he got no call from Dundee. The next time Dundee came to Louisville with a fighter, Clay, puzzled at being ignored, went to him. "How come you never approached me to handle me?" he asked the fight manager.

"It's this simple," Dundee replied. "You know my business

is boxing. That's all I do. I have a gym in Miami Beach and if you ever want to become a fighter, come down and see me and I'll work with you."

Taken aback, Cassius answered, "You must be some kind of a nut. Everybody approaches me, offers me all kinds of money, cars. And you, all you offer me is to come down to Miami Beach."

Taken aback, in turn, Dundee responded simply, "Certainly. What I'm offering you is what talent I have! I'm sure I can do a good job with you. *You've* got to be some sort of a nut."

The exchange had been blunt, to say the least, but Cassius went to Miami Beach, and Dundee worked with him. As a matter of fact, he has been working with him ever since. Of course, Cassius had wanted "to become a fighter." Four years after his conversation with Dundee, he was one—to a superlative degree. In fact, he was heavyweight boxing champion of the world.

Neither on the road to the championship, nor after he had won it for that matter, did Cassius' loudmouth tactics change. Such tactics were not only good for the gate. They were psychologically damaging to his opponents, causing them to lose their tempers and throw punches savagely, trying to flatten this brash young man with a single blow. And that, of course, was playing into this skillful boxer's hands. Goading and taunting the other man in the ring, Cassius would dance out of the reach of angry blows with the speed of light, jab, jab, jab with his powerful left, move and hit again before his furious and befuddled opponent could get set for a counterpunch. And when he was set, Cassius was elsewhere, out of range, hitting again with his long reach.

The tactics were effective, so Cassius kept them up in and out of the ring. Meeting the European champion Henry Cooper on the road to the heavyweight title, Cassius called him "a tramp, a bum, and a cripple, not worth training for." Aging

Archie Moore was "the old man." Floyd Patterson he called "the Rabbit" and, insultingly, took a bunch of carrots to the fighter's training camp. Confronting Doug Jones in the ring at the start of a bout, having predicted in rhyme—falsely, as it turned out—that he would fall in four rounds, Cassius asked him, "How tall are you?" And when Jones asked him why he wanted to know, Cassius responded, "So I'll know how far to step back when I knock you out in the fourth."

Naturally, his antics antagonized large segments of the sports world and the press. Then, in 1964, before the championship fight with Liston, Cassius invited Malcolm X to his training camp. It was bad enough for a fighter to express contempt for his opponents. But for a boxer to consort with a radical critic of society itself—that was unthinkable. What would he do next? What Clay did, in fact, was join the Nation of Islam as a follower of the black separatist Elijah Muhammad, changing his name to Muhammad Ali and announcing, "I don't have to be what you want me to be. I am free to be who I want."

There was a hysterical outcry in the press. A campaign was initiated to strip Ali of the title. Ed Lassman, president of the World Boxing Association, called Ali "a detriment to the boxing world" and suggested that he was "setting a very poor example for the youth of the world."

Ali responded by pointing out that he had won an Olympic gold medal for the United States and that he had won the heavyweight title "fair and clean. Honestly. . . . Furthermore," he said, "I don't smoke or drink, and I don't fool around with women. I'm a clean fighter. I've never been in jail and I carry no pistol. I'm an example for the youth of the whole world."

Indeed, he was, as his triumphant visit to Africa and the Muslim world in 1964, shortly after his marriage to Sonji Roi in Chicago, demonstrated. And he was a *world* champion, defending his title not only against former champions Sonny Liston (in a return match in May 1965) and Floyd Patterson and a host of

American contenders, but also against challengers from all over
the globe—Henry Cooper and Brian London of England;
Koko "Duke" Sabedong from Hawaii; Oscar Bonavena, the
indestructible Argentinian; Karl Mildenberger of Germany;
and the iron-chinned Canadian George Chuvalo, among others.

It was not in the ring but out of it that Ali lost the
championship. He lost it by doing what thousands of his
countrymen were doing at the time—expressing their opposition to one of the most unpopular wars in American history, the
Vietnam War. On April 28, 1967, Ali refused induction into the
army on religious grounds. He was a minister in the Nation of
Islam. Perhaps as much to the point was his observation,
frequently quoted at the time and expressive of an attitude
widely held. He said, "I ain't got no quarrel with them Viet
Congs. They don't call me nigger."

Ali not only lost the championship but also the right to box
as a professional when the World Boxing Association took his
title from him. For three and a half years he was not allowed to
practice his craft. Divorced from Sonji, to whom he paid
alimony, and married again, to Belinda Boyd, Ali needed
money both for his personal expenses and for court costs. His
recourse was to the college lecture circuit, where he was
extremely popular. And he fought imprisonment for draft
evasion all the way to the U.S. Supreme Court, where he was
finally vindicated on June 28, 1971, by a unanimous decision.

After three and a half years of forced retirement, during
what should have been the peak years of his career, Ali's
attempt at a comeback in professional boxing was checkered
with victories and defeats. He won impressive victories over
Jerry Quarry and Oscar Bonavena. The latter fight, especially,
showed Ali's ability to take punishment for fifteen rounds as the
aggressive Bonavena, with his great strength and unorthodox
boxing style, pressed Ali hard to the last round. Then,
seemingly exhausted by the long, grueling fight, Ali caught the
Argentinian with a wicked left hook that knocked him down.

Flooring Bonavena twice more in the last round, Ali won a TKO—three knockdowns in one round constitute a technical knockout and automatically end the fight. Even skeptics who had questioned the strength of Ali's punch and doubted his ability to endure punishment, who had thought of him as a lucky trickster who had escaped defeat through speed and luck, were now convinced that he would win back the title.

Ali, too, was confident that he would reclaim the championship from Smokin' Joe Frazier. On the day of the fight, March 8, 1971, he rhymed:

> *Joe's gonna come out smoking*
> *And I ain't gonna be joking,*
> *I'll be picking and a-poking*
> *Pouring water on his smoking.*
> *This might shock and amaze ya,*
> *But, I'm gonna re-tire Joe Frazier.*[2]

Wrong in his predictions before, he was disastrously wrong this time. Overconfidence, which led him to stand in his corner showing off instead of sitting down during the intervals between early rounds, contributed to his defeat. And although he had Joe Frazier bleeding from the mouth and his head monstrously swollen from punches, Ali couldn't stop him. Both boxers absorbed tremendous punishment in a fight that seesawed back and forth, with one fighter then the other taking the beating. Finally, in the fifteenth round Frazier hit Ali with a left hook that smashed against his jaw, knocking him down. Gamely, Ali struggled to his feet at the count of three, his jaw ballooning out of shape from the blow. With Frazier too exhausted to find the range again, Ali tried to fend him off and stay on his feet to the end. He did so, but to no avail. The fight was Joe's.

The fight was Joe's, but Ali had shown great courage and staying power. Indeed, Budd Schulberg, in his biography of Ali

---

[2] Quoted in José Torres' . . . *Sting Like a Bee: The Muhammad Ali Story.*

written after the championship bout, called it *Loser and Still Champion: Muhammad Ali*. The pretty boy with the dancing feet, whose speed had kept him out of danger in previous fights, had shown that he could take terrible punishment and keep going. On January 28, 1974, he proved that he could climb back from defeat by winning a unanimous decision in twelve rounds over Frazier. Of course, by this time Frazier had himself been dethroned by George Foreman, who had scored a second round TKO over him at Kingston, Jamaica, on January 22, 1973. But the victory was no less sweet for Ali, who at thirty-two was able to overcome his own conceit and, seemingly, time itself, in a superb exhibition of boxing skill against his most powerful and determined adversary.

Ali's victory was no fluke either, as he demonstrated conclusively on October 30, 1974, in Kinshasa, Zaire, when he knocked out George Foreman in the eighth round to regain the World's Heavyweight Boxing Championship. It was a feat only one other fighter, Floyd Patterson, had ever accomplished before. Moreover, Ali won his astounding victory—his forty-fifth in forty-seven fights—without using his customary dancing tactics. He stood flat-footed in the ring, taking everything Foreman could hit him with, chipping away at his opponent a punch at a time. Then with Foreman arm-weary and exhausted, Ali cut him down with a right-hand chop to the side of the head that dropped him like a log.

Ali's victory brought him $5 million and the world championship. He was still "The Prettiest. The Wittiest. The Greatest," in the words of that best authority on the subject: Muhammad Ali.

INDEX